Chautauqua Cooks

A Century of Recipes
from Chautauqua County Kitchens

Joanne L. Schweik

Chautauqua Region Press
Westfield, New York
2000

Cover photograph: "Dinner at Ellery," ca. 1910.
Lewis, Clark and Pickett families. Photo Jack T. Ericson

International Standard Book Number: 0-9658955-4-8

Book Design and Production by:
Carol Mellors
Classic Design • Westfield, New York
Printed in the United States of America

Chautauqua Region Press
19 Spring Street
Westfield, New York 14787

Table of Contents

ABOUT THIS COOKBOOK

With these words this little book is submitted just as it is.
May it lessen the perplexities and cares of those who travel
the daily round of household duties, and stimulate that just
pride without which work is a drudgery and excellence
impossible.

The Philergian Cookbook, 1888

Jack Ericson's idea for *Chautauqua Cooks* may have had nothing whatever to do with the fact that a century was coming to an end. Nevertheless, during the last decade or so, Jack, who is Archivist and Curator of Special Collections at Reed Library at the State University of New York College at Fredonia, has been quietly and purposefully building a collection of cookbooks published in Chautauqua County.

Beginning with Kate Cook's interesting and quite comprehensive *Cook Book*, first published in 1882, with revisions in 1886, 1889 and 1896, that collection now numbers more than 150 cookbooks. Every year another church or philanthropic group publishes a fundraising cookbook. Such books are still very popular and always manage to come up with new and interesting recipes.

Jack's idea was to do a comprehensive digest of recipes culled from county cookbooks through the century from 1882. In order to include some good examples and to record minor changes in eating habits, we have extended the scope of the book through the 1990s. Our purpose is to provide an appetizing sample of what Chautauqua County cooks have been preparing in their kitchens as the years have progressed.

Some things drew on our culinary memory: Kate Cook's very frequent instruction to "take butter the size of an egg," for example; or the widespread use of cream, before milk was homogenized and the necessity to use the cream from the top of the bottle no longer applied. There were also surprises: to learn that Triscuits — the still-popular base for dips and spreads — were manufactured in Niagara Falls, early in the century; and that German Sweet Chocolate was available as early as 1927-28. Campbell's soups, Jell-o, and other never-fail ingredients for quick and easy cooking also made their debuts in the first quarter of the 1900s.

It is not exactly possible to track the history of Chautauqua County cooking decade by decade. However, predictably, depression recipes were light on meat, because meat prices were high. Wartime cookbooks featured sugarless and meatless recipes because of food rationing. Casseroles began to dominate the cookbook pages in the 1950s. By the 1980s dips, spreads and other appetizer concoctions were popular. And in the 1990s, when food trends seemed to be on a fast track in large part because of the new celebrity status and creativity of restaurant chefs, we began to see a geographical

iv

widening of our cuisine repertoires and increased interest in new flavors.

On the whole, this collection of recipes is varied, interesting and appetizing. We have included representatives of most of the ethnic groups in Chautauqua County as they were represented in the cookbooks.

The selection of recipes was completely random, the only criterion being did it "sound good" and was it the best recipe for the dish of those available. The final compilation depends on nothing but that criterion. In preparing the book to be useful and attractive to prospective Chautauqua County cooks, we have edited all the recipes carefully to be sure that they work, that the directions are clear, and that the book has a necessary consistency in style.

Special Note: Since the recipes, still, after editing, come from different sources, take care to read the recipe through, *before* you start to cook.

It is our fervent hope that you take as much pleasure out of the book as we have had in preparing it. And, of course, in the American way of saying it: Good eating!

ACKNOWLEDGEMENTS

I wish to thank several people who helped bring this book to publication. First, Jack Ericson, who collected the books in the first place, and invited me to take on the project. Jack helped in innumerable ways as the work progressed.

Also Carole Somerfeldt, Secretary, Archives and Special Collections, Reed Library at the State University College at Fredonia, for her daily help through several months. I enjoyed working with Aaron Dux, a student at the College at Fredonia, who took on the rather formidable task of photocopying materials as I needed them, and who earned my admiration and gratitude thereby.

Fenton Historical Society and Reed Library are to be thanked for providing many of the photographs used throughout this book.

When I was ready to start editing recipes and making decisions on which would be included, Jeanne Keefe, my friend of many years, agreed to help. Because of her, the project came to fruition months earlier than it might otherwise have done. I couldn't have survived without her cheerful and excellent work. And my sincere thanks to three generous women who loaned precious cookbooks from their own collections to fill in gaps: Carmela Frame and Ruth Mohney, both of Fredonia, and Marty Hegner of Dunkirk.

For his patience, tolerance, good humor, love and support throughout, and for help in many ways, special thanks to Bob Schweik, my lifelong partner.

Finally, many, many thanks to Carol Mellors, who typeset and designed the book. A great deal of the credit for the way it is and the way it looks belongs to her.

In the end, though, any and all mistakes or problems, should they occur, are mine.

Joanne L. Schweik
Spring 2000

KATE COOK

(1843 - 1900)

APPETIZERS

What we today call "appetizers" were not unknown in 1882, when Kate Cook first published her *Chautauqua Cook Book*. At that time such things were served — some, like cucumber sandwiches and stuffed celery, frequently — but they were served as first courses, or as what were known as "canapés," a term we tend to use quite loosely in our time, or as accompaniments to afternoon tea.

The idea of a separate party, with drinks and small pick-up foods of many kinds, probably evolved during prohibition, when the illegality of buying liquor in public places gave rise to the home cocktail party.

During the great depression (1930 - 1939) and the deprivation years of the second World War, when meat, butter, sugar, clothing, gasoline and other necessities were rationed, big-splurge parties were rare, and in most homes appetizers, or whatever they were called, were uncommon.

Beginning with the 1950s, though, appetizers assumed a legitimate place among food categories. They have become increasingly popular as the century has passed, until now it is not only common to have parties where appetizers, or hors d'oeuvres, including canapés, star; but it is also usual practice to serve one or two preliminary foods as appetizers, with drinks, at nearly every entertainment occasion that involves a meal.

It has been fun to notice, in our perusal of county cookbooks, when certain appetizers appeared or seemed to be popular, and which ones achieved such status. You will find nearly all the popular ones in this book: the tomato soup-based shrimp mousse and the baked artichoke dip, for instance, both of which appeared in just about every book since the 1960s. And, of course, other dips, from avocado (Guacamole) to the layered Tex-Mex taco dip. Also, the seafood melanges, with clams, crab, shrimp, lobster or smoked fish, often mixed with cream cheese and heated.

In a wonderfully readable and fascinating book published in 1997, the *American Century Cookbook*, the experienced cookbook author Jean Anderson takes us through the 20th century, detailing when the most popular American recipes entered our culinary repertoire, which ones were most popular, and how they varied or did not vary from one region to another. Anderson's survey is amply corroborated by 100 years of Chautauqua cookbooks.

In preparing this book it became obvious that recipes that were popular in the Midwest or the South or the far West eventually worked their way to Chautauqua County, or vice versa, and appeared in cookbooks published by the various groups in this area. As you read through this book — and, we hope, cook from it — you'll recognize many of your own favorites; or, if you are young enough, you'll find many that will *become* your favorites.

A toast to the appetizer! Long may it thrive.

1

ARTICHOKE HEARTS SUPREME

4 artichoke hearts, (fresh, frozen or canned in water)
4 round bread rolls (Pepperidge Farm French rolls work
   nicely)
butter
1 cup (or more) grated Swiss cheese
1 egg
2 Tbsps. milk
salt and pepper

If using fresh or frozen artichoke hearts, cook in boiling, salted water and lightly sauté them in butter. For canned hearts, rinse with water and sauté.

Cut the rolls in half and cut a hole in each half of the roll the size of the artichoke heart. Do not cut through the crust of the roll. Remove bread from roll halves and brush with melted butter.

In each cavity, place 1 artichoke heart. Mix the grated cheese with the egg, milk, salt and pepper. Spoon the mixture on the artichoke hearts. Brush with butter and bake in a hot oven, 400°, for about 20 minutes, or until golden and crisp. Serve immediately.

Lesley Mucha
Centennial Cookbook...
(1987)

ASPARAGUS ROLLS

1 can asparagus spears
1 loaf Arnold thin bread
8 oz. package cream cheese
4 oz. blue cheese
1 egg
margarine, melted

Beat together until smooth, cream cheese, blue cheese and egg. Roll bread with rolling pin. You may remove crusts if you prefer. Spread cheese mixture on bread and top each with asparagus spear. Roll up from one long side to the other. Put three toothpicks in each roll and cut into three pieces. Freeze after cutting until ready to use. Brush with melted margarine and brown in broiler; turn after five minutes. Serve hot, makes about 50.

Kris Michaels
Cook Book
Silver Creek
(1977-78)

AVOCADO DIP

3 avocados, chopped finely or puréed
1 Tbsp. salt
$^3/_4$ tsp. garlic powder
2 Tbsps. lemon juice
$^1/_3$ cup green onions, sliced
$^1/_3$ cup celery, chopped
$^1/_3$ cup mayonnaise
$^1/_2$ tsp. chili powder
Dash Tabasco sauce
1 medium tomato, peeled and chopped (or canned)
$^1/_2$ green pepper, diced
$^1/_4$ cup mushrooms, finely chopped
jalapeno pepper, fresh or canned, minced to taste
   (optional)

   Blend avocado puree with mayonnaise, seasonings and lemon juice. Fold in remaining ingredients. Chill thoroughly.

   Shirley Slater
   Chautauqua Motet
   (1985)

DEVILED EGGS

Hard-boil 8 eggs. Mash the yolks fine; add 1 tsp. salt, $^1/_2$ tsp. dry mustard, large pinch of paprika, 1 large Tbsp. oil or 2 large Tbsps. melted butter, 3 Tbsps. weak vinegar, and 4 Tbsps. fine bread crumbs. Mix well. Spread mixture into egg white halves.

   Mrs. Pratt
   The Fredonia Cook Book
   (1899)

TEN STEPS TO HEAVEN

1. Toast a thin slice of bread lightly on one side
2. With toasted side down, cut out a circle with a glass
3. With toasted side up, put on a matching slice of
   peeled tomato
4. Add a thin slice of the center of a hard boiled egg
5. Add a thin slice of canned artichoke heart
6. Cover with a layer of black caviar
7. Cap with mayonnaise thinned with cream
8. Sprinkle grated egg yolk over top
9. Serve with knife and fork on individual plates
10. Wash down with dry champagne

   George Crile, Jr., M.D.
   Chautauqua Celebrity . . .
   (1980)

JEZEBEL SAUCE

18-oz. jar pineapple jam
18-oz. jar apple jelly
$5^1/_2$-oz. jar horseradish (drained)
1 small can dry mustard, or to taste (Be careful, it's hot!)
1 Tbsp. fresh ground pepper

   Stir all together. Serve over cream cheese. (Sauce may be frozen). Delicious hors d'oeuvre. Serve with Triscuits or crackers.

   Jeanne Lyons
   CSEA Cookbook
   (1988)

CAVIAR CANAPÉS

To Russian caviar, add half as much lemon juice. Spread on toast and garnish with stuffed olives or pickles. Sift over with riced hard-boiled eggs. Dot with pearl onions.

CHICKEN CANAPÉS

Sprinkle mustard over buttered toast and cover with minced chicken. Garnish with stuffed olives, capers, or minced truffle.

LOBSTER CANAPÉS

Cut bread in circular pieces and sauté in butter. Soften finely chopped, well seasoned lobster meat to a paste with creamed butter and Worcestershire sauce. Make mounds of this mixture on the rounds of bread and garnish with olives.

CHEESE CANAPÉS

One cup grated cheese to 6 slices bread. Salt and pepper to taste. Sprinkle cheese over bread cut in any shape desired. Toast until cheese is melted. Serve hot.

TOMATO AND BACON CANAPÉS

Cut bread in circular pieces. Toast and butter. Layer sliced tomatoes and strips of fried bacon on each piece. Spread with a little mayonnaise and garnish with cross strips of red and green peppers.

SARDINE CANAPÉS

Shape slices of bread with a circular fluted cutter, sauté in butter and spread each piece with sardine butter which is made by smashing the sardine with a fork and mixing with creamed butter. Season with lemon juice and cayenne. Garnish each canape with finely chopped egg white and a tiny shred of pimiento. In the center of each half put a stuffed olive.

Cook Book
Jamestown
(1920s)

APPETIZER CHEESECAKE

3 cups shredded sharp cheese
2 cups cottage cheese, drained
2 Tbsps. prepared horseradish
$^1/_2$ cup mayonnaise
2 Tbsps. Dijon style mustard
6 slices bacon, cooked, crumbled
1 small onion, minced
$^1/_4$ cup butter, melted
Salt and pepper, to taste
Garnishes (see below)

Combine Cheddar cheese, cottage cheese, mustard, horseradish, mayonnaise, bacon, onion, salt, pepper and butter in a large bowl. Will combine well in a food processor. Beat until blended but not completely smooth. Press into an ungreased 8" springform pan. Cover with foil; refrigerate at least 4 hours. Remove cover and sides of pan. (Pretty if served on cake pedestal type dish.) Garnish top with any or all of the following: alternate rings of olives, pimiento, green onions and radishes. Cut into thin slices or wedges. Serve on assorted crackers. Makes 35 servings.

Jean Lloyd
Crèche Cooks
(1986)

CHILE-CHEESE SQUARES

2 (4 oz.) cans green chiles
1 (8 oz.) package Cracker Barrel cheese, grated
3 eggs, beaten
1 tsp. prepared mustard
dash of Worcestershire sauce
dash of salt and pepper
dash of garlic salt
paprika

Butter a square pan. Rinse green chiles in cold water and remove seeds. Spread chilis in bottom of pan. Grate cheese. Combine with eggs, mustard, Worcestershire sauce, salt and pepper, and garlic salt. Place mixture on top of chilis. Sprinkle with paprika. Bake in a 350° oven for 25 to 30 minutes. Cut into small squares.

Mary McCroskey
"Someone's in . . ."
(1980s)

As popular as a recipe could ever be — these appetizers were everywhere for a couple of decades. Michael Hudson, a popular local caterer, gave out the recipe only a few times — to special friends.

MICHAEL'S CHEESE PUFFS

1 cup Kraft Parmesan cheese (use only Kraft)
1 cup Hellmann's mayonnaise (only Hellmann's)
1 cup minced onion
1 Tbsp. milk
2 packages party bread (rye or pumpernickel)

Mix cheese, mayonnaise, onion, and milk. Use only these ingredients. Any other brands will make the puffs very oily. Put spread on party bread and broil in broiler till golden. Serve warm.

This recipe can be easily cut in half or doubled as needed. *Enjoy!*

Betsy Hudson
Warm Your Heart . . .
(1987)

HOT RYES

8 oz. finely grated sharp cheese
$^1/_2$ cup cooked, well-drained bacon
$^1/_2$ cup chopped black olives or stuffed olives
$^1/_2$ cup finely sliced green onions or chives
2 tsps. Worcestershire sauce
$^1/_2$ tsp. salt
1 tsp. dry mustard
1 tsp. poppy seed
$^1/_2$ to $^3/_4$ cup Miracle Whip or mayonnaise

Put bacon in blender for tiny bits. Mix all ingredients well. May be stored in covered jar 10 days in refrigerator. Put rounded teaspoon on rye or pumpernickel cocktail bread. Bake on ungreased baking sheet, 350° for 10 minutes. Serve hot. Can also be an open-face sandwich for lunch with soup.

Virginia Wareham Dean
First Presbyterian . . .
(1986)

GOLDEN CHICKEN CHUNKS

3 whole chicken breasts, skinned, boned and cut into
   bite-sized chunks
1 cup grated Parmesan cheese
2 tsps. basil
$1/_2$ cup butter or margarine, melted
$1^1/_2$ cups seasoned bread crumbs
$1/_2$ tsp. salt.

In a bowl, combine the bread crumbs, cheese, salt, and basil. Dip chicken into melted butter and then cover with the bread crumb mixture. Spread chunks out on a cookie sheet with a lip or edge. Bake at 400° for 20 minutes or until golden brown. Check after 10 minutes and turn the chunks over if needed.

Joe Crupi
Chautauqua Motet . . .
(1985)

SLOW-BALL DIP

1 large round loaf, French, Italian or other unsliced
   crusty bread
2 (8 oz.) packages cream cheese, softened
3 ($6^1/_2$ oz. each) cans chopped clams, drained
   (reserve $1/_4$ cup liquid)
2 Tbsps. grated onion
2 Tbsps. beer
2 tsps. Worcestershire sauce
2 tsps. lemon juice
1 tsp. hot-pepper sauce (or to taste)
$1/_2$ tsp. salt

With sharp knife cut top from bread; set aside. Hollow loaf, leaving a 1-1/2 to 2-inch thick shell. Cut removed bread into cubes. Set both aside.

In large bowl, beat cream cheese until smooth; stir in clams, reserved clam liquid, onion, beer, Worcestershire sauce, lemon juice, pepper sauce and salt until well blended. On baking sheet, make a cross with 2 sheets of aluminum foil, each long enough to cover loaf. Center bread shell on foil. Pour clam mixture into shell. Cover with top of bread. Wrap loaf with foil.

Bake in preheated oven, 250°, for 3 hours for flavors to blend and clam mixture to get piping hot. Remove top; sprinkle dip with parsley if desired. Serve loaf on large platter surrounded by bread cubes that have been toasted in oven during last 5 minutes of baking time. Fill platter with raw vegetables for dipping. When empty, bread shell may be torn apart (or cut) and eaten.

Earlene Steger
Centennial Cook Book (1987)

CRAB QUICHE

1 pie shell (9 inch)
$^3/_4$ cup Swiss cheese, shredded
8 ounces crabmeat (canned or frozen)
2 green onions, sliced
3 eggs
1 cup half and half
$^1/_2$ tsp. salt
$^1/_2$ tsp. grated lemon rind
$^1/_4$ tsp. dry mustard
dash of pepper
$^1/_4$ cup sliced almonds

Line a 9-inch quiche dish or pie pan with pastry. Bake at 400° for 3 minutes; remove from oven and gently prick with fork. Bake 4 minutes longer and let cool. Sprinkle cheese in shell. Place crabmeat on top of cheese and sprinkle with onions. Beat eggs; add half and half, salt, lemon rind, dry mustard and pepper. Pour into pastry shell and sprinkle with almonds. Bake at 325° for 1 hour or until set. Let stand 10 minutes before serving.

Lucille Piper
Chautauqua Motet . . .
(1985)

ARTICHOKE DIP

1 can artichoke hearts (in water)
1 cup Hellmann's mayonnaise
1 cup grated Parmesan cheese

Drain artichokes and press out remaining water. Chop coarsely. Blend with mayonnaise and cheese. Bake in a shallow casserole at 350° for 15-20 minutes or until bubbly. Serve hot with crackers or party rye bread.

Cindy Coon
Cooking by Degrees
(1985)

Note: This appetizer appeared in many of the cookbooks reviewed. Suggested variations:
Add 1 can crab meat and mix well before baking.
Add juice of $^1/_2$ lemon and red pepper (cayenne) to taste.
Add garlic powder to taste.

LUNA PASTE

3 eggs, beaten
3 Tbsps. vinegar
3 Tbsps. sugar
Combine and cook until thick. Add: $^1/_2$ lb. cream cheese
1 green pepper - cut fine
1 small grated onion
1 pimiento - cut fine

Mix thoroughly. Delicious as a spread on crackers or bread.

Margaret Mastrian
What's Cooking (II)
(1966)

HOT MUSTARD DIP

$^1/_2$ cup wine vinegar
1 egg, beaten
3 Tbsps. sugar
3 Tbsps. dry mustard
1 tsp. flour
2 Tbsps. butter

In saucepan, heat vinegar till hot. In small bowl, mix remaining ingredients, then add to hot vinegar. Stir until thick. Remove from heat. Add butter. Cool. Serve with pretzels. *Hot but good.*

Betsy Hudson
Warm Your Heart . . .
(1987)

SPINACH BALLS

2 (10 oz.) packages frozen chopped spinach
1 stick margarine
1 small box herb or chicken stuffing mix
$^1/_2$ cup grated Romano or Parmesan cheese
4 beaten eggs

Cook spinach; drain well. While still hot, stir in margarine until melted. Add stuffing mix (including herb package), cheese and eggs. Mix together well. Leave in refrigerator several hours or overnight. Mold into small balls and bake on a lightly greased cookie sheet at 350° for 15 minutes. Serve warm.

Verna Ann Pappalardo
A Cappella Choir . . .
(1986)

TUNA MOUNTAIN

1 cup butter or margarine
2 (6$^1/_2$ - 7 oz.) cans tuna, drained
1 (8 oz.) package cream cheese
2 Tbsps. chopped green onions
1 Tbsp. lemon juice
$^1/_4$ tsp. salt
$^1/_4$ tsp. dried tarragon, crushed
dash of pepper
$^1/_4$ cup finely snipped parsley, dried
1 hard cooked egg, sieved

Cream together cream cheese and margarine. Beat in other ingredients through pepper. On plate, shape into a mountain. Sprinkle parsley on sides. Chill. Sprinkle sieved egg on top part. If desired, mix with a little mayonnaise. Serve as spread for crackers or rye bread.

Margaret Rector
East Dunkirk . . .
(Date unknown)

HOMMUS - HORS D'OEUVRE SPREAD

1 can chick peas
$^3/_4$ cup sesame seed or peanut oil
3-4 garlic cloves
1 tsp. Lawry's seasoned salt
$^1/_8$ tsp. cayenne pepper
1-2 tsps. lemon juice

Drain chick peas. Combine the chick peas with the oil, garlic, salt, cayenne pepper, and lemon juice. Mash until very smooth in blender. Taste for seasoning and chill. Serve with crisp crackers or party bread as a spread.

Barrie Sanford Greiff, M.D.
Chautauqua Celebrity . . .
(1980)

UNBELIEVABLE BRIE

1 wedge of Brie cheese
Honey
Sliced almonds

Place Brie in ovenproof serving dish with sides. Pour honey over Brie, so that Brie is covered and a small amount has run onto surface of serving dish. Sprinkle with sliced almonds. Heat at 300° (uncovered) about 20 minutes, or until brie is hot and runny. Serve immediately with assorted crackers.

Jeanne Henderson
Crèche Cooks
(1986)

FRITTATAS

$^1/_2$ cup olive oil
2 medium onions, peeled and thinly sliced
2 potatoes, peeled and thinly sliced
8 mushrooms, sliced
10 asparagus tips, steamed
1 red pepper, seeded and sliced
1 zucchini, thinly sliced
12 eggs, beaten
salt and pepper

3 (8") baking dishes. 400° oven. 15 to 20 minutes.

Divide olive oil among 3 baking dishes. Arrange some onion slices on the bottom of each baking dish and bake for 6 minutes. Cover with potatoes and bake for 8 minutes. Arrange remaining vegetables in a decorative pattern and bake 5 minutes. Pour the eggs over vegetables and season with salt and pepper. Bake till center is set and sides are puffy and golden. Reduce the oven temperature if eggs brown too quickly. Let cool slightly before slicing into small wedges. Makes 24 single servings.

Pam Fagerstrom Russo
A Cappella Choir . . .
(1986)

QUICHE PETITES

1 cup flour
$^1/_2$ cup butter
3 oz. cream cheese
1 egg
$^1/_2$ cup milk
$^1/_4$ tsp. salt
$^1/_2$ lb. mushrooms, diced
1 cup grated Swiss cheese
$^1/_2$ cup bacon, fried and crumbled
1 small onion, grated (optional)

Cream butter and cream cheese. Work in flour. Roll into 24 balls and press into miniature muffin pans. Sauté diced mushrooms and onion. Spread into tins. Divide Swiss cheese and bacon bits into the tins. Pour mixture of egg, milk and salt over the above. Bake at 350° for 30 minutes. Can freeze.

Michelle Johnson
Cooking by Degrees
(1985)

LOBSTER QUICHE

1 medium onion, minced
$^1/_2$ stick butter
6 eggs
6 oz. Swiss cheese, ground or finely chopped
2 oz. Parmesan cheese
1 cup chunked lobster meat
pinch of nutmeg
pinch of pepper
1 cup heavy cream (adjust amount according to
   consistency)
deep 9-inch unbaked pie shell

Sauté onion in butter until clear; combine with next 7 ingredients until well blended. Pour into pie shell and bake at 350° for 35-45 minutes or until egg has set well. Serve immediately. Serves 8.

Lucille Petrella
Westfield Jayncees . . .
(1983)

EASY HOSTESS MUSHROOMS

2 - 3 lbs. mushrooms
2 sticks margarine
2 tsps. minced onion
$^1/_2$ tsp. minced garlic
1 tsp. Worcestershire sauce
$^1/_2$ tsp. rosemary leaves
1 tsp. salt, if needed
fresh ground pepper

Wipe mushrooms clean with dampened paper towels. In 13" x 9" x 2" cake pan melt margarine in slow oven (250°F.). Add seasonings and mix well; add mushrooms and mix well; increase oven temperature to 325°F. Bake 40-45 minutes turning several times to cover all mushrooms. Serve warm in fondue pot. You may need to double or triple recipe for a big party.

Connie Swanson
Favorite Hometown . . .
(Date unknown)

STUFFED MUSHROOMS
(microwave)

SPINACH STUFFED:
1 (10 oz.) package frozen spinach souffle, thawed
   and well-drained
$^1/_3$ cup grated Parmesan cheese

SAUSAGE STUFFED:
$^1/_4$ cup bulk pork sausage
dash of paprika

HAM AND CHEESE STUFFED:
1 (3 oz.) package cream cheese, softened
$1^1/_2$ tsps. margarine or butter, softened
$^1/_4$ cup finely chopped ham
2 Tbsps. bread crumbs
2 Tbsps. finely chopped onion
$^1/_2$ tsp. Worcestershire sauce
$^1/_4$ tsp. salt

Wash mushrooms and remove stems. Prepare stuffing and heap into mushroom caps. Arrange stuffed mushroom caps on plate lined with paper towel. Microwave on High (100%) for 3 to 4 minutes.
"Cookin' from . . ."
(1987-88)

APPETIZER PIE
1 (8 oz.) package cream cheese, softened
2 Tbsps. milk
1 ($2^1/_2$ oz.) jar dried beef, finely snipped ($^3/_4$ cup)
$^1/_2$ cup minced onion (or 2 Tbsps. instant minced onions)
2 Tbsps. finely chopped green peppers
$^1/_8$ tsp. pepper
$^1/_2$ cup sour cream
$^1/_4$ cup chopped walnuts

Blend cream cheese and milk. Stir in next 5 ingredients. Spoon into 8-inch pie plate or similar dish. Sprinkle nuts on top. Bake at 350° for 15 to 20 minutes. Serve with crackers or vegetables. About 40 servings.
Gerda Morrissey
Sue Seaman
Centennial Cook Book
(1987)

PARTY PORK BALLS

1 pound ground pork
1 (8 oz.) can water chestnuts
$^1/_2$ cup minced green onions
1 tsp. minced fresh or preserved ginger
$^3/_4$ tsp. salt
1 Tbsp. soy sauce
1 egg, lightly beaten
$^1/_2$ cup bread crumbs
cornstarch
3 Tbsps. vegetable oil
sweet and sour sauce

SWEET AND SOUR SAUCE:
$^1/_2$ cup cubed sweet green pepper
$^1/_2$ cup cubed sweet red pepper
2 large carrots, thinly sliced
2 Tbsps. vegetable oil
1 (20-oz.) can pineapple chunks
$^1/_4$ cup vinegar
1 Tbsp. soy sauce
2 Tbsps. sugar
$^1/_2$ cup beef broth
2 tsps. minced fresh ginger
2 Tbsps. cornstarch
$^1/_2$ cup water

Combine pork, water chestnuts, onions, ginger, salt, soy sauce, egg and bread crumbs in a large bowl. Mix well. Shape into 36 balls. Roll in cornstarch to coat lightly.

Brown in oil in a large skillet. Remove balls as they brown to a roasting pan. Cover loosely with foil.

Bake in a moderate oven, 350°, for 20 minutes, or until thoroughly cooked. Combine with sweet and sour sauce.

Sauté peppers and carrots in oil for 3 minutes, or until tender. Stir in pineapple with juice, vinegar, soy sauce, sugar and broth, and ginger. Combine cornstarch with water and stir into above mixture. Cook, stirring constantly, until mixture thickens.

Mrs. Alfred G. Ford
Post-Journal Cookbook
(1984)

TIP

To test fresh eggs, drop the egg into a deep saucepan of cold water; if fresh, it will sink at once; if it stands nearly upright, it is not fresh, but can still be used; if it floats on the surface, it is not good.

What's Cooking I (1954)

STUFFED PICKLES

3 to 4 large dill pickles, depending on size
1 (8 oz.) package cream cheese
$^1/_3$ cup stuffed olives, finely chopped
dash of garlic salt
dash of onion salt

Cut both ends off of dill pickles. Scrape inside of pickles out with vegetable peeler or long thin knife. Leave some of the meat on the outer part. Gently squeeze juice out. Wrap with paper towel and refrigerate until cold (about 1 hour). The paper towel will help draw out additional juice.

Meanwhile soften cream cheese, season with garlic salt and onion salt. Mix well. Add chopped stuffed olives.

Stuff pickles with cheese mixture. Push mixture into center of pickles, work in until pickles are stuffed firmly with mixture. Refrigerate several hours until nice and firm. Slice pickles into $^1/_2$- to $^3/_4$-inch slices.

Note: Excellent for the holidays. The appetizers will look like Christmas wreaths with the red and green mixtures. Also can be made with chopped walnuts instead of stuffed olives.

Donna Jordan
Post-Journal Cookbook
(1987)

GIOZA

1 lb. hamburger
1 tsp. ground ginger
1 Tbsp. dried onion bits
1 egg
$^1/_2$ c. cornflake crumbs
3 eggs
3 Tbsps. water
$1^1/_4$ to $1^1/_2$ cups flour
salt as desired
pepper as desired

Mix together thoroughly the hamburger, salt, pepper, ginger, onion, 1 egg and cornflake crumbs. Set aside. Mix together 3 eggs with 3 Tbsps. water. Mix in flour, $^1/_2$ cup at a time to make a workable dough. Roll out $^1/_2$ of the dough at a time. Roll out fairly thin. Cut into 3 inch circles. Place teaspoonful of meat mixture on noodle circles. Wet on edge, fold and pinch together to seal. Put small amount of water in a frying pan. Fry giozas in water until lightly browned; turn and fry on other side. Keep covered in frying pan while frying. Add small amounts of water as needed.

May be frozen and reheated in oven, tightly covered with a small amount of water on the bottom of the pan.

Serve with a spicy mustard or tangy sauce, if desired.

Leslie Wagner
Centennial Cook Book
(1987)

SHRIMP SNACK PUFFS

$^1/_2$ cup sifted all-purpose flour
$^1/_4$ tsp. salt
$^1/_4$ cup shortening
$^1/_2$ cup water, heat to boiling
2 eggs
$^1/_4$ cup shrimp, finely chopped

FILLING:
1 cup shrimp, cooked and chopped
8 ripe olives, chopped
$^1/_2$ cup celery, chopped
1 egg, hard-cooked and chopped
1 Tbsp. mayonnaise
$^1/_4$ tsp. Worcestershire sauce

Sift flour and salt together. Melt shortening in boiling water, add dry ingredients all at once to boiling liquid, stirring constantly. Cook until mixture leaves sides of pan in smooth ball. Remove from heat; cool 1 minute. Blend in eggs, one at a time, beating until smooth. Add chopped shrimp and drop by teaspoonfuls onto greased baking sheets. Bake in hot oven (450°) 10 minutes, then at 400° for 5-10 minutes. Prick with fork during last 5 minutes. Cool. Fill split puffs with olive-shrimp filling.

Combine all ingredients and mix well. Makes 5 dozen puffs.

Mrs. Richard Cline
Post-Journal Cookbook
(1987)

SHRIMP TOAST

1 lb. cooked, thawed shrimp (small size)
1 cup Hellmann's mayonnaise
$^1/_2$ c. shredded Colby cheese
dash of curry powder
1 loaf party rye bread

Mix shrimp, mayonnaise, cheese, and curry powder. Place 1 Tbsp. on each slice of rye bread. Broil till brown and bubbly. Serve immediately.

Laurel K. Clawson
Food for . . .
(1987)

SHRIMP TOAST

Toast thin round pieces of bread and butter while hot. Mash 1 cupful of canned shrimp, add to them 1 Tbsp. chopped parsley, 1 Tbsp. melted butter, 1 tsp. of French mustard, $^1/_4$ tsp. of salt and a dash of pepper. Mix until thoroughly smooth. Spread over the toast, stand a few moments in the oven and serve.

E.W.M.
Needlework . . .
(1907)

COCKTAIL SHRIMPCAKES

1 cup pancake mix
$1/_4$ cup corn meal
$1^1/_2$ cups milk
1 egg, beaten
1 Tbsp. melted shortening

FILLING:
2 Tbsps. mayonnaise
2 Tbsps. cream cheese
1 tsp. prepared horseradish
1 tsp. grated onion
dash of catsup
1 (6 oz.) can of shrimp, drained,
    rinsed, and chopped fine

Combine pancake mix with corn meal. Stir in milk. Beat in egg and shortening. Pour 1 Tbsp. of batter for each pancake onto hot, lightly greased griddle. Bake 2 or 3 minutes on each side or until golden brown turning once. Makes 28 small cakes.   Fill and roll pancakes with Shrimp Filling.

Mix ingredients together. Spoon a little on each pancake. Roll and fasten with a toothpick. Heat under broiler for 2 minutes or sauté lightly in a little butter in chafing dish. Serve hot.

This may be prepared well in advance (even frozen) up to the final stage. Also may vary with fillings of your choice.

Anna Mae Hutchinson
Post-Journal Cookbook
(1987)

SHRIMP MOUSSE

1 can tomato soup
2 (3-oz.) packages cream cheese
2 Tbsps. gelatine
$1/_2$ cup cold water
1 cup mayonnaise
$1^1/_2$ cups chopped celery
1 green pepper, chopped
chopped onion to taste
2 cans of shrimp, drained

Melt cheese. Dissolve gelatin in cold water and let stand for 10 minutes. Beat gelatine mixture into cheese. Add heated soup. Cool. Add remaining ingredients. Pour into fish-shaped (or other) mold and refrigerate until set. Serve with party rye bread or crackers.

Edna Blom
To the Town's Taste
(1964)

SMOKED FISH LOG

1 lb. smoked fish, flaked
1 (8 oz.) package cream cheese
2 Tbsps. grated onion
1 Tbsp. lemon juice
1 Tbsp. prepared mustard
$^1/_4$ tsp. salt

Mix together and blend well. Shape into log. Wrap in foil and chill. Roll log in 1/2 cup each of chopped parsley and chopped pecans. Serve with rye bread or crackers.

Dorothy Kokocinski
Sharing Our Best
(1987)

SPANAKOPITTA

(Spinach Pie)
2 packages frozen chopped spinach
2 tsps. butter
2 tsps. parsley
1 tsp. dill
$^1/_4$ tsp. pepper
3 eggs
$^1/_2$ lb. phylo (filo) pastry
1 cup melted butter
1 small onion, chopped
$^1/_4$ cup chopped scallions
1 tsp. salt
$^1/_4$ cup milk
$^1/_4$ lb. feta cheese

Thaw spinach and drain. Sauté onions in 2 Tbsps. butter and add scallions; add spinach and seasonings. Toss. Remove from heat and add milk. Beat eggs and add cheese and add to spinach mixture. Coat bottom and sides of 11"x7"x2" pan with butter. Line with 8 sheets of phylo, brushing each sheet with butter. Do not trim overhang. Pour in mixture and fold overhang sections. Top with 8 more greased sheets of phylo. Fold ends over. Brush top with butter and score into squares or diamonds. Bake at 350° for 45 minutes. Let stand 10 minutes before serving. Makes about 20 appetizer servings.

Iris Hilton
Chautauqua-Allegheny Cookbook
(1990)

SOUPS

Of course Kate Cook made soups, as did, probably, every other Chautauqua County cook before and after her.

Not surprisingly, the soup repertoire in 1882 was not too far from what it is in the 1990s, beginning with recipes for "white" (made from veal bones) and "brown" stock (made from beef). Chicken stock was there, too, but we found no mention of vegetable stock in the early cookbooks; moreover, it wasn't until 1978 that a cookbook included the rule for achieving a rich, dark-colored stock: browning the beef and vegetables at high heat in the oven before adding water and beginning the long simmer (see Phillip Lord's recipe on page 21 of this chapter).

Down through the years, the soup recipes represented in the cookbooks illustrated three things apparently known to good cooks no matter when they lived: first, that soup is a healthful, nutritious way to feed a family well and inexpensively—serve a big, hearty bowl with a good bread and a fruit dessert and you have a satisfying meal; second, that just about anything lends itself to being turned into soup—vegetables, of course, such as the first asparagus in spring (real soul food) and the perfectly ripe tomato in late summer (yes, it's a fruit, but used as a vegetable), meat, poultry, fish, and even fruit (see the Swedish fruit soup and Carol Adams's plum soup on page 28); and third, that hot soups warm your body in the winter and cold soups refresh and relax in the summer and both are equally delicious. All of the soups that follow deserve attention.

GENERAL DIRECTIONS

Lean beef, mutton, or veal is the basis of all good rich soups, but fresh bones and those from cooked meat and poultry, with trimmings of meats and odds and ends of vegetables, cooked or raw, make very good stock where economy is desired.

In seasoning soup the general rule is to use, for every quart of water used to cover the meat, a teaspoonful of salt, one of pepper, a quarter teaspoonful of celery salt, a little parsley, and half a pint of vegetables. In making stock it is a safe rule to use a quart of water to every pound of bones. Soup should always be boiled slowly. The stock will probably be reduced nearly one-half by cooking, and may be diluted for the table. Strain through the colander, and put aside to let the fat harden before removing it. To color soups brown, add a tablespoonful of caramel (browned sugar) to a pint of stock. Clear soups are dinner soups; cream soups are more appropriate for luncheons. Part beef and veal, or mutton, combined makes a better flavored stock than beef alone.

A stock stronger and more palatable than the common one we call a consommé, and it serves as the foundation of soup for a formal dinner. The following directions are intended only for a very rich soup.

RICH CONSOMMÉ

A veal shank weighing about two pounds, five pounds of beef and bones, a chicken (a hen will do), two carrots, one onion, half a turnip, one stalk of celery, three quarts of water, and salt and pepper to taste.

Put the beef and veal in the pot with the cold water and boil slowly, skimming until clear. After half an hour's boiling add the vegetables, and let boil for two hours;

then take the veal out of the pot, as all the juices will have been extracted from it, put in the fowl, and let boil slowly for three hours more. Skim again, then remove from the fire. After it has cooled, take off any fat that has come to the top of the stock.

A more economical consommé, and one quite good enough for everyday purposes, is as follows.

CLEAR SOUP OR CONSOMMÉ

Take a good-sized shank of beef, chopped in several pieces; put it into a very large pot or divide it and put it into two smaller pots. Cover it well with cold water, leaving just room enough to let it boil. As soon as it comes to a boil set it back on the stove so that it will boil *very slowly*, but keep it boiling. After it has boiled three hours have ready a couple of turnips, three or four carrots, three large onions sliced, and two stalks of celery. After washing these well, add them to the pot or pots. Let the stock boil slowly for three hours more and then strain through a colander and put away to cool until the next day. When it is quite cold, and the fat has risen to the top, skim it off, add pepper and salt to taste, about half a grated nutmeg, a tablespoonful each of mushroom and anchovy sauce, and tomato catchup(sic); put it all back on the stove in a clean pot, and add the white of three eggs well beaten. *Do not skim.* Let it boil five minutes, set aside a moment, then strain through a cloth laid in a sieve. This will keep for days. Heat it as you need it, and be sure that it is served very hot.

The fat skimmed from the stock is excellent for frying potatoes.

Wholesome Cooking
(Date unknown)

BROWN STOCK

2 lbs. each meaty beef and veal bones
2 onions, cubed
1 carrot, cubed
pinch of thyme
1$\frac{1}{2}$ tsp. salt

BOUQUET GARNI:
4 sprigs parsley
2 stalks celery
1 small bay leaf

In a flat pan, spread bones which have been cracked into small pieces along with onions and carrot. Brown on all sides in moderately hot 375° oven. Transfer to a kettle and add 3 quarts water, salt, thyme and bouquet garni. Bring water slowly to a boil, skimming fat from surface when necessary. Cook slowly for at least 4 hours or until reduced to 2 quarts. Strain stock through fine sieve or cheesecloth.

Father Phillip Lord
Favorite Recipes
from Our Best Cooks
(1978)

JELLIED BOUILLON

1$\frac{1}{2}$ Tbsps. unflavored gelatin
$\frac{1}{2}$ cup cold water
2 cups canned beef bouillon
1 cup canned chicken bouillon
1 onion, sliced
1 small bunch celery
$\frac{1}{2}$ tsp. salt
dash pepper
1 hard cooked egg, sliced

Soak gelatin in cold water 5 minutes. Combine remaining ingredients except egg, heat to boiling point, simmer 10 minutes. Add gelatin mixture and stir until dissolved. Let stand 5 minutes, strain. Pour into bouillon cups, set until firm. Just before serving, draw fork through to break up jelly. Garnish with egg slice. Also lemon wedge, catsup or horseradish. Serves 6.

To the Town's Taste
(1964)

ASPARAGUS SOUP

2 quarts chicken stock.
2 bunches of asparagus
2 Tbsps. butter
1 quart milk
2 Tbsp. flour

Cut the heads off the asparagus and save in a cup; cut up stalks and put in stock and boil one hour.

Boil heads in 1 cup of salted water. Melt butter and flour in a stew pan and stir in milk until it cooks; strain stock; stir in milk mixture, and season thoroughly with salt and pepper. Before serving put in $1/_2$ cup of cream and asparagus heads.

Mrs. Joseph Brown
The Fredonia Cook Book
(1899)

SPICY BLACK BEAN SOUP

4 carrots, chopped
2 onions, chopped
1 garlic clove, minced
2 Tbsps. olive oil
2 Tbsps. ground cumin
$1/_2$ tsp. cayenne or to taste
1 tsp. mace
4 cups beef broth
2 (16 oz.) cans black beans, including liquid
$1/_2$ cup rice
$1/_2$ cup sherry

In a kettle cook the carrots, onions and garlic in the oil over moderate heat until the vegetables are softened. Stir in the spices and cook, stirring for a minute. Add the broth and the beans, with the liquid. Bring to a boil and simmer for 15 minutes. Add rice and simmer for 15 to 20 minutes or until the rice is tender. In blender, puree half the mixture and return to the mixture in kettle. Stir in sherry and salt and pepper to taste.

Claire Davis
Soup and Salad
(1989)

SPANISH BEAN SOUP

3 qts. water
1 ham hock
1 small beef soup bone
1 (1 lb. 4 oz.) can of tomatoes
3 (15 oz.) cans Garbanzo beans
2 onions, chopped
1 green pepper, chopped
1 clove garlic, minced
$1/4$ tsp. saffron
6 potatoes, peeled and cubed
Salt and pepper to taste

Bring ham, soup bone and tomatoes to a boil in the water and cook slowly 1 hour. Add beans and continue cooking slowly for another hour. Remove meat from bones. Return meat to pot, add onions, pepper, garlic, saffron, and potatoes. Simmer until meat is tender, 45 minutes. Before serving add salt and pepper to taste. Serves 8.

With a green salad and toasted French or garlic bread this makes a delicious meal.

This recipe came from the famous Spanish restaurant, Los Novadades in Ybor City, the Cuban section of Tampa, Florida.

Mrs. George Hiles
Wonderful Cooking . . .
(Date unknown)

CRAB BISQUE

3 cans tomato soup
3 cans consommé
3 cans green pea soup
3 cans crabmeat
$1^1/_2$ tsps. curry powder
4 cups light cream
$1/_2$ cup sherry
1 cup whipped cream
chopped parsley

Heat tomato, pea and consommé soups together with the light cream and curry powder. Add sherry and crabmeat a few minutes before serving. Top with a tablespoon of whipped cream and chopped parsley. Serves 12.

Hazel Nixon
St. Peter's . . .
(1979)

BOUILLABAISSE

$1/2$ lb. boiled shrimp
1 boiled lobster, or 1 large can lobster meat
$1/2$ lb. mushrooms, sliced
1 doz. clams—frozen O.K. (optional)
2 doz. fresh oysters
$3/4$ cup sliced onions
2 cloves garlic, minced
$1/2$ cup olive oil
$3/4$ cup cooked strained tomatoes
$1/2$ cup dry white wine
2-3 lbs. fish fillets (sole, perch, flounder) each fillet cut
    into 2 or 3 pieces
4 cups fish stock (water in which shrimp and lobster
    were cooked)
1 bay leaf
4 peppercorns
2 cloves
1 small slice lemon rind
1 tsp. salt
$1/2$ tsp. paprika

Sauté onion and garlic in olive oil until soft. Add tomatoes, fish stock, bay leaf, peppercorns, cloves, lemon rind, salt and paprika. Simmer for $1/2$ hour in covered pan. Add fish and mushrooms. Simmer for 10 minutes. Add shellfish and simmer for 5 minutes. Add wine. May be served in 2 dishes—soup in one, fish in other—or in one tureen, with 2 Tbsps. chopped parsley over top. Serves 8.

Mrs. Alaric C. Bailey
Wonderful Cooking . . .
(Date unknown)

From the Athenaeum Hotel, a landmark owned by Chautauqua Institution.

CREAM OF CHICKEN SOUP - LORRAINE

1 Tbsp. butter
2 Tbsps. chopped onion
2 Tbsps. chopped green pepper
2 Tbsps. chopped celery
1 quart chicken stock
1 Tbsp. chicken base
2 Tbsps. flour
1 Tbsp. cornstarch
4 oz. water
$1^1/_2$ cups diced chicken
4 oz. evaporated milk

Sauté onion, green pepper and celery in butter until soft but not brown. Add chicken stock combined with chicken base. Bring to a slow boil for 30 minutes. Make a smooth paste of cornstarch and flour in 4 ounces of water, add to chicken stock. Simmer for 5 minutes, remove from heat, add diced chicken and evaporated milk. DO NOT BOIL but let chicken get warm in hot mixture and serve. Makes 6 portions.

Athenaeum Hotel
Chautauqua Celebrity . . .
(1980)

CARROT-BROCCOLI SOUP

2 Tbsps. minced onion
3 Tbsps. butter or margarine
3 Tbsps. flour
3 cups milk
3 cups chicken broth
1 package broccoli (frozen), chopped and slightly
  thawed
2 cups thinly sliced carrots
salt and pepper to taste

In large saucepan, sauté onion in butter until tender. With whisk stir in flour and 1-1/2 teaspoons salt, gradually add milk, stirring constantly, and bring to boil. Add broth, broccoli and carrots. Cook over low heat (do not boil), stirring occasionally, about 25 minutes or until tender and flavors blended. Add salt and pepper to taste. Serve hot. Makes 2 quarts.

Family Favorites
(1989-90)

CREAM OF CAULIFLOWER WITH SAVORY

1 Tbsp. butter
$1/2$ med. onion, coarsely chopped
1 small leek, or scallion, coarsely chopped
1 stalk celery, coarsely chopped
1 Tbsp. flour
4 cups stock: chicken or beef
1 head fresh cauliflower, trimmed and cored
  (about 1 lb.)
$1/2$ tsp. salt (can be omitted)
$1/4$ tsp. pepper
1 cup light cream (or evaporated milk)
1 Tbsp. parsley or chives finely chopped
$1/2$ tsp. savory

Melt the butter in a large saucepan and sauté the chopped onions, leek and celery for about 5 minutes. Sprinkle the flour over the vegetables and mix. Add the stock, bring to a boil, lower the heat, and simmer uncovered for 15 minutes. Trim the head of cauliflower and break or cut the florets into small pieces and add to the soup, cover and simmer for another 15 minutes. Pour the mixture into a blender and puree until smooth (you will probably have 2 blender loads). Strain through a fine sieve, into a clean saucepan. Add the cream and reheat but do not boil. Garnish with chopped parsley or chives. Garnish with grated cheese. Serves 4 to 6

Connie Francis
Cooking by Degrees
(1985)

BEST BOSTON CLAM CHOWDER

2 (10 oz.) cans whole baby clams
2 cups diced raw potatoes (do not have to peel)
2 Tbsps. chopped onions
2 Tbsps. chopped red peppers
2 Tbsps. flour
$1/2$ tsp. Old Bay seasoning
$1/2$ cup carrots, diced
$1/3$ cup diced celery
3 cups chicken broth
4 tsps. butter
$1/2$ cup cream
pepper to taste

Drain clams, reserve liquid. Boil carrots, potatoes and celery in enough of the chicken broth to cook properly in microwave or on stove top. Sauté clams, onion, peppers in butter. Blend in flour. Add broth and vegetables gradually. Stir constantly to keep smooth. Add the clam broth, cream and seasonings. Reheat to just boiling. Makes about 8 cups. This recipe may be halved successfully.

Jeannette Winner
Home Made . . .
(1989)

CORN CHOWDER

(In a slow cooker)
4 slices raw bacon, diced
1 large onion, coarsely diced
   (can be fried first with bacon)
3 cups peeled and diced potatoes
3 cups water
3 Tbsps. margarine
2 cups milk mixed with $1/4$ cup flour
2 cups diced ham or weiners
2 (12 oz.) cans whole kernel corn, undrained
2 tsps. salt
$1/2$ tsp. pepper
2 Tbsps. dried parsley flakes

Dump everything into cooker, and let cook all day or at least several hours.

Evelyn A. Button
Women's Committee
County Fair
(1979)

George and his wife, Ellie, discovered this soup at a friend's home in London, England.

CREAM OF CELERY AND WALNUT SOUP

1 head celery
1 medium onion
1 oz. butter (1/4 stick)
2 pints chicken stock
celery salt
freshly ground black pepper
2 oz. shelled walnuts
1/2 to 1 cup heavy cream

Remove and reserve some of the celery leaves for garnish. Roughly chop the celery. Peel and chop the onion. Melt 1 Tablespoon butter in a saucepan, add the celery and onion and cook over a low heat, stirring every now and then, until the onion is soft and transparent. Add the stock, bring to the boil, season with salt and pepper and simmer for about 30 minutes until the celery is soft. Puree the soup through a fine sieve, a food mill, blender or food processor.

Mince or very finely chop the walnuts. Heat the remaining butter in a clean pan. Add the walnuts and cook over a medium heat for three minutes; stirring, add the pureed soup, check seasoning and heat through. Stir in the cream and serve with a garnish of finely-chopped celery leaves.

George Shearing
Chautauqua Celebrity . . .
(1980)

CHILLED CUCUMBER SOUP

2 cups chicken stock
3 cucumbers, peeled, seeded, sliced
1 Tbsp. chopped onion
1 tsp. snipped fresh dill, or 1/2 tsp. dried
salt and pepper, to taste
2 cups plain yogurt
1/2 cup finely chopped walnuts
thin slices unpeeled cucumbers, for garnish
snipped fresh dill, for garnish

In a 4 quart saucepan combine stock, cucumbers and onion. Bring to a boil; reduce heat and simmer until cucumbers are just tender, about 5 to 7 minutes. Cool. In a food processor or blender, puree soup, dill, salt and pepper until smooth (in batches if necessary). Add yogurt and walnuts. Chill and adjust seasonings. Serve cold with garnish. Serves 8.

Carole Sellstrom
Crèche Cooks
(1986)

SWEDISH FRUIT SOUP
"Equally good as a first course or dessert"
Set out a large sauce pan having a tight fitting cover. Put in:
1 cup (about 6 oz.) dried apricots
1/2 cup (about 3 oz.) dried peaches (optional)
Cherries and/or dried pears may be added
3/4 cup (about 3 oz.) dried apples
1/2 cup (about 3 1/2 oz.) prunes, pitted
1/2 cup (about 2 1/2 oz.) dark seedless raisins
Cover and soak fruits briefly in 2 quarts water, if desired.
Add:
1/4 cup sugar
1 (3 inch) stick of cinnamon
1 tsp. grated orange peel
3 Tbsps. quick-cooking tapioca
1 cup red raspberry fruit syrup

Bring mixture to boiling; reduce heat; cover and simmer about 20 min. or until fruit is tender. Do not overcook. Remove from heat and stir in red raspberry fruit syrup. Chill soup in refrigerator. Serve with whipped cream (or Cool Whip), slivered blanched almonds, as desired. Serves 12+. Can be frozen.

Florence L. Erickson
Cooking by Degrees
(1985)

PLUM SOUP
1 lb. ripe plums, pitted
3 cups water
juice of 1 lemon
3 whole cloves
1/2 cup dry red wine
1/3 cup honey
2/3 Tbsp. almond liqueur
1 cup sour cream
1/2 cup halved pitted cherries

Boil plums in the water, with the lemon juice and cloves until the plums are tender. Remove the cloves and puree the plum mixture in a blender. Add the wine and honey and refrigerate. Just before serving, add the liqueur and sour cream and cherries.

Carol Adams
First United . . .
Dunkirk
(1978)

GAZPACHO ANDALUZ
(Cold Andalusian Vegetable Soup)
4 large, very ripe tomatoes
1 large green sweet pepper
1 cucumber
$1/2$ cup fine bread crumbs
$1/4$ tsp. cumin
2 cups chicken broth
$1/2$ cup olive oil
$1/4$ cup red wine vinegar
1 tsp. salt
freshly ground black pepper
3 or more cloves of garlic
Garnish: 1 small pepper, chopped
Cucumber, chopped
1 medium tomato, chopped
onion, chopped

Cut tomatoes into wedges and blend a few seconds in a blender. Add cut up cucumber, pepper and bread crumbs, blending a few seconds after each addition so that the ingredients are coarsely chopped. Place crushed garlic, cumin, chicken broth, olive oil, vinegar and salt and pepper to taste in a separate bowl and whisk thoroughly. Combine with vegetable mixture and stir. Chill at least 3 to 4 hours before serving. Top each individual serving with croutons and pass small dishes of garnish. Serves 8-10.

Danny Duff
Favorite Recipes from
Our Best Cooks
(1978)

LIFESAVER SOUP
$1^1/_2$ cups tomato juice
2 beef bouillon cubes
1 medium head cabbage, chopped
3-4 stalks celery, chopped
1 tsp. horseradish (opt.)
1 tsp. Worcestershire sauce
1 pint stewed tomatoes
salt and pepper to taste
2 cups water
1 cup mushrooms and juice

In large kettle, cook all ingredients until cabbage and celery are tender. (Very low calorie.)

Debbie Simpson
Westfield Jayncees . . .
(1983)

A Southern family recipe which has been passed down from one generation to the next . . .

GUMBO

1 2-lb. shank bone (beef)
1$\frac{1}{2}$ - 2 lbs. okra, stem and tip removed
2 stalks celery (cut very fine)
2 large onions, chopped fine
3 buds garlic, chopped
2 Tbsps. parsley, chopped
2 bay leaves
$\frac{1}{4}$ tsp. thyme
1 large can tomatoes
1 can tomato sauce
$\frac{1}{2}$ - $\frac{3}{4}$ lb. raw shrimp
1 can crab meat and juice
1 jar oysters and juice
salt and pepper

Simmer bone in six quarts of salted water (1 Tbsp. salt) for two hours or until meat is tender. While this is simmering prepare vegetables. Lift out bone and add the cans of tomato; let this simmer while frying okra and onions in separate pans in bacon fat or butter until golden brown, add to soup. Put in chopped garlic, vegetables, meat and herbs and seasoning, and cook about 1/2 hour. Clean backs of shrimp and put in raw. Simmer 15-20 minutes until tender. Add crab just long enough to heat. Oysters with juice can be added for a minute or two until edges curl. Season to taste with salt and pepper. Serve, passing a bowl of rice, if desired. Serves 12.

Robert N. Bellah
Chautauqua Celebrity . . .
(1980)

SPRING SOUP

3 leeks, washed & chopped
3 Tbsps. butter or margarine
2 medium sized potatoes, peeled and quartered
$\frac{1}{4}$ cup uncooked rice
12 stalks asparagus
1 onion, chopped
1 carrot, sliced
pinch of salt
2 quarts water
1 lb. fresh spinach
$\frac{1}{2}$ cup cream

Melt butter in large pan. Cook leeks and onions in butter until golden. Add potatoes, carrot, salt and water. Simmer for 15 minutes and add rice, asparagus (tender parts only) cut into pieces, and spinach, washed and coarsely chopped. Cook 10 to 15 minutes longer. Add salt and pepper to taste and add cream. Heat gently until ready to serve. Makes 6 servings.

Shari Vance
Chautauqua-Allegheny Cookbook
(1990)

MINESTRONE WITH PESTO SAUCE

1 cup dried white beans (Great Northern)
2 (10³/₄ oz.) cans condensed chicken broth
1 small head cabbage
4 carrots
1 can Italian-style tomatoes
2 medium onions
¹/₄ cup olive oil
1 stalk celery
2 zucchini
1 large fresh tomato
1 clove garlic
¹/₄ tsp. pepper
¹/₄ cup chopped parsley
1 cup broken thin spaghetti

PESTO SAUCE:
¹/₄ cup butter, softened
¹/₄ cup Parmesan cheese
¹/₂ cup finely chopped parsley
1 clove garlic, crushed
1 tsp. dried basil leaves
¹/₂ tsp. marjoram leaves
¹/₄ cup olive oil
¹/₄ cup chopped pine nuts or walnuts

Cover beans with cold water overnight; drain. Add water to broth to make 1 quart. Pour in 8-quart kettle with 2 more quarts water and beans. Bring to boil, then simmer 1 hour. Slice cabbage and carrots. Add to soup with canned tomatoes; cook ¹/₂ hour longer. Sauté onions, zucchini (cubed), tomato and celery (sliced) in olive oil slowly, about 20 minutes. Add to bean mixture with parsley and spaghetti. Cook slow 30 minutes.

Blend butter with cheese, parsley, garlic, basil and marjoram. Gradually add oil, beating constantly. Add nuts. Serve hot soup topped with spoonful of Pesto Sauce.

Mary Jane Begert
Soup and Salad
(1989)

To remove floating fat from the surface of hot soup stock, use clean white blotting paper.
Cool soup or meat soup stock uncovered, otherwise it may sour.
TIP *To add a rich color and flavor to meat soups, always melt a teaspoon of granulated sugar until browned in the soup kettle, before putting in the meat.*

What's Cooking I (1954)

BEEF AND BARLEY VEGETABLE SOUP

1 can (1 lb. 12 oz.) tomatoes
1 1/2 - 2 lbs. boneless chuck, cut into 1 1/2" pieces
1 1/2 Tbsps. salt
1/2 tsp. pepper
celery tops from 1 bunch
1/2 cup regular barley
1 can tomato juice
1 (10 oz.) package frozen cut green beans
1 cup chopped peeled rutabaga
3 cups coarsely chopped cabbage
1 cup sliced carrots
1 cup sliced celery
1 cup thinly sliced onion

Drain tomatoes, reserving juice. Add enough water to juice to make 2 quarts. Place liquid, meat, salt, pepper, and celery tops in a large kettle. Cover and cook slowly for at least 1 hour.

Add barley and cook 1 hour longer. Remove celery tops, discard. Add tomato juice, tomatoes, beans, rutabaga, cabbage, carrots, celery, and onion. Bring to a boil; reduce heat and cook about 45 minutes. Makes 5 quarts.

This soup can be frozen in containers according to the size you require and reheated as needed.

Reuel and Valeta Howe
Chautauqua Celebrity . . .
(1980)

MUSHROOM BISQUE

1 lb. fresh mushrooms
1 qt. chicken broth
1 medium onion, chopped
6 Tbsps. butter
6 Tbsps. flour
3 cups milk
1 cup heavy cream
white pepper
tabasco sauce
2 Tbsps. sherry

Chop mushrooms and stems very fine. Simmer, covered, in broth with chopped onion, 30 minutes. Melt butter in saucepan. Add flour and stir with whisk until blended. Meanwhile, bring milk to a boil and add all at once to flour mixture, stirring vigorously until sauce is thick and smooth. Add cream. Combine mushroom-broth mixture with sauce and season to taste. Can freeze. Yield: 2 quarts

James Kulwicki
Warm Your Heart . . .
(1987)

WASHINGTON CHOWDER

4 oz. salt pork
$1/4$ lb. onions (medium dice)
3 oz. flour
oil
1 quart chicken stock
2 lbs. potatoes ($1/4$ inch dice)
$1 1/4$ lbs. frozen whole kernel corn
6 oz. celery (medium dice)
$1 1/2$ oz. diced green peppers
21 oz. canned tomatoes, chopped
$3/4$ Tbsp. baking soda
$1/2$ Tbsp. sugar
$1/2$ Tbsp. salt
$1/4$ tsp. white pepper
pinch of cayenne pepper
pinch of thyme
pinch of basil
$2 1/2$ quarts milk

Fry diced salt pork in soup pot until partially rendered. Add onions and finish cooking salt pork, browning onions lightly. Add flour to make roux. Add as much oil as necessary for proper consistency. Cook 3-4 minutes. Add stock gradually, blending roux well. Stir until smooth and bring to a boil. Add potatoes, corn and celery; simmer until potatoes are nearly tender. Add green peppers and cook until tender. Add tomatoes and baking soda. Add seasonings and simmer 5 minutes. Remove from heat. Heat milk and add to soup. Let flavors blend before serving. Makes 25 portions. (Recipe from Culinary Institute of America.)

Hazel Nixon
St. Peter's . . .
(1979)

FRENCH ONION SOUP

1 lb. onions
3 Tbsps. butter
2 ($10 1/2$ oz.) cans beef consommé
1 ($10 1/2$ oz.) can chicken broth
1 ($10 1/2$ oz.) can cold water
1 Tbsp. salt
1 Tbsp. Ac´cent
1 Tbsp. Worcestershire sauce

Slice onions very thin and brown well in butter. Add broth, consommé, water, salt, pepper, if desired, Ac´cent and Worcestershire. Simmer until onions are tender. Pour into earthen jar or casserole. Arrange toasted croutons on top, sprinkle with grated Parmesan cheese and place under broiler until cheese melts and browns. Casserole or toast may be rubbed with a cut clove of garlic. Makes 2 quarts.

Cease Commissary
Recipe Roundup
(1954)

SWEDISH PEA SOUP
(Arter med flask)

2 cups yellow dry peas
6 cups water
1 lb. fresh side pork
2 tsps. salt
1 tsp. ginger

Rinse peas and soak overnight. Put in cold water, let come to a boil slowly, cooking vigorously until skins come off. Skim the skins off as they come to the surface. Add pork cut in pieces, after the peas have been boiled 1 hour.

Simmer 2 hours longer. Add ginger just before serving.

Edith Stohlbrost
From Allen Park . . .
(1960s)

SPLIT PEA AND SPINACH SOUP

2 cups chopped onions
2 Tbsps. oil
1 pound yellow or green split peas, picked over and rinsed (2 cups)
2 quarts water
2 bay leaves, crumbled
1 tsp. basil
1 (10 oz.) package frozen chopped spinach
2 tsps. salt
$1/2$ tsp. pepper
$1/8$ tsp. ground cloves
$1/4$ cup grated Parmesan cheese

In Dutch oven or kettle, sauté onions in oil until tender. Add peas, water, bay leaves and basil. Cover and simmer about one hour or until peas are tender. Add spinach, cover and simmer, stirring occasionally, about eight minutes longer or until done. Season with salt, pepper and cloves. Serve sprinkled with Parmesan cheese. Very good with pumpernickel bread.

Mrs. Dorothy Harte
Post-Journal Cookbook
(1986)

A. Johnson's store, Second Street, Jamestown, ca. 1914.

TOMATO CHOWDER

5 Tbsps. finely minced salt pork
1 clove garlic, minced very fine
3 medium sized onions, sliced very thin
1 green pepper, sliced thin
1 cup small cubes of raw potato
1 cup leeks, thinly sliced
enough cold water to cover generously
1 large bay leaf
6 or 7 sprigs parsley
1 sprig thyme
2 whole cloves
3 cups fresh, raw tomatoes, peeled, seeded,
   and cut into small pieces
salt to taste
dash of cayenne pepper
2$^1/_2$ cups scalded milk
2$^1/_2$ cups scalded thin cream (or evaporated milk or
   whole milk)
1 Tbsp. flour
minced parsley
frankfurter slices, if desired

Fry salt pork and garlic in soup kettle until garlic is fragrant. Add onions and green pepper and cook for 4 or 5 minutes, stirring constantly. Add potatoes, leeks, and water to cover. Bring to a boil, then add bay leaf, parsley sprigs, thyme, cloves, tomatoes, salt and cayenne pepper.

Lower the flame and allow to simmer gently until the potatoes are tender. Moisten 1/4 tsp. baking soda with few drops of cold water and add to the soup. Continue simmering for about 20 minutes longer (the water should be almost evaporated).

Bring milk and cream to a boil in a separate pan and thicken with the 1 Tbsp. flour. Pour milk mixture into tomato-potato mixture, stirring constantly and heat if necessary to serving temperature, but do not allow to boil again. Serve in soup bowls, garnishing the top with minced parsley and a few frankfurter slices, if desired.

Mrs. William Welch
American Legion . . .
(1945)

To add zest to various soups . . .

. . . a slice of lemon in black bean soup will sharpen the flavor as well as enhance the looks of the cup of soup.

. . . rub the bottom of the soup cup with a sliced whole garlic to accent the flavor of navy bean soup.

. . . add sliced pimientos (without the liquid) to asparagus soup just before removing from fire to serve. Do not cook pimientos in soup for this will destroy the asparagus flavor.   *What's Cooking III (1965)*

TURKEY CARCASS SOUP

1 turkey carcass
4 quarts water
6 small potatoes, diced
4 large carrots, diced
2 stalks celery, diced
1 large onion, chopped
1½ cups shredded cabbage
1 (7½ oz.) can tomatoes, drained and chopped
½ cup uncooked barley
1 Tbsp. Worcestershire
1½ tsps. salt
1 tsp. dried parsley flakes
1 tsp. dried basil
1 bay leaf
¼ tsp. pepper
¼ tsp. paprika
¼ tsp. poultry seasoning
pinch of dried thyme

Place turkey carcass and water in large Dutch oven; bring to a boil. Cover, reduce heat and simmer 2 hours. Remove carcass from broth, and remove meat from bones. Return meat to broth and add remaining ingredients. Simmer 1 hour or until vegetables are tender. Remove bay leaf. Makes 5 quarts.

Sharon Golm
Soup and Salad
(1989)

ZUCCHINI SOUP

3 young zucchini, sliced
1 green pepper, chopped
3 medium onions, chopped
2 cloves garlic
6 cups chicken broth
3 Tbsps. butter
salt and white pepper
dash of thyme
dash of basil
1 cup heavy cream

Sauté sliced zucchini, onions and peppers in butter. Add garlic, salt, pepper, thyme and basil. Stir in broth. Simmer, uncovered, for 15 minutes. Cool broth slightly. Puree in blender. Stir in cream. Chill well.

Barbara Roberts
*Favorite Recipes from
    Our Best Cooks*
(1978)

BREAD

In Kate Cook's time, and for a long time after, breadmaking was a way of life. Every cook expected to make some sort of bread — biscuits, gems (muffins), pancakes, loaves — almost on a daily basis. There were bakeries, of course, in the larger communities; but the opportunity to get to them was not always available. Bread being the staff of life, then as now, it had to be baked.

It was harder in Kate's time, moreover, because, among other things, they probably made their own yeast, which was perhaps not always reliable. Very much different from our easy days now, with several kinds of excellent yeast readily available, with our bread machines, and with our convenience bakeries close at hand. But good cooks still love to make bread. It is one of the most satisfying activities in life.

Because of the difficulty of choosing among all the recipes in the cookbooks we consulted, we left out completely rules for making white bread, wheat breads, and other commonplace loaves on the grounds that such recipes can be found everywhere. But we left in a great variety. There is a sampling of "heirloom" breads such as graham bread and graham gems, both of which appeared in nearly every cookbook from the first half of our hundred years, and even in several from the 1980s; and also good recipes for oatmeal bread and a multi-grain "Colonial" bread. There is a considerable range of fruit and nut breads — those much-loved little loaves which are so easy to make and so welcome with coffee or tea, for breakfast and for snacks. And, with a bow to Chautauqua County's ethnic populations, there are international specialties, such as Swedish Limpa Rye Bread, Danish, German, Polish and Swedish coffeecakes, and more.

The chapter begins with a page from Kate Cook's *Chautauqua Cook Book*, to illustrate her style. Then go on and bake through the rest — definitely an attractive bread sampler.

RUSK

Stir one pint of lukewarm milk, after being boiled, and one-half cup yeast, into flour enough to make it like bread sponge. Set in a warm place and let rise until light; beat three eggs a little, add two-thirds cup sugar, one-half cup of lard and butter; beat thoroughly together; add this to the sponge; work enough flour with it to make it the same as biscuit dough; then put back in pan and let rise again. When light, shape into rusks, put in biscuit pans, let rise until light and bake twenty minutes. This sponge should be set in the morning; work up stiff and set to rise again two hours before tea. On taking from the oven, varnish them with a glazing made of two tablespoons of milk and a teaspoon of sugar. Brush over the top of the rusk, lightly, and place in the oven a few minutes to dry. Rusk should be baked a dark brown.

CURRANT BUNS

Break one egg into a cup and fill with sweet milk; mix with it one-fourth cup yeast, half cup butter, three-fourths cup sugar, enough flour to make a soft dough; flavor with nutmeg. Let rise till very light, then mold into biscuits with a few currants. Let rise a second time in pan; bake, and when nearly done, glaze with a little molasses and milk. Use the same cup, no matter about the size, for each measure.

WHEAT FLOUR GEMS

Two cups buttermilk, one tablespoon butter, one teaspoon soda, one-half teaspoon salt, one teaspoon sugar. Stir into this enough flour to make a batter that will drop from a spoon, dissolve soda in a teaspoon of warm water and add to milk before stirring in flour; add the melted butter last; set gemirons on a hot stove and let them get smoking hot; grease well, fill nearly full of batter and bake in a hot oven fifteen minutes.

BUTTERMILK GEMS

Two cups rich buttermilk, two tablespoons molasses, one teaspoon soda dissolved in a teaspoon of warm water and added to the milk, one-half teaspoon salt; stir in enough Graham flour to make a batter that will drop off the spoon nicely; have gem-irons very hot, grease well, put in the batter and bake in a hot oven; bake until a nice brown, be sure and do not make any of these too thick.

Kate Cook
Chautauqua Cook Book
(1882)

APPLE CREAM COFFEE CAKE

$^1/_2$ cup chopped walnuts
2 tsps. cinnamon
$1^1/_2$ cups granulated sugar
$^1/_2$ cup butter or margarine
2 eggs, beaten
1 tsp. vanilla
2 cups sifted all purpose flour
1 tsp. double acting baking powder
1 tsp. baking soda
$^1/_2$ tsp. salt
1 cup sour cream
1-2 apples

Mix walnuts, cinnamon and $^1/_2$ cup sugar. Heat oven to 375°. Beat butter (margarine) until creamy. Add 1 cup sugar gradually and beat until light and fluffy. Add eggs, then vanilla, beat until blended. Sift flour and other dry ingredients. Beat mixture into batter with sour cream. Spread $^1/_2$ of batter into well-greased 9-inch tube pan with removable bottom. Top with thinly sliced apples, sprinkle with half of walnut mixture. Add remaining batter, apples and walnut mixture. Bake 40 minutes or until cake tester (toothpick) comes out clean.

Remove from oven and let stand in pan 30 minutes. Loosen cake, lift tube and let cool completely on wire rack.

Regina Goodrich
First United . . .
(1978)

BUNDT KUCHEN - GERMAN COFFEE CAKE

$1^1/_2$ cups milk, scalded
2 cups flour, sifted
2 yeast cakes
1 Tbsp. sugar
$^3/_4$ cup sugar
3 eggs, well-beaten
1 tsp. mace and 1 tsp. lemon extract
$^1/_2$ cup butter, creamed until fluffy
$1^1/_2$ cups sifted flour
$^1/_2$ tsp. salt
$^1/_2$ cup seedless raisins

Scald milk and cool to lukewarm. Dissolve yeast and 1 Tbsp. sugar in warm milk. Add 2 cups flour; beat until smooth. Set in warm place to rise until light. Meanwhile, cream butter, adding sugar gradually. Add well-beaten eggs, and the rest of the ingredients. Put mixture in greased tube pan. The pan should be large enough so it is half filled. Cover and set in warm place to rise until double in bulk. Bake in moderate oven, 350°, for 45 minutes. When done, remove from pan by inverting pan on bread board. Dust Kuchen with Confectioners' sugar.

Mrs. Elizabeth Durk
What's Cooking VII . . .
Mayville
(Date unknown)

DANISH PUFF COFFEE CAKE

FIRST LAYER:
$1/2$ stick butter or margarine
2 Tbsps. water
1 cup flour

Blend softened butter with flour. Add water and mix to form ball. Divide into two parts. Spread on ungreased cookie sheet forming 2 rectangles (5" x 12").

SECOND LAYER:
$1/2$ cup butter or margarine
2 tsps. almond extract
3 eggs
1 cup water
1 cup flour

Bring butter and water to rolling boil and remove from heat. Quickly add flour and extract, mixing well. Blend in one egg at a time. Dough will become elastic. Spread evenly over each first layer rectangle. Bake 55-60 minutes at 350°. Ice with confectionery glaze and sprinkle with slivered almonds.

GLAZE:
$1^1/_2$ cups powdered sugar
2 Tbsps. margarine
$1^1/_2$ tsps. vanilla
1-2 Tbsps. warm water

Mix all ingredients until smooth
Douglas Swanson,
JCC Alumni...
(Date unknown)

GRAPENUT BREAD

$1/2$ cup grapenuts
1 cup sour or sweet milk
$3/_8$ cup sugar
$1/4$ cup melted shortening
1 egg, well-beaten
$1/2$ tsp. soda
2 tsps. baking powder
2 cups flour
$1/2$ tsp. salt

Combine grapenuts and milk. Let stand half hour. Add sugar, shortening and egg. Sift flour, measure and sift with salt, baking powder and soda. Add to first mixture and mix thoroughly. Pour into well-greased loaf pan. Bake in slow oven (325°) 10 minutes and continue in moderate oven (350°) about one hour
Mary L. Blystone
Victory Cook Book
(1940s)

GOSHUT KIPPSEL

1/2 lb. butter
5 eggs, separated
1 cup sugar
1 1/2 rounded cups flour
1 tsp. baking powder
rind of 1 lemon
1/2 cup sugar
1/2 cup chopped nuts
1/2 tsp. cinnamon

Cream 1/2 lb. butter. Add egg yolks one at a time. Beat well. Add 1 cup sugar. Beat well. Add flour, sifted with baking powder. Add rind of one lemon, grated. Stir in.

Beat 5 egg whites until stiff. Fold into butter mixture. Put into 8" x 12" well-greased pan. Before you bake it, mix 1/2 cup chopped nuts, 1/2 cup sugar and 1/2 tsp. cinnamon in bowl. Put this on top of unbaked mixture. Bake 35 minutes at 350°.

Theresa Janisch
Cooking Favorites
Dunkirk
(1960s)

PLACEK

2 sticks plus 1 Tbsp. margarine, melted
1 cup scalded milk
1/2 cup water (105°-115°)
2 pkgs. yeast
1 cup plus 1 Tbsp. sugar
1 Tbsp. salt
5 eggs, beaten
1 Tbsp. vanilla
7 to 8 cups flour

CRUMB TOPPING:
1 stick soft margarine
1 1/2 cups flour
3/4 cup sugar

Combine scalded milk and margarine; let cool. Combine water, yeast and 1 Tbsp. sugar. This mixture will become very frothy after a few minutes. Put these 2 mixtures together in mixing bowl; add 1 cup sugar, salt, beaten eggs, vanilla and 3 cups of the flour. Mix with mixer until smooth. Add remaining flour and stir (dough very moist). Do not knead; just let rise in mixing bowl until doubled. Divide into 4 parts. Roll out into rectangles; sprinkle with cinnamon. Roll up and pinch ends together; place in well-greased bread pans. Sprinkle generously with crumb topping. Let rise. Bake at 350° F. for 25-30 minutes. Makes 4 loaves.

Connie Aikens
Our Country...
(Date unknown)

GRANDMA WASHBURN'S KRINGLE

2 cups flour
$1^1/_2$ Tbsps. sugar
$^1/_2$ tsp. salt
$^1/_2$ cup soft shortening - part margarine
$^1/_2$ cup milk, scalded
1 egg, separated
$^1/_4$ cup warm water
1 pkg. yeast

FILLING CHOICES:
$^1/_4$ cup butter
$^1/_2$ cup brown sugar
1 cup chopped pecans

$^1/_4$ cup butter
$^1/_2$ cup brown sugar
1 cup chopped apples

$^1/_2$ cup brown sugar
1 cup chopped dates, nuts

$1^1/_2$ cups chopped prunes
3 Tbsps. lemon juice
$^1/_2$ tsp. lemon peel
$^1/_4$ cup sugar

$^1/_4$ cup soft butter
$^1/_2$ cup brown sugar
$^1/_2$ cup almond paste

Cool milk; stir in egg yolk; add to first four ingredients. Soften yeast in warm water. Add. It will be very soft; cover; chill but not longer than 48 hours. Prepare fillings.

Divide dough in half; return one half to refrigerator. Beat egg white; grease baking sheets. Roll dough into 6"x18" rectangle; spread 3" center strip with beaten egg white, then filling. Fold over one side of dough, $1^1/_2$" lap to cover filling. Repeat with other half of dough.

Arrange on sheet. Let rise 30 to 45 minutes. Bake at 350 ° for 25 minutes. When cool, ice with 1 cup confectioners' sugar, $^1/_2$ Tbsp. milk and $^1/_2$ tsp. vanilla, mixed well.

Virginia Barden
Home Cooking . . .
Ripley
(Date unknown)

ORANGE-BUTTER COFFEE CAKE

1 pkg. dry active yeast
2 beaten eggs
1 cup sugar
$1/_2$ cup dairy sour cream
$1/_2$ cup butter or margarine, melted
1 tsp. salt
$2^3/_4 - 3^1/_4$ cup flour
1 cup flaked coconut
2 tsps. grated orange peel

GLAZE:
In saucepan, combine:
 $1/_2$ cup sugar
$1/_2$ cup dairy sour cream
$1/_4$ cup orange juice
$1/_4$ cup butter or margarine

In a bowl soften yeast in $1/_4$ cup warm water (110° to 115°). Stir in eggs, $1/_4$ cup sugar, the sour cream, 6 tablespoons butter or margarine and salt. Stir in $2^3/_4$ cups flour. On a floured surface, knead in enough flour to make a moderately soft dough that is smooth and elastic (3-5 minutes). Place in a greased bowl, turn once. Cover, let rise till double ($1^1/_2$ hours). Punch down. Turn onto floured surface; divide in half. Shape each half into a ball. Cover. Let rest 10 minutes. Roll each half into 12" circle. Brush each with 1 tablespoon remaining butter. Combine remaining sugar, $3/_4$ cup coconut and the orange peel. Sprinkle over circles. Cut each circle into 12 wedges. Roll up wedges starting at wide end. Arrange rolls, pinwheel fashion, in two greased 9" round pans. Cover. Let rise till double (30 minutes). Bake in a 350° oven for 25-30 minutes. Immediately remove from pans. Place on wire racks over waxed paper. Top with glaze and remaining $1/_4$ cup coconut. Makes 2 coffee cakes.

Stir over medium heat until sugar dissolves. Bring to boiling. Boil 3 minutes, stirring constantly.

Deborah Johnson
Favorite Recipes
Mayville
(1982)

To keep egg yolks which have been separated from the whites, drop in a small cup and cover with cold water.
To insure a white film over the yolk when frying eggs, add a few drops of water to the frying pan, and cover with a lid.
What's Cooking I (1954)

TIP

PINEAPPLE CREAM CHEESE COFFEE CAKE

DOUGH:
1 pkg. dry yeast
$1/4$ cup evaporated milk, warmed
1 Tbsp. sugar
1 cup margarine
$2^1/_2$ cups sifted flour
$1/4$ tsp. salt
4 egg yolks (slightly beaten)
1 egg white (slightly beaten)

FILLING:
1 lb. cream cheese
1 egg
1 cup sugar
1 tsp. vanilla
1 (8 oz.) can crushed pineapple (well drained)
chopped nuts

Dissolve yeast in milk and add sugar. Set aside. Mix together flour and margarine (like for pie crust). Add beaten egg yolks to yeast mixture and stir well. Combine flour mixture and yeast mixture. After mixing well, divide dough in half.

Roll each half to fit 9" x 13" x 3" baking pan. Line bottom of pan with one-half of dough. Whip filling ingredients until fluffy and pour into pan. Sprinkle with well drained crushed pineapple.

Cover with top crust. Spread egg white over top and garnish with nuts. Let stand at room temperature for 2 hours. Bake at 350° for 30 minutes.

Kitty Mistretta
Favorite Hometown...
(Date unknown)

TWIN MOUNTAIN BLUEBERRY COFFEE CAKE

2 cups enriched flour
1 cup sugar
3 tsps. baking powder
$1/4$ tsp. salt
$1/2$ cup shortening
2 eggs, beaten
1 cup milk
$1^1/_2$ cups cultivated blueberries
1 can ($1^1/_3$ cups) flaked coconut

Mix and sift flour, sugar, baking powder, and salt. Cut in shortening with pastry blender. Combine eggs and milk. Stir into dry ingredients. Fold in blueberries. Divide batter between 2 greased 9" layer cake pans. Sprinkle coconut evenly over tops. Bake at 375° for 25 minutes.

Jean Beale
Warm Your Heart...
(1987)

SNOW-FROSTED COFFEE CAKE

FIRST MIX:
1$\frac{1}{4}$ cups milk, scalded
$\frac{1}{4}$ cup shortening
$\frac{1}{4}$ cup sugar
1 tsp. salt
1 cake fresh or 1 pkg. granular yeast
1 egg
4 cups flour

SECOND MIX:
1 cake fresh or 1 pkg. granular yeast
3 Tbsps. milk, scalded
3 egg yolks
$\frac{1}{4}$ cup shortening, melted
1$\frac{1}{2}$ tsps. vanilla
$\frac{1}{2}$ cup finely chopped candied fruit

First Mix: Combine the milk, shortening, sugar, and salt in large mixing bowl. Cool to lukewarm. Soften yeast in this mixture. Stir in egg, then 2 cups flour; beat thoroughly. Stir in remaining flour. Turn out on lightly floured surface. Cover and let rest 10 minutes. Knead 8 to 10 minutes until dough is smooth and elastic. Place in greased bowl; cover with damp cloth. Let rise in warm place until double.

Second Mixing: Dissolve yeast in milk. Add egg yolks, cooled shortening, vanilla and fruit. Add mixture to 1st mixture when it has doubled. Beat vigorously until shiny, 10 min. in an electric mixer. Pat dough into well greased 10-inch Angel Food Cake pan. Cover with damp cloth. Let rise until double. Bake in a 375° oven, 25 to 30 minutes. Turn out of pan and cool. Sprinkle with sugar, through a sieve.

Art/Dunkirk
(1960s)

GRAHAM GEMS

1 cup graham flour
1 cup white flour
$\frac{3}{4}$ tsp. salt
4 tsps. baking powder
1 cup milk
1 egg
2 Tbsps. molasses or sugar
3 Tbsps. shortening

Mix together dry ingredients, add milk, beaten egg, molasses and melted shortening, and mix until just blended. Bake in greased gem pans* in hot oven (400°) about 25 minutes.
*small muffin pans

Eleanor Wise
Cooking Favorites . . .
Fredonia
(1960s)

APRICOT NUT BREAD

Wash $1^1/_2$ cups dried apricots, cut them up with scissors.
Boil in small amount of water for 5 minutes.
Cream together
2 Tbsps. butter
$^1/_2$ cup sugar
Add 1 beaten egg and
1 cup sour milk
Add $2^1/_2$ cups flour sifted
with 5 tsps. baking powder
$^1/_2$ tsp. salt
$^1/_8$ tsp. soda

Fold in apricots and $^1/_2$ cup chopped nuts. Bake in 2 loaf tins in moderate oven (350°) for 45 minutes.

Mrs. D. Neil Fleek
Come Out...
(Date unknown)

BLACK WALNUT BREAD

1 egg
1 cup brown sugar, firmly packed
$1^1/_2$ Tbsps. melted butter
2 cups sifted flour
$^1/_2$ tsp. soda
$^3/_4$ tsp. baking powder
$^1/_4$ tsp. salt
1 cup buttermilk
$^1/_2$ cup chopped black walnuts

Beat egg and brown sugar together. Add butter and blend. Sift together dry ingredients. Add to egg mixture alternately with the buttermilk, and stir until mixed. Add nuts. Pour into greased loaf pan and bake in 350° oven 1 hour.

Alice H. Salhoff
To the Town's Taste
(1964)

BONANZA BREAD

1 cup sifted all-purpose flour
1 cup whole wheat flour
$1/2$ tsp. salt
$1/2$ tsp. baking soda
2 tsps. baking powder
$1/2$ cup nonfat dry milk powder
$1/3$ cup wheat germ
$1/2$ cup firmly packed brown sugar
$1/4$ cup chopped walnuts
$1/2$ cup unsalted dry roasted peanuts, chopped
$1/2$ cup raisins
3 eggs
$1/2$ cup vegetable oil
$1/2$ cup molasses
$3/4$ cup orange juice
2 medium bananas, mashed (1 cup)
$1/3$ cup chopped dried apricots

Combine flour, salt, soda, baking powder, dry milk, wheat germ, sugar and nuts and raisins in a large bowl. Blend thoroughly with pastry blender or fork.

Whirl eggs in container of electric blender until foamy. Add oil, molasses, orange juice and bananas, whirling after each addition. Add apricots, whirl just to chop coarsely.

Pour mixture into bowl with dry ingredients, and just mix. Pour into two greased loaf pans.

Bake in a slow oven (325°) for 1 hour, or until center is firm when pressed lightly with fingertip. (Watch closely so it doesn't get too brown. It may take less than 1 hour.) Cool slightly in pan on a wire rack, then remove from pan and cool completely. When cool wrap tightly and store overnight to mellow flavors.

Can be baked in greased muffin cups at 350° for 20 minutes, or until muffins test done. One-half recipe makes 18 muffins.

Joanne L. Schweik
The Artful Kitchen
(1987)

CHEESE, DATE & NUT LOAF

$3/4$ cup boiling water
$1 1/4$ cups finely cut dates
2 Tbsps. butter
$1 3/4$ cups flour
1 tsp. soda
$1/4$ tsp. salt
$1/2$ cup sugar
1 egg, beaten
1 cup sharp grated cheddar cheese
1 cup chopped nuts

Grease 1 large loaf pan. Heat oven to 325° (300° for glass). Pour boiling water over dates and butter. Let stand 5 minutes. Sift dry ingredients into mixing bowl. Add date mixture, beaten egg, cheese and nuts. Mix until just blended. Spread in prepared pan. Let stand 20 minutes. Bake 50 to 60 minutes. Remove from pan when done and cool on wire rack.

Laura Crowell
Favorite Hometown...
(Date unknown)

CHOCOLATE DATE NUT BREAD

2 (1oz.) squares unsweetened chocolate
1 cup hot water
1 cup chopped dates
$1/_2$ cup chopped nuts
1 tsp. vanilla
2 cups sifted flour
$1/_4$ tsp. soda
$1/_4$ cup shortening
1 cup sugar
$1/_2$ tsp. salt
1 egg

Melt chocolate in water over low heat; add dates, nuts and soda; mix will. Cool. Cream shortening, sugar, salt, egg and vanilla. Add flour alternately with chocolate mixture to creamed mix. Beat well. Spoon into two (1 lb. 13 oz.) cans greased and floured. Bake at 350° for 65 minutes.

Betty Morse
Cooking Favorites
Arkwright
(1963)

FRUIT 'N OAT BREAD

$2^1/_2$ cups all purpose flour
$1^1/_2$ tsps. baking powder
1 tsp. cinnamon
1 tsp. salt
1 tsp. soda
$1/_2$ tsp. nutmeg
1 cup quick or old fashioned oats, uncooked
$3/_4$ cup firmly packed dark brown sugar
$1/_2$ cup chopped dates
$1/_2$ cup broken walnuts
1 cup applesauce
$1/_2$ cup milk
$1/_2$ cup vegetable oil
2 eggs

Combine flour, baking powder, cinnamon, salt, soda and nutmeg; stir in oats, sugar, dates and nuts. Add applesauce, milk, oil and eggs; mix just until dry ingredients are moistened. Pour batter into well-greased 9"x5" loaf pan. Bake in pre-heated oven, at 350° for 1 hour and 15 minutes or until wooden pick inserted in center comes out clean. Cool 10 minutes, and remove from pan. Slice when cool. Makes 1 loaf.

Lylla Berndt
Chautauqua- Allegheny Cookbook
(1990)

ORANGE NUT BREAD

2¹/₄ cups flour
2¹/₄ tsps. baking powder
¹/₄ tsp. soda
³/₄ tsp. salt
1 cup sugar
³/₄ cup chopped nuts
1 egg beaten
2 Tbsps. oil
³/₄ cup orange juice
1 Tbsp. grated orange rind

Sift together dry ingredients; add nuts. Combine egg, oil, orange juice and rind; pour into flour mixture. Stir only until smooth. Bake in loaf pan 60-65 minutes. If loaf is covered with aluminum foil for the first 20 minutes of baking it is less likely to crack on top

Hildegarde Ball
Cooking Favorites
Arkwright
(1963)

PINEAPPLE ZUCCHINI LOAF

3 eggs
2 cups sugar
1 cup oil
3 Tbsps. vanilla
2 cups peeled, grated and well-drained zucchini
3 cups all-purpose flour
1 tsp. baking powder
1 tsp. baking soda
1 tsp. salt
1 (8 oz.) can crushed pineapple, undrained
1 cup chopped pecans or walnuts
¹/₂ cup raisins (optional)

Preheat oven to 350°. Grease and flour 2 (9x5 inch) loaf pans.

Beat eggs until fluffy. Add sugar, oil and vanilla and blend well. Add zucchini. Sift together flour, baking powder, soda and salt and add to batter. Stir in pineapple, nuts and raisins and mix well. Turn into pans and bake until toothpick inserted in center comes out clean, about 1 hour. Cool on wire rack before removing from pans. Wrap and store overnight to develop flavors before slicing.

Mrs. Larry Serrone
First United...
(1978)

PEAR BREAD

3/4 cup brown sugar
1/2 cup shortening
2 eggs
1/3 cup peeled and mashed ripe pears
2 Tbsps. lemon juice
1 tsp. vanilla
2 cups flour
1 1/2 tsps. ginger
1 tsp. mace
1/2 tsp. cinnamon
1 tsp. soda
1 tsp. salt
2 cups coarsely chopped pears
1/2 cup chopped nuts
Sugar Topping

In large mixer bowl, combine brown sugar, shortening, eggs, 1/3 cup peeled and mashed pears, lemon juice and vanilla. Beat until smooth. Combine flour, ginger, mace, cinnamon, soda and salt and stir into creamed mixture. Gently fold in chopped pears and nuts. Pour into 2 greased and floured 8 1/2" x 4 1/2" x 2 1/2" loaf pans. Sprinkle with Sugar Topping. Bake in a 350° oven until tests done with wooden pick (about 60 minutes). Remove from pans. Cool. Store in refrigerator. Makes 2 loaves.

SUGAR TOPPING:
1/4 cup sugar
1 1/2 tsps. butter
Combine to make a crumbly mixture

Ange Fedor
Our Daily Bread
(1988)

PRUNE BREAD

1 cup sugar
2 Tbsps. melted butter
1 egg (well-beaten)
1 cup cooked prunes cut in pieces
1/2 cup prune juice
1 cup sour milk
1 tsp. soda
1 cup wheat flour or rye flour
2 cups flour
1/4 tsp. baking powder
1/2 tsp. salt

Cream butter and sugar. Add egg, prune juice, prunes and wheat or rye flour. Mix and sift dry ingredients and add alternately with sour milk to first mixture. Beat thoroughly and pour into buttered bread pan (large) or two small ones. Bake 60 to 70 minutes in moderate oven (350°).

Mary Kidder
Come Out...
(Date unknown)

RHUBARB BREAD

$1^1/_2$ cups brown sugar
$2/_3$ cup vegetable oil
1 egg
1 tsp. soda
1 cup buttermilk
$1/_2$ tsp. vanilla
1 tsp. salt
$1^1/_2$ cups raw rhubarb
$1/_2$ cup walnuts (optional)
$2^1/_2$ cups flour

TOPPING:
$1/_4$ cup sugar
1 Tbsp. butter or margarine

Combine sugar, oil and eggs and mix well. Dissolve soda in buttermilk and add to sugar mixture. Add vanilla and stir in. Stir flour and salt into batter. Fold in rhubarb and nuts. Pour into greased bread pan. Bake at 350° for 50 minutes. Test with toothpick. For topping, mix sugar with butter until crumbly and sprinkle over loaf while warm. Cool in pans for 10 minutes before removing. Makes 2 small loaves or 1 large loaf.

Barb Brown
Westfield Jaycees . . .
(1983)

GREEN TOMATO BREAD

8 - 10 medium green tomatoes
$2/_3$ cup seedless raisins
$2/_3$ cup boiling water
$1^1/_2$ cups sugar
$2/_3$ cup shortening
4 eggs
$3^1/_2$ cups flour
1 tsp. salt
1 tsp. cinnamon
1 tsp. cloves
$2/_3$ cup chopped pecans
2 tsps. soda
$1/_2$ tsp. baking powder

Core tomatoes, remove some seeds, run in blender until smooth (2 cups). Pour boiling water over raisins; let cool. Cream shortening and sugar. Add eggs, tomatoes, raisins and water. Beat. Combine dry ingredients. Add 1 cup at a time. Stir after each addition. Makes 2 regular size loaves. Bake 1 hour and 10 minutes at 350°. (Grease and flour pans.) Freezes well.

Debbie Simpson
Westfield Jaycees . . .
(1983)

CRISP BREAD WITH ROBUST BUTTERS
3 loaves Brown and Serve French Bread. Brush top of each loaf with a robust butter. Bake according to package directions. Slice bread and let guests select desired robust butter for spreading.

CHEESE-GARLIC BUTTER
Blend 1/2 cup (1 stick) softened butter
1/4 tsp. garlic powder
1/4 cup grated Parmesan Cheese
Yield: 1/2 cup

CHILI-OLIVE BUTTER
Blend 1/2 cup (1 stick) softened butter
1/4 tsp. chili powder
2 Tbsps. finely chopped ripe olives
Yield about 1/2 cup

CHIVY BUTTER
Blend 1/2 cup (1 stick) softened butter
1 Tbsp. minced chives
1/2 tsp. Worcestershire Sauce
Yield: 1/2 cup

Mrs. Barbara Wise
Home Bureau . . .
(1972)

OATMEAL BREAD
(Raised Yeast Bread with a satisfying nutlike flavor)
1 cup uncooked old-fashioned or quick-cooking oatmeal
1 cup milk, scalded
1/2 cup boiling water
1/3 cup shortening
1/2 cup brown sugar, firmly packed
1/2 cup lukewarm water
5 cups sifted all-purpose flour
2 tsps. salt
2 pkgs. dry yeast

Put oatmeal in large bowl, stir in milk and boiling water. Add shortening, sugar, salt. Let stand until lukewarm. Sprinkle yeast into lukewarm water, stir until dissolved. Stir into oatmeal mixture, add half the flour. Beat until smooth. Add remaining flour a little at a time and mix until dough comes away from the sides of the bowl. Turn out on a lightly floured board and knead about 7 min. until smooth and elastic. Place dough in a greased bowl. Turn once to bring greased side up. Cover with damp cloth and let rise in warm place until double in size, about 1 1/2 hour. Knead down, divide into two parts, shape each into a loaf. Place in greased bread pans, let rise again, about 45 min. Bake in hot oven 400° for 10 min. then reduce heat to 350°. Bake 40 minutes.

Mrs. Violetta Coons
Kiantone Cookbook (1969)

LINDA ERICKSON'S SWEDISH RYE BREAD (LIMPA)

3 cups Quaker Oats
1 pkg. yeast dissolved in 1/4 cup lukewarm water
1 tsp. sugar added to yeast and water
1 cup milk
2 cups all-purpose white flour
2 eggs
Rinds of 2 oranges, grated
Juice of one orange
$1/2$ cup molasses
$1/2$ cup brown sugar
3 Tbsps. bacon fat
7 (more) cups flour ($1/2$ rye, $1/2$ all-purpose)
Fennel seed (palm of hand full)
1 Tbsp. salt

Mix thoroughly the Quaker Oats, yeast and sugar mixture and cup of milk with 2 cups of flour. Let rise 2 hours.

Add and mix thoroughly eggs, orange rind and juice, salt, molasses, brown sugar, bacon fat and fennel seeds. Add rest of flour gradually.

Let rise again, 2 hours in a warm place (like a heating pad). Knead on a flat surface over light flouring. Form into loaves using margarine or butter on hands. Pat into buttered Pyrex dish or equivalent. Pierce with a fork. Cover with thin cloth or cheese cloth; let rise 1 hour plus (until double in bulk). Bake until brown (approximately 1 hour) at 425° for about 15 minutes, then at 300°.

Florence Erickson
First United . . .
(1978)

GRAHAM BREAD

1 cup white flour
2 cups graham flour
$1/2$ tsp. salt
$1/2$ cup sugar
$1/2$ cup dark molasses
2 cups buttermilk
2 tsps. soda
1 egg slightly beaten

Mix together in a bowl, buttermilk, molasses and egg. Place other ingredients in a separate bowl and mix together. Make a well in center of dry ingredients and add liquid. Mix together until moistened. Pour into greased 9" x 5" pan and bake at 325° for about 60 minutes.

Mary Ann McKinley Williamson
Matthews Knapp
Pioneer . . .
(1987)

Horse wagons ca. 1890, Clarke Bakery Co., 707 N. Main Street, Jamestown.

Jamestown Bread Co., 1921.

Sunrise Bread, Jamestown, ca. 1950.

COLONIAL BREAD

$^1/_2$ cup yellow corn meal
$^1/_3$ cup brown sugar
1 Tbsp. salt
2 cups boiling water
$^1/_4$ cup cooking oil
2 packages active dry yeast
$^1/_2$ cup lukewarm water
$^3/_4$ cup whole wheat flour
$^1/_2$ cup rye flour
$4^1/_4$ to $4^1/_2$ cups sifted unbleached white flour

Thoroughly combine corn meal, brown sugar, salt, boiling water and oil. Let stand about 30 minutes, until lukewarm. Soften yeast in lukewarm water. Stir into the cornmeal mixture. Add whole wheat and rye flour; mix well. Stir in enough white flour to make a moderately stiff dough. Turn out on lightly floured board and knead until smooth and elastic (8 to 10 minutes). Place in a greased bowl, turning once to grease surface. Cover and let rise in warm place until doubled in bulk. Punch down; turn out on lightly floured board and divide in half. Cover and let rest 10 minutes. Shape into loaves. Place into greased 9"x5"x3" bread pans. Let rise again until almost doubled. Bake in 375° oven for about 45 minutes. Remove from pans to cool. Delicious with sweet butter and honey. Makes 2 loaves.

Don Raupp
What's Cooking . . .
Lily Dale
(1980)

JANE HARTLEY'S BATH BUNS

1 cup milk, scalded
$^1/_4$ cup butter
1 tsp. salt
$^1/_2$ cup sugar
3 egg yolks, well-beaten
1 Tbsp. lemon extract
1 cake yeast
4 cups flour
$^1/_2$ cup raisins, scalded & drained

Scald milk. Add butter and salt and cool to lukewarm. Stir in 1 cup flour. Add yeast (softened in a little warm water). Add second cup flour, then raisins, eggs, sugar and lemon extract. Then add remainder of flour. Stir well. Let rise until doubled in bulk. Put on well-floured board and fold in about 6-12 times. Let rise 15 minutes. With a sharp knife cut off pieces the size of an egg and fold to make round ball. Let rise 15 minutes more. Dip in $^1/_3$ cup milk and 1 tsp. lemon extract and roll in granulated sugar. Place on greased cookie sheet. Let rise until double. Bake at 300° for 20 minutes or until light brown.

Violetta Coons
Kiantone Cookbook (1989)

"HILLBILLY" BREAD

(makes 2 loaves)
2 env. yeast
$1\frac{1}{2}$ cups boiling water
1 cup rolled oats (for smooth textured bread put oats through blender to make a fine meal, or leave as is for coarse textured bread)
1 cup cornmeal
$\frac{1}{2}$ cup molasses
2 Tbsps. honey
$\frac{1}{3}$ cup shortening
1 Tbsp. salt
$5\frac{1}{2}$ to $6\frac{1}{2}$ cups sifted unbleached flour
2 eggs, slightly beaten

Soften yeast in $\frac{1}{2}$ cup warm (not hot!) water. Meanwhile, combine the $1\frac{1}{2}$ cups boiling water, oats, cornmeal, molasses, honey, shortening, and salt. Cool to lukewarm. Stir in 2 cups of the flour.

Add eggs and beat by hand. Add softened yeast and beat. Add rest of flour, 2 cups at a time to make a moderately stiff dough. Knead on floured surface about 5 minutes. Place dough in greased bowl; turn once to grease surface. Cover with clean dish towel and let rise in a warm place until double. Punch down. Form into 2 balls and let sit 10 minutes. Form into 2 loaves and place in greased bread pans. Cover and let rise until double. Bake at 375° about 40 minutes. If you prefer a soft crust, brush tops of loaves with butter while still warm from the oven. This bread slices well and is great for sandwiches or toasted and spread with homemade jam!

Mary Lou Short
Our Favorite Recipes
Jamestown
(Date unknown)

BAKED FRENCH TOAST

$\frac{1}{4}$ cup butter
$\frac{1}{3}$ cup sugar
$\frac{1}{4}$ tsp. cinnamon
1 Tbsp. orange rind
4 eggs, slightly beaten
$\frac{2}{3}$ cup orange juice
bread slices

Melt butter in 10" x 15" pan. Mix sugar, cinnamon, rind; sprinkle over butter. Mix eggs, juice. Dip bread in egg mixture, soaking well. Arrange over butter mixture in pan. Bake at 400° for 30 minutes.

Esther Barden
Cookbook
Westfield
(1986)

WHITE CLOUD BISCUITS

2 cups sifted flour
1 Tbsp. sugar
4 tsps. baking powder
$^1/_2$ tsp. salt
1/2 cup shortening
1 egg, beaten
$^2/_3$ cup milk

Cut shortening into flour and add other dry ingredients. Combine egg and milk, add to dry ingredients and mix just until dough holds together. Turn onto floured board. Knead gently 20 strokes with heel of hand. Roll dough and cut with biscuit cutter or glass rim. Bake on ungreased tin, at 450° for 10 to 14 minutes.

Helen Berndt
Stella Kazmierczak
Jane Wagner
Chautauqua Allegheny Cookbook
(1990)

GARLIC CHEESE BISCUITS

2 cups flour
4 tsps. baking powder
3 tsps. garlic powder, divided
$^1/_2$ tsp. baking soda
1 tsp. chicken bouillon granules, divided
$^1/_2$ cup butter-flavored shortening
$^3/_4$ cup shredded cheddar cheese
1 cup buttermilk
3 Tbsps. butter or margarine, melted

In a bowl, combine flour, baking powder, 2 tsps. garlic powder, baking soda and $^1/_2$ tsp. bouillon. Cut in shortening until mixture resembles coarse crumbs. Add cheese. Stir in buttermilk, just until moistened. Drop by heaping tablespoonsful onto a greased baking sheet. Bake at 450° for 10 minutes. Combine butter and remaining garlic powder and bouillon. Brush over biscuits. Bake 4 minutes longer or until golden brown. Serve warm. Makes about 12.

Ronda Reynolds
Post-Journal Cookbook
(1998)

Remove bread and biscuits from the baking pan as soon as they are taken from the oven or "sweating" will spoil the crispness of the bottom crust.

TIP

Cook Book
Jamestown (1920s)

WHOLE WHEAT BISCUITS

$^{7}/_{8}$ cup all-purpose flour
2 tsps. double-acting baking powder
$^{1}/_{2}$ tsp. baking soda
2 tsps. sugar (optional)
$^{3}/_{4}$ tsp. salt
1 cup whole wheat flour
$^{1}/_{3}$ cup margarine or shortening
1 cup yogurt or sour cream

Preheat oven to 400°. Mix together all-purpose flour, baking powder, baking soda, sugar and salt. Add and mix well 1 cup whole wheat flour. Cut into the flour with a pastry blender $^{1}/_{3}$ cup margarine or shortening. When mixture has a fine-crumb texture, stir in with a fork 1 cup yogurt or sour cream. Turn onto floured board. Knead gently and quickly 8-10 times. Pat out evenly with floured hands. Cut into desired shape and bake on ungreased sheet until lightly browned 12-15 minutes. Yields 24 biscuits.

Linda Austin
Westfield Jayncees . . .
(1983)

NEW YORK HOT CROSS BUNS

1 cup milk (scalded)
$^{1}/_{4}$ cup sugar
$^{1}/_{2}$ yeast cake dissolved in $^{1}/_{4}$ cup lukewarm water
$^{3}/_{4}$ tsp. cinnamon
3 cups flour
2 Tbsps. butter
$^{1}/_{2}$ tsp. salt
1 egg
$^{1}/_{4}$ cup raisins or currants.

Add butter, sugar and salt to the milk. When lukewarm, add dissolved yeast cake, cinnamon, flour and well-beaten egg. When thoroughly mixed add raisins, cover and let rise overnight. Then shape into forms of large biscuits, place in pan 1" apart, let rise, brush over with beaten egg and bake at 350° for 20 minutes. Cool, and with white icing make a cross on top of each bun.

Cook Book
Jamestown
(1920s)

SOPAIPILLAS (FRITTERS)

2 cups flour
2 tsps. baking powder
1 tsp. salt
2 Tbsps. shortening
$^3/_4$ cup cold water
oil or fat for frying

Sift all dry ingredients together; cut in the shortening with a pastry blender or 2 knives till mealy; work in the water gradually to form pastry-like dough. Turn onto a lightly floured board and knead until smooth. Roll as thin as possible and cut into 2 inch or 3 inch squares and fry one by one in the hot fat (370°). The sopaipillas should puff up as they brown and should be turned during the frying so the second side can also puff. Drain on paper towels. Makes 20-30 according to size. These fritters, which look like little fat pillows, are excellent served with soup, or with guacamole or any other dip. They will stay nicely puffed, if refrigerated, and can be reheated in the oven. Use as a dessert, with syrup or honey or sprinkled with sugar and cinnamon.

Barbara Mackowiak
Favorite Hometown . . .
(Date unknown)

SWEDISH OVEN PANCAKE

Sift together and set aside
1 cup sifted flour
1 Tbsp. sugar
$^1/_2$ tsp. salt
Blend together 2 eggs, slightly beaten
2 cups milk
1 Tbsp. melted bacon fat or butter

Gradually add the milk mixture to the dry ingredients, stirring until well blended. Set aside. Grease a baking dish or frying pan with bacon grease. Add batter and bake at 400° 40 to 45 minutes or until mixture is browned. Serve with maple syrup, canned raspberries or lingonberries.

Phil Wicklund
Good Cooking
(1950s)

CROISSANTS

1 cup (2 sticks) butter
1$^1/_4$ cups milk
4 tsps. sugar
1 tsp. salt
3 to 4 cups unsifted flour
$^1/_3$ cup cornstarch
$^1/_3$ cup warm water
1 pkg. active dry yeast
$^1/_4$ cup peanut oil
1 egg, beaten
1 tsp. water

Divide butter into 3 equal portions. Wrap each in plastic wrap. Chill. Scald milk; add sugar and salt. Cool to lukewarm. Combine flour and cornstarch; set aside. Measure warm water into large, warm bowl. Add yeast. Stir until dissolved. Add milk mixture, peanut oil, and flour to make a soft dough. Knead about 5 minutes on a lightly floured board. Cover; let rise until doubled.

Punch down; turn onto floured board. Roll into 16"x12" rectangle with long side toward you. Dot center third with one portion of chilled butter. Cover butter with right-hand third of dough. Fold left-hand third under butter section. Seal edges; wrap in plastic wrap. Chill 30 minutes. Repeat procedure two times.

Cut chilled dough in half. Roll out each half into a 16" circle. Cut each into 12 pie shaped wedges. Roll up each wedge, beginning with the wide end. Place on greased baking sheets with points underneath. Curve to form crescents. Cover; let rise until doubled (about 1 hour). Combine egg and 1 teaspoon water. Brush gently on rolls. Bake at 425°F. about 15 minutes. Makes 2 dozen .

Linda Hodorowicz
Our Own Cookbook (1986)

ONION-MUSTARD BUNS

1 package active dry yeast
$^1/_4$ cup warm water
2 cups milk, scalded
4 cups flour, about
1 egg, slightly beaten
2 Tbsps. sugar
1 Tbsp. prepared mustard
Scant $^1/_2$ tsp. pepper
2 Tbsps. instant minced onion
2 Tbsps. oil

Dissolve yeast in water and set aside.

In a large bowl combine the sugar, mustard, pepper, minced onion and oil. Add the scalded milk and cool to lukewarm. Add 2 cups flour, beating until smooth. Add yeast mixture and egg. Stir in enough flour to make a soft dough. Turn onto floured surface and knead until smooth, about 5 minutes. Place in a greased bowl, cover and let rise until doubled, about one and one-half hours. Punch down.

Divide dough into 2 equal parts, let rest for 10 minutes. Pat each portion into a 9-inch square.

Cut each portion into 9 squares. Tuck corners under to form buns. Flatten with palm of your hand. Let rise until doubled, about 30 minutes. Meanwhile, combine 2 Tbsps. more minced onion and $^1/_4$ cup water and let stand 5 minutes. Brush rolls with a glaze of 1 beaten egg and 2 Tbsps. water, then sprinkle with onion. Bake at 375° for 20 minutes.

Serve at once. Or split and toast and spread with cream cheese. Makes 18 buns.

Sally Bulger
Adventures in Food (1977)

BROCCOLI QUICHE MUFFINS

1 (10 oz.) package frozen chopped broccoli,
   thawed and drained
1 medium onion, chopped
$^1/_2$ cup diced cooked ham
$^1/_2$ cup grated Parmesan cheese
6 eggs
$^1/_2$ cup vegetable oil
$1^1/_4$ cups all-purpose flour
1 Tbsp. baking powder
1 tsp. dried oregano
1 tsp. dried parsley flakes
$^1/_4$ tsp. garlic powder
$^1/_4$ tsp. salt
$^1/_4$ tsp. dried thyme

Combine the broccoli, onions, ham and cheese, set aside. In a mixing bowl, beat eggs until frothy. Add oil, mix well. Combine dry ingredients, add to egg mixture, just until moistened. Fold in broccoli mixture. Fill greased muffin cups $^2/_3$ full. Bake at 375° for 18-22 minutes or until muffins are tested done. Remove from pan to a wire rack. Makes $1^1/_2$ dozen.

Millee Bush
Post-Journal Cookbook
(1998)

PARIS PUFFINS

$^1/_3$ cup soft shortening
1 egg
$1^1/_2$ tsps. baking powder
$^1/_4$ tsp. nutmeg
$^1/_3$ cup butter, melted
$^1/_2$ cup sugar
$1^1/_2$ cup flour
$^1/_2$ tsp. salt
$^1/_2$ cup milk
$^1/_2$ cup sugar
1 tsp. cinnamon

Heat oven to 350°. Grease 12 medium muffin cups. Mix thoroughly shortening, $^1/_2$ cup sugar, and egg. Blend flour, baking powder, salt and nutmeg; add alternately with milk. Fill muffin cups $^2/_3$ full. Bake 20 to 25 minutes. Immediately roll in melted butter, then in a mixture of $^1/_2$ cup sugar and 1 tsp. cinnamon. Serve hot.

Diane Osborn
Culinary Delights
(1988-89)

HERBED POPOVERS

3 eggs
1 cup milk
1 cup all-purpose flour
$^1/_2$ tsp. celery salt
3 Tbsps. butter or margarine, melted
1 tsp. dried thyme, sage or basil, crushed

Preheat oven to 450°. Grease 8 (6 ounce) custard cups; set aside. In blender container mix eggs, milk, flour, butter or margarine, thyme and celery salt. Cover and process at low speed until smooth.

Spoon about $^1/_3$ cup batter into each greased custard cup. Bake 15 minutes. Reduce heat to 375° and bake 30 minutes longer or until browned. Serve immediately. Makes 8 popovers.

Luci Petrella
Westfield Jayncees . . .
(1983)

CARAWAY PUFFS

1 package active dry yeast
$^1/_4$ tsp. baking soda
$1^1/_3$ cups sifted all-purpose flour
1 cup cream-style cottage cheese
1 Tbsp. butter or margarine
$^1/_4$ cup water
2 Tbsps. sugar
1 tsp. salt
1 egg
2 tsps. grated onion
2 tsps. caraway seed

Combine in a bowl the yeast, the baking soda and the flour.

Put the cottage cheese, butter or margarine, water, sugar and salt in a small saucepan and heat together until the butter melts. Add the heated mixture to dry ingredients in the bowl and mix. Add the egg, grated onion and caraway seed. Beat all at low speed of electric mixer for $^1/_2$ minute. Then beat 3 minutes at high speed. stir in 1 cup more flour. Place in greased bowl, turning once. Cover; let rise until double, $1^1/_2$ hours. Divide among 12 well-greased muffin wells. Cover; let rise about 40 minutes. Bake in a 400° oven for 12-15 minutes. Makes 12 delicious puffs.

Gwen Haskin
St. Peter's . . .
(1979)

SFINGE PUFFS FOR ST. JOSEPH'S DAY

2 cups water
1 Tbsp. sugar
2 Tbsps. margarine
2 cups flour
4 tsps. baking powder
2 tsps. vanilla
2 tsps. whiskey
6 extra-large eggs
deep fat for frying

In good-sized pan bring water to a boil and add sugar and margarine. Mix together baking powder and flour. Add all at once to mixture in saucepan and stir in quickly. (Mixture should leave sides of pan.) Cool a bit and add eggs 1 at a time, beating after each addition. Add vanilla and whiskey and beat again.

Have fat heated to 375°. Drop teaspoonfuls of dough into hot fat and fry until golden brown. Fry only a few at a time—pan should not be crowded. Drain on paper towels and sprinkle with powdered sugar or drizzle with honey. These puffs turn out hollow in center, light and crisp.

Connie Laurie
Home Cooking
Forestville
(1960s)

CHEESE-STUFFED BREAD

1/2 cup mayonnaise
1 cup. grated sharp cheese (4 oz.)
3/4 cup finely chopped onions
    (or 6-8 scallions)
few drops Worcestershire sauce
20-inch-long French bread
sprinkle top with paprika

Split the French bread down the center. Do not go through the bread. Wrap the bread in aluminum foil leaving the top open.

Mix mayonnaise, cheese, onions, and Worcestershire sauce and spread inside the bread. Sprinkle top with paparika. Bake at 350° for 20-25 minutes.

Kaye Butcher
Favorite Recipes
Mayville
(1982)

GERMAN SOUR CREAM TWISTS

$3^1/_2$ cups sifted flour
1 tsp. salt
2 tsps. ground cardamom
$^1/_2$ cup butter
$^1/_2$ cup margarine
1 pkg. dry yeast
$^1/_4$ cup warm water
$^3/_4$ cup sour cream
1 egg
2 egg yolks, well-beaten
1 tsp. vanilla
1 cup sugar

Sift flour, salt and cardamom into bowl. Cut in shortening. Dissolve yeast in water. Stir into flour mixture with sour cream, egg and egg yolks and vanilla. Mix well. Cover with damp cloth and refrigerate at least 2 hours (or overnight). Roll $^1/_2$ of the dough on sugared board (use the 1 cup sugar for this) into oblong 8"x16". Fold ends toward center, ends overlapping. Sprinkle with sugar; roll again to same size. Repeat a third time. Roll about $^1/_4$" thick. Cut into strips 1"x4". Twist ends in opposite directions, stretching dough slightly. Put in shape of horseshoe on greased cookie sheet, pressing ends to keep shape. Repeat with rest of dough. Bake at 375° 15 min. Remove from cookie sheet immediately. Makes 75. Extra hints: Work as fast as possible or dough will get sticky. Use enough sugar (as you would flour) so it won't stick to hands or board. Keep part of dough in refrigerator while rolling out first half; refrigerate until ready to bake after rolled out.

Hazel and Violet Young
100 Years of Cooking . . .
Jamestown (1986)

ROZKI, FILLED PASTRIES

4 cups flour
1 lb. margarine
1 tsp. salt
1 package dry yeast
3 Tbsps. sugar
1 cup warm milk
3 egg yolks
1 lb. walnuts, ground fine
2 Tbsps. melted margarine
1 egg
$^1/_4$ cup sugar
$^1/_2$ tsp. vanilla
2 lbs. dried prunes
pancake syrup
1 tsp. cinnamon
$^1/_2$ cup sugar

Blend flour, salt, and margarine as for pie crust. Mix 3 Tbsps. sugar and yeast in warm milk, add to this beaten egg yolks. Add milk mixture to flour mixture and mix well; dough will be sticky. Let rise 3 hours. Work dough on floured board only enough to roll out like pie crust. Cut in 2 inch squares. Place teaspoon nut or prune filling in center of squares. Fold 2 corners over filling and pinch together. Bake on lightly greased cookie sheet at 350°, 15 to 20 minutes or until lightly browned.

NUT FILLING: Mix together ground walnuts, 2 Tbsps. melted margarine, 1 egg, $^1/_4$ cup sugar, $^1/_2$ tsp. vanilla and enough pancake syrup to make moist.

PRUNE FILLING: Cover 2 lbs. dried prunes with water and bring to boil. Cover and let cool. Remove pits and grind in medium dice. Add $^1/_2$ cup sugar and 1 tsp. cinnamon and mix well.

Shirley Sventek
Favorite Recipes
Sherman
(Date unknown)

HOMEMADE HAMBURGER ROLLS

$1^1/_2$ cups lukewarm water or potato water
$^1/_2$ cup sugar
$1^1/_2$ tsps. salt
2 packages dry yeast dissolved in $^1/_2$ cup warm water
1 egg
1 cup soft shortening
$5^1/_2$ to $5^3/_4$ cups flour
$^1/_3$ cup dry skim milk

Combine lukewarm water or potato water, sugar and salt, and mix. Add the dissolved yeast, egg and soft shortening and mix well. Stir in about half of the flour which has been well mixed with the dry milk. Then add just enough of the remaining flour to make the dough soft and easy to handle. Turn dough onto a lightly floured board and knead until smooth and elastic.

Place ball of dough in a greased bowl, brush top with a soft shortening and cover bowl tightly. Place in refrigerator until ready to use. As dough rises in the refrigerator, punch it down. Dough will keep for a couple of days.

To make 24 hamburger rolls, divide dough into two portions, roll each portion about $^1/_3$ inch thick and cut into 12 rounds with a $3^1/_2$" cutter. Place rolls on lightly greased baking sheet, gently pressing down on the pan. Prick tops of rolls. Let rise covered in a warm place until double in bulk. Bake in a hot oven (400°) 12 to 15 minutes. Remove from oven and brush tops with soft butter.

Mrs. Janice Brown
Home Bureau . . .
(1972)

SWEDISH TEA LOGS

1 package dry yeast
$^1/_4$ cup water
$2^1/_4$ cup flour
2 Tbsps. sugar
1 tsp. salt
$^3/_4$ cup butter
$^1/_4$ cup evaporated milk
1 egg, unbeaten
$^1/_4$ cup raisins or currants
$^1/_2$ cup brown sugar, firmly packed
$^1/_2$ cup chopped pecans

Soften yeast in warm water. Sift flour, sugar, salt into mixing bowl. Cut in $^1/_2$ cup butter, into fine meal. Add milk, egg, raisins, and softened yeast. Mix well. Cover. Chill 2 hours or overnight.

Cream $^1/_4$ cup butter; add brown sugar, creaming well. Stir in pecans. Divide dough in halves. Roll out one part on floured surface to 12" x 6" rectangle. Spread with $^1/_2$ of nut filling. Roll up starting with 12" side; seal. Place, crescent shaped, on baking sheet lined with foil. Make cuts along outside edge 1" apart to within $^1/_2$" of center. Turn cut pieces on sides. Repeat with remaining dough. Let rise in warm place until light. Bake at 350° for 20 to 25 min. until a deep golden brown. Glaze while warm.

GLAZE: Melt and brown 2 Tbsps. butter. Add 1 cup confectioners' sugar and $^1/_2$ tsp. vanilla. Add 1 to 2 Tbsps. evaporated milk. Spread on crescents.

Mrs. Violetta Coons
Kiantone Cookbook
(1969)

ENTRÉES

In the early cookbooks from Chautauqua County, recipes for meat, poultry and fish entrees were what we might have expected: roasts, stews, long-braised dishes like pot roasts, and, of course, recipes for using leftovers.

The most interesting of these latter dishes to us in the 1990s are those for what we never see these days, for what were called "pressed" meats, with good reason. Cooked meat, fish or chicken was shredded and mixed with gelatinous broth and seasonings, pressed down in a loaf pan or similar utensil, then weighted down with another heavy pan and covered and chilled. Then it was sliced and served cold for lunch or supper with, of course, bread and, probably, pickles or relish. It seemed a good idea to resurrect those recipes for our time, since they are still tasty and they will fit well into our eating style.

In this long chapter — for it was, of course, difficult to choose among the hundreds of entrée recipes in all these books — we also revisited dishes that have been popular almost throughout the 100 years. These include stuffed cabbage and meatballs, in many ethnic guises; ham loaves, other meat loaves and salmon loaves; casseroles using cooked chicken or turkey or canned tuna fish, several of which appeared often, attesting to their popularity. Among these are the "No-Peek" Chicken casserole and the "Mock Lobster," both of which are included here.

Also here are several out-of-the-ordinary dishes, usually reflecting the ethnic heritage of county groups or souvenirs of travel in, especially, the latter half of the century. Dishes like Bouillabaisse (Provencal), Chicken Cacciatore (Italian), String Beans with Lamb (Greek), and Saté (Satay), from Indonesia.

Finally, there's a recipe for Escalloped Muskellunge, as it was served to President Theodore Roosevelt for breakfast when he visited Chautauqua Institution.

There are many much-loved familiar dishes here, but all with a special twist. And there are just as many new things to try.

EGGS, CHEESE, PASTA AND RICE

CHEESE PATTIES

3 Tbsps. butter
$^1/_2$ cup milk
1 egg, beaten
3 Tbsps. flour
$^1/_2$ lb. grated cheese (2 cups)
$^1/_2$ tsp. salt
1 cup soft stale bread crumbs
$^1/_4$ tsp. pepper
1 egg
2 Tbsps. water
$^1/_2$ cup dry bread crumbs
1 tsp. Worcestershire sauce

Melt butter in top of double boiler, add flour, stir well, add milk and cook over hot water until sauce is smooth and thick, stirring all the time. Add beaten egg, cheese, stale bread crumbs and seasonings. Cook until cheese is melted, then chill. Form into 8 thin flat patties. Roll in dried bread crumbs, then in egg and water which have been beaten together with a fork. Roll again in crumbs and fry in a small amount of fat (2 Tbsps.) until brown on both sides.

Serve with tomato sauce if desired. Serves 4.

Odette's War Recipes
(1940s)

GOLDEN BINK

Beat 1 egg in a small saucepan. Add to it 5 ounces of soft domestic cheese broken into bits, 1 level Tbsp. of butter, $^1/_3$ tsp. salt, a grain of cayenne, a tsp. of mustard and 5 Tbsps. of milk (beer or ale may be substituted for the milk). Put in chafing dish with the hot water pan underneath and stir until the cheese is almost creamy. Have 5 slices of toast and 5 eggs that have been poached in salted water hot and ready. Spread cheese mixture on the toast and put an egg on top. Serve at once. Instead of the egg a slice of broiled bacon is very nice.

Isabella Sheldon
Needlework....
(1910)

CHILES RELLENOS CASSEROLE

6 beaten eggs
3 cups cream-style cottage cheese
$^3/_4$ cups crushed Ritz crackers
1 (4-oz.) can El Paso green chiles, chopped
3 oz. ($^3/_4$ cup) shredded Cheddar cheese
3 oz. ($^3/_4$ cup) shredded Monterey Jack cheese

Combine eggs, cottage cheese, cracker crumbs, chiles and $^1/_2$ of cheeses. Turn into a 10x6x2" baking dish and bake for 45 minutes at 350°, or until set. Sprinkle remaining cheese on top and return to oven for 5 minutes. Remove from oven and let stand for 5 minutes before serving. Cut into squares and lift out with spatula. Great served with other Mexican favorites.

Julie Poppleton
Sts. P. And P. Family . . .
(1988)

EGG AND MUSHROOM CASSEROLE

2 Tbsp. butter
2 Tbsp. flour
2 cups milk
salt
$^2/_3$ of 8 oz. package sharp cheddar cheese, cut up
2 pimientos
1 lb. mushrooms
6 eggs (hard-boiled)
buttered crumbs

Make a cream sauce of butter, flour and milk and salt. Add cheese and pimientos cut in pieces. Slice mushrooms and sauté in butter 5 minutes. Do not let them get brown. Slice hard-boiled eggs. Place layers of mushrooms, eggs and cream sauce in casserole and cover with buttered crumbs. Bake 20 minutes at 350° until brown.

Edna Blom
To the Town's Taste
(1964)

FOO YUNG

4 eggs, well-beaten
1 can bean sprouts, drained
$1/_3$ cup thinly sliced onions
1 cup cooked crab, shrimp or chicken, chopped or flaked
$1/_2$ tsp. salt
$1/_8$ tsp. pepper
$1/_8$ tsp. garlic powder

Mix all ingredients. Heat oil in frying pan using just enough to coat pan. Use $1/_4$ cup of the mixture for each. Fry patties as you would pancakes, turning once. Cook until set and lightly browned. Remove to hot platters and pour the Foo Yung sauce over.

FOO YUNG SAUCE: In a saucepan combine 1 tsp. cornstarch, 1 tsp. sugar, 2 tsps. soy sauce and 1 tsp. vinegar. Stir in $1/_2$ cup regular strength chicken broth. Cook until thickened. May use leftover gravy instead of broth.

Alverna Holmlund
Kiantone Cookbook
(1989)

POTATO OMELET WITH TOMATO SAUCE

3 Tbsps. butter or margarine
$2^1/_2$ cups raw potatoes, very finely chopped or shredded
1 tsp. salt
Dash of pepper
3 Tbsp. onion, finely chopped
6 eggs
5 Tbsps. milk or light cream
$2^1/_2$ cups whole canned tomatoes
$1^1/_2$ Tbsps. cornstarch
2 Tbsps. water
1 Tbsp. sugar
$1/_4$ tsp. celery salt

Melt butter in a large skillet; add potatoes, $1/_2$ tsp. salt, pepper and onion. Cover and cook over medium heat, stirring occasionally, for 10 minutes, or until potatoes are tender. Beat eggs slightly; add cream or milk and remaining salt; pour over potatoes. Cover and cook over low heat for 8 to 10 minutes or until omelet is firm. Meanwhile, heat tomatoes in saucepan. Combine cornstarch, water and sugar; add to tomatoes and cook, stirring constantly, until mixture is thickened and clear. Stir in celery salt. Serve directly from pan with tomato sauce or fold over and turn out whole omelet on platter, pour tomato sauce over it. Makes 4 servings.

Mrs. Donald Newlove
recipe from France
Jamestown International...
(1960s)

BAKED STUFFED EGGS

CHEESE SAUCE:
2 Tbsps. butter
2 Tbsps. flour
$1^3/_4$ cups milk
$^1/_2$ tsp. salt
dash of pepper
1 cup grated Swiss or Cheddar cheese
· $^1/_2$ cup heavy cream

EGG STUFFING:
6 hard-cooked eggs
3 oz. can mushrooms, drained
1 medium onion
$^1/_2$ green pepper
2 Tbsps. butter
$^1/_2$ tsp. salt
dash pepper
fine dry bread crumbs

Make cream sauce, add cream and $^3/_4$ cup grated cheese. Set aside while stuffing eggs. Chop mushrooms, onions and green pepper very fine. Fry in butter a few minutes; season with salt and pepper. Cut eggs in half lengthwise. Scoop out yolks and mash. Mix yolks with enough cheese sauce and all the mushroom mixture to make a thick paste. Stuff eggs and place in shallow baking dish. Pour remaining sauce over eggs. Sprinkle with remaining cheese and crumbs. Bake 20 to 30 minutes at 375°. This may be prepared in advance, refrigerated and baked the second day.

Monica Link
Out of Silver Creek . . .
(1962)

PERFECT MACARONI

Get perfectly cooked macaroni or noodles every time by bringing salted water to a rolling boil, add macaroni and stir until it begins boiling again. Cover and turn off heat. Let stand for 20 minutes and drain. Result: perfect macaroni!

Mrs. Neva Frankson
Kiantone Cookbook
(1989)

BAKED MACARONI AND CHEESE

4 oz. package macaroni or egg noodles
1 cup soft bread crumbs
1 cup grated American cheese
3 eggs, beaten
1 pimiento, chopped
1½ cups hot milk
¼ cup butter
1 Tbsp. chopped parsley
1 Tbsp. chopped onion
1 tsp. salt

Cook macaroni or noodles, drain and rinse with water. Scald milk and add the rest of the ingredients. Bake in buttered dish or ring mold for 40 min. at 350°. Take out of mold and serve on platter. Fill center with creamed peas, mushrooms, tuna fish or chicken.

Mrs. Olga Van Guilder
Kiantone Cookbook
(1969)

MACARONI AND CHEESE

2 cups uncooked macaroni
2 beaten eggs
1½ cups sharp white Cheddar cheese, cubed
½ tsp. salt
½ tsp. dry mustard
1½ cups Half and Half
½ oz. white wine (Chablis or Rhine)
½ can (2 oz.) chopped green chiles
½ cup bread crumbs mixed with
2 Tbsps. butter

Combine all ingredients, except crumbs, in a buttered casserole. Sprinkle top with crumbs. Bake covered at 350° for 50 minutes. (Note: uncooked macaroni is correct.)

Joyce M. Mathews
Favorite Recipes
Mayville
(1982)

RING OF PLENTY

1$\frac{1}{2}$ cups cooked macaroni
1 cup diced sharp cheddar cheese
1 cup soft bread crumbs
1 Tbsp. minced parsley
3 Tbsps. minced pimiento
3 Tbsps. melted butter
1 Tbsp. minced onion
1 cup scalded milk
2 eggs well beaten
1 tsp. salt
$\frac{1}{8}$ tsp. pepper

Combine ingredients in order given. Transfer to ring mold rubbed with butter. Place mold in pan of hot water. Bake in moderate oven 375° about 45 minutes. Unmold and let stand about 5 minutes. Serve hot. Cover with cream sauce dressing with mushrooms, or with creamed chicken or creamed tuna.

Irene B. Clark
Victory Cook Book
(1940s)

SPAGHETTI MARCO POLO

$\frac{2}{3}$ cup chopped walnuts
$\frac{1}{2}$ cup chopped black olives
$\frac{1}{2}$ chopped red pepper
$\frac{1}{3}$ cup chopped parsley
1 tsp. fresh basil
$\frac{1}{4}$ tsp. salt
$\frac{1}{4}$ tsp. pepper
1 lb. spaghetti
3 Tbsps. olive oil
1 pressed garlic clove

Cook spaghetti and mix with olive oil and garlic. Combine remaining ingredients and add to spaghetti. Mix and serve with grated Parmesan cheese.

Joyce Frazeur
Dames in the Kitchen
(1975)

FETTUCINI AND BROCCOLI

Meatless main dish or side dish
1 lb. wide fettucini
$^1/_2$ cup salad oil
1 large onion, chopped finely
2 cloves garlic, crushed
2 pkgs (20 oz. each) frozen chopped broccoli,
　　thawed and drained
1 cup canned condensed chicken broth, undiluted
　　(I dissolve 2 bouillon cubes in 1 cup water as a
　　substitute)
1 tsp. basil or oregano
$^1/_2$ cup chopped parsley
$^1/_2$ cup grated Parmesan
2 cups cottage cheese
1 tsp. salt
$^1/_2$ tsp. pepper

Cook and drain noodles. Reserve for last step. In hot oil, sauté garlic and onion. Add thawed broccoli to oil mixture and continue cooking five to eight minutes. Add remaining ingredients. Blend over low heat about two minutes. Quickly toss with noodles. May serve with additional cheese. Serves 6-8.

Arlene Maler
Cooking by Degrees
(1985)

PASTA A LA CAPRESE

(Good For Summer)
4 large tomatoes (ripe), sliced thin, lengthwise
3 small garlic cloves, smashed
1 long, thin red sweet pepper, sliced thin
Fresh basil, torn (20 leaves)
$^1/_2$ cup olive oil
1 tsp. salt
6 twists of pepper from mill
8 oz. mozzarella, cubed
Parmesan cheese, grated
1 lb. ziti (or rigatoni)

At least $^1/_2$ hour before serving, combine tomatoes, garlic, pepper, basil, oil, salt and pepper in a large bowl. Let stand at room temperature. Cook and drain ziti. Add mozzarella to pasta, stir a little bit, then add sauce and mix quickly and well. Serve immediately with parmesan sprinkled on top. Serves 6 to 8.

Julianne Ventura
A Cappella Choir
(1986)

PASTA BELLA

2 cups broccoli flowerets
1 cup carrot slices
$^1/_4$ cup margarine
2 cups summer squash slices
$^1/_2$ lb. asparagus spears, cut into 1 inch pieces
$^3/_4$ cup half and half
$^3/_4$ lb. Velveeta cheese, cubed
1 tsp. oregano
2 cups bow noodles, cooked
$^1/_3$ cup grated Parmesan cheese
$^1/_4$ lb. pepperoni (chopped) (optional)

In large skillet, stir-fry broccoli and carrots in margarine 3 minutes. Add squash and asparagus; stir-fry until crisp-tender. Reduce heat to medium. Add Velveeta cheese, half and half and oregano. Stir until cheese is melted. Add remaining ingredients; mix lightly. 6 servings. May use any available vegetables desired.

Leslie Wagner
Centennial Cookbook
(1987)

PIZZA PASTA PIE

1 Tbsp. toasted wheat germ
3 oz. spaghetti, cooked and drained
2 eggs
1 (10 oz.) pkg. frozen chopped spinach,
 thawed and drained
$^3/_4$ cup cottage cheese
$^1/_2$ cup finely shredded carrots
$^1/_2$ tsp. basil
dash of garlic powder
1 Tbsp. margarine
$^1/_4$ cup grated Parmesan cheese
1 (8 oz.) can pizza sauce
1 ($2^1/_2$ oz.) jar mushrooms, drained
$^1/_2$ tsp. oregano
$^1/_2$ cup Mozzarella cheese

Grease $^3/_4$ quart baking dish. Sprinkle with wheat germ; set aside. In a small mixing bowl stir margarine into hot spaghetti. Beat 1 of the eggs and add to spaghetti with half of Parmesan cheese and $^1/_8$ tsp. salt. Mix well. Form spaghetti mixture into a crust. Using paper toweling, squeeze excess liquid from drained spinach; spread the spinach over pasta crust. Drain the cottage cheese. Beat remaining egg; add drained cottage cheese and remaining Parmesan cheese. Spoon cottage cheese over the spinach layer. In a bowl combine pizza sauce, shredded carrot, chopped mushrooms, herbs and garlic powder. Spoon over cottage cheese layer. Top with Mozzarella cheese. Bake, uncovered at 350° for 30 to 35 minutes.

Debbie Pasquale
Treasured Recipes
(1988)

STUFFED SHELL CASSEROLE

Cook 1 (12 oz.) package giant shells al dente.
$1/2$ lb. Italian sweet sausage
1 small chopped pepper
1 small chopped onion
1 (32 oz.) jar Ragu spaghetti mushroom sauce
2 (10 oz.) pkgs. frozen chopped spinach, thawed
2 eggs
1 lb. Ricotta cheese
$1/2$ lb. Mozzarella cheese, shredded or diced
$1/2$ tsp. nutmeg
1 tsp. garlic powder
1 tsp. oregano
1 tsp. onion salt
2 Tbsps. Parmesan cheese

Drain shells in colander and rinse in cold water. Slit sausage casings; peel off. Crumble and brown in large skillet; add onion and pepper. Brown. Add spaghetti sauce, oregano, and Parmesan cheese. Place thawed spinach in a strainer and press moisture out. Place in bowl; add beaten eggs, Ricotta, Mozzarella cheese, onion salt, garlic and dash of nutmeg.

Stuff shells with spinach mixture. Pour about $1/2$ cup of sausage sauce mixture in bottom of 3 quart casserole dish (enough to cover bottom of dish). Add shells and rest of mixture (sauce) over the shells. Sprinkle Parmesan cheese over top. Bake at 350° for 30 minutes. Serves 6.

Kathy Goodell
Our Own Cookbook
(1986)

LINGUINE FINE WITH FRENCH LENTILS, ESCAROLE AND ASIAGO

4 Tbsps. extra virgin olive oil
1 large red onion cut into $1/8$ julienne
1 medium head escarole (about $3/4$ pound) chopped in $1/2$" pieces, washed and spun dry to yield 3 cups
1 cup cooked tiny green French lentils
1 pound linguine fine pasta
1 cup freshly grated asiago cheese

Bring 6 quarts water to boil and add 2 Tbsps. salt.
In a 12" to 14" sauté pan, sauté onion in olive oil until translucent (about 7 to 8 minutes). Toss in escarole and cook over medium heat until wilted yet still bright green. Add lentils and toss to heat through. Season with salt and pepper and remove from heat.

Drop linguine into water and boil according to package instructions until al dente. Drain in colander over sink and pour hot pasta into pan with escarole. Toss, stirring well to mix, over medium high heat about 1 minutes. Add grated asiago and toss to mix. Pour into heated serving dish and serve immediately. Serves 4.

No name given
C.I.A.O. Italian Traditions Cookbook (1980s)

PIEROGGE

4 egg yolks*
1 whole egg*
$^3/_4$ tsp. salt
2 cups water
6 cups unbleached white flour

Fill each with one of the following fillings:
CHEESE:
1 lb. cottage cheese
2 egg yolks
2 Tbsps. sugar
2 Tbsps. onion
flour to stiffen

Beat egg and egg yolk, salt and water and add flour gradually and mix well until mixture is no longer sticky. Add small amount of extra flour if necessary. Turn out on floured board. Knead a few times; divide in half and roll rope style. With a sharp knife, cut in $^1/_4$" rounds; roll each slice to about 4" diameter.

Mix well. Add 1 Tbsp. to round of dough and finish as usual.

SAUERKRAUT: 1 pkg. (2 lb.) sauerkraut, rinsed in cold water; 1 large onion (1 cup chopped); $^1/_2$ cup mushrooms, chopped; 4 Tbsps. butter (or 2 Tbsps. oil and 2 Tbsps. butter); garlic powder, salt, pepper to taste. Place rinsed sauerkraut in sauce pan, cover with water and cook for 30 minutes. Drain and squeeze out water. Meanwhile, sauté onion and mushrooms; add seasonings. Combine with sauerkraut. Mixture must be cooled before filling dough.

FINISH: Fold together, pinch edges or use fork to press together. Be sure the edges are well sealed. Heat water in large kettle to boiling point. Drop pierogge (12 to 15) into boiling water and cook until they float to the top, cooking 2-3 minutes. Do not crowd them. Remove from water with slotted spoon, place in large bowl and moisten with melted butter or oil to keep from sticking if they are to be stored for a short time. They may be frozen. They also can be fried in butter until lightly brown. Serve with plain sour cream or a sour cream and fried onion sauce.

OTHER FILLINGS: Seasoned mashed potatoes (mixture of mashed potatoes and farmers' cheese or ricotta cheese) or sweetened plums.

Ann M. Padlo
Chautauqua Allegheny . . .
(1990)

Ruth Mackowiak
Home Town Recipes
(1989)

*Egg whites or frozen egg substitute may be substituted for yolks and whole egg. Use some yellow food coloring if only whites are used.

POORMAN'S PIEROGGE

1 lb. spiral macaroni
1 large can sauerkraut
5 medium onions, sliced (when cooked,
    about the same amount as sauerkraut)
2 Tbsps. oil
2 cans mushroom soup
2 small cans mushrooms, undrained

Drain sauerkraut (set aside juice). Rinse sauerkraut with cold water. Sauté onions in oil in large pan; when onions are partially cooked, add sauerkraut and cook until tender. A little water or sauerkraut juice may be needed to finish cooking. Cook spiral macaroni in salted water and drain. To sauerkraut and onions add mushroom soup, mushrooms, salt and pepper to taste and macaroni. Mix well. Makes large amount; ingredients may be cut in half.

Janyce Tunney
Centennial Cookbook
(1987)

AUNT MARY LOU'S BRUNCH EGGS

10 to 12 slices cubed white bread
1 lb. bacon, fried and crumbled
1 lb. smoked link sausage, cut up (or 2 cups cubed ham)
2 cups shredded American cheese
1 cup Monterey Jack cheese, shredded
10 eggs
$3^1/_2$ cups milk
1 tsp. salt
1 tsp. dry mustard
2 cups corn flakes
1 cup Rice Krispies
$^1/_2$ cup butter, melted

Layer first 5 ingredients in buttered 9"x13" pan. Beat eggs until fluffy. Add milk, salt and mustard. Pour over layers; refrigerate overnight. Before baking, top with the cereals, mixed with the butter. Bake in preheated 350° oven for 1 hour.

Ruth Anne Morales
Sts. P. And P. Family . . .
(1988)

PIZZA BIANCA

CRUST:
1 cup warm water, 105° to 115°
1 env. active dry yeast
Pinch of sugar
About 3 cups all-purpose flour
$1/_2$ tsp. salt, optional
3 Tbsps. olive oil
1 (15-oz.) container light or part-skim ricotta cheese
1 cup shredded part-skim Mozzarella cheese
$1/_2$ cup grated Romano cheese
1 Tbsp. fresh lemon juice
$1/_2$ tsp. dried oregano, crumbled
$1/_4$ tsp. pepper, or to taste
Ground red pepper, to taste
$3/_4$ cup thinly sliced scallions
1 red bell pepper, cut in $1/_4$" wide strips

CRUST: Mix water, yeast and sugar in small bowl, let stand 5 to 10 minutes until foamy. Mix flour and salt in a large bowl. Add yeast and oil. Stir, adding more flour if needed, until dough leaves side of bowl and forms ball. Knead dough on a lightly floured surface 5 minutes or until smooth and elastic. Put in oiled bowl and turn dough until coated. Cover and let rise in a warm place 45 minutes or until doubled. Punch down dough and divide in half (wrap and freeze half up to 3 months). Form remaining dough into ball. On lightly floured surface, roll dough into 13" circle. Transfer to round 12" pan. Form a thick rim by folding dough over around edge. Cover crust lightly and let stand 15 minutes. Mix cheeses, lemon juice, oregano and red and black peppers in a bowl. Place one oven rack in lowest position in oven. Heat oven to 450°. Bake crust 10 minutes. Spread on cheese mixture, sprinkle with scallions. Arrange bell pepper strips on top. Bake 15 minutes or until filling starts to turn golden. Cool 5 minutes before cutting.

Sally Galati
Here's What's Cookin' . . . *(1988)*

BROWN RICE CASSEROLE

4 Tbsps. melted butter or margarine
$1/_2$ cup small noodles (uncooked)
1 cup brown rice (uncooked)
1 can beef bouillon
1 can sliced mushrooms (save liquid)
$1/_2$ onion, grated or diced
$1/_2$ tsp. salt
$1/_4$ tsp. pepper
$1/_2$ cup diced celery
$1/_3$ cup diced green pepper
2 cups water

Melt margarine; add mushrooms, celery, onions, green pepper, noodles, rice, bouillon, salt and pepper. Bring to a boil and put in a casserole. Add 1 cup water (use mushroom liquid as part). During baking, add 1 more cup water. Do not cover. Bake for $1 1/_2$ hours at 350°. Delicious with tossed salad and bacon or ham.

Mary Shopland
Saint Peter's . . .
(1979)

ALPINE ASPARAGUS QUICHE

1 (9 inch) unbaked pie shell
1 (10 oz.) pkg. asparagus (spears or cut up)
$^3/_4$ cup milk
$^3/_4$ cup half and half
$^1/_2$ cup finely chopped onion
1 tsp. salt
$^1/_4$ tsp. nutmeg
Dash of pepper
3 eggs, slightly beaten
1 cup shredded Swiss cheese

Bake pie shell at 400° for 8 to 10 minutes. Prepare asparagus as directed on package; drain. Combine milk, cream, onion, salt, nutmeg, and pepper in saucepan. Bring to boil. Simmer 1 minute. Stir hot mixture into eggs. Sprinkle $^2/_3$ of cheese into partially baked pie shell. Arrange asparagus over cheese, trimming spears if necessary. Pour in egg mixture. Sprinkle remaining cheese over top. Bake at 375° for 20 to 25 minutes or until silver knife inserted 1 inch from center comes out clean. Makes 8 servings.

Betty Sikorski
Warm Your Heart . . .
(1987)

ZUCCHINI - EGGPLANT QUICHE

2 small zucchini ($^1/_2$ lb.), sliced thin diagonally
$^1/_2$ small eggplant ($^1/_2$ lb.) in $^1/_2$ inch dice
1 green onion, sliced
$^1/_4$ cup butter or margarine
1 clove garlic, minced
1 small tomato, peeled and chopped
1 small green pepper, chopped
$^1/_2$ tsp. salt, or to taste
$^1/_8$ tsp. pepper
$^1/_4$ tsp. each basil and thyme
9 inch pastry shell
3 eggs
$^1/_2$ cup heavy cream
$^1/_2$ cup grated Parmesan cheese

Sauté zucchini, eggplant, onions and garlic in butter for 5 minutes, stirring occasionally. Stir in tomato, green pepper, salt, pepper and herbs. Cook over low heat for 10-15 minutes or until vegetables are tender and liquid has evaporated. Spread mixture evenly in shell. Beat eggs and cream until mixed, but not frothy; pour into shell. Sprinkle with Parmesan cheese. Bake in a pre-heated 375° oven for 30-35 minutes or until set.

Elaine Horton
Saint Peter's . . .
(1979)

KUSHERIE

(Egyptian Rice and Lentils)
2 Tbsps. oil
1¼ cups lentils
3 cups boiling water or stock
1 tsp. salt
Dash pepper
1½ cups rice
1 cup boiling water
SAUCE:
3/4 cup tomato paste
3 cups tomato juice or sauce
1 green pepper, chopped
Chopped celery leaves
1 Tbsp. sugar
½ tsp. salt
1 tsp. cumin
¼ tsp. cayenne pepper

Heat 2 Tbsps. oil in heavy saucepan. Add lentils, brown over medium heat 5 minutes, stirring often. Add 3 cups boiling water or stock, salt, pepper. Cook uncovered 10 minutes over medium heat. Stir in rice and 1 cup boiling water (or stock). Bring to boil, reduce heat to low, cover and simmer 25 minutes without stirring.

SAUCE: In a saucepan, heat together tomato paste, tomato juice or sauce, green pepper, celery leaves, sugar, salt, cumin, cayenne pepper. Bring sauce to boiling, reduce heat and simmer 20 to 30 minutes.

Browned onions: Heat in small skillet 2 Tbsps. oil. Saute over medium heat until brown, 3 onions, sliced, 4 cloves garlic, minced. To serve, put rice-lentil mixture on a platter. Pour tomato sauce over. Top with browned onions. (Don't omit the onions!)

Hazel L. Roth
Culinary Delights (1988-89)

BAKED RICE WITH PEAS, CELERY AND ALMONDS

1 small onion, chopped
½ stick butter
2 stalks celery, cut in ¼" slices
1 cup long-grain or converted rice
2 cups simmered chicken stock
⅓ cup sliced almonds
1 cup thawed frozen peas

Cook onion in 3 Tbsps. butter until softened. Add celery and rice. Cook until rice is well coated. Stir in stock. Bring to boil. Pour into covered casserole dish. Bake in preheated 375° oven for 15 minutes. While this is baking, sauté almonds in 1 Tbsp. butter until golden. Stir almonds, peas, salt and pepper into rice and bake another 15 minutes, or until rice is tender and all moisture is absorbed. Let stand 5 minutes, then fluff with fork. Serves 6.

Helen Schaefer
Sts. P. And P. Family . . .
(1988)

CHICKEN CHEESE STRATA

8 slices white bread, diced
3 Tbsps. salad oil
1 medium bunch broccoli, cut into bite-size pieces
1 medium onion, chopped
$^1/_2$ lb. mushrooms, sliced
3 cups cooked chicken or turkey (diced)
1 pkg. (8 oz.) cheese slices (American, Muenster,
    mild Cheddar)
6 eggs
4 cups milk
$^1/_2$ tsp. mustard
1 tsp. salt

Line bottom of greased 9"x13" baking dish with half of diced bread. In skillet over medium heat, cook broccoli, onion, mushrooms in salad oil until crisp- tender. Place over bread cubes. Place cheese slices over vegetables.

Layer with remaining bread cubes and cover with diced chicken. In large bowl, beat eggs, milk, mustard and salt until blended. Carefully pour egg mixture over cheese and chicken in baking dish. Bake 45 minutes or until knife inserted in center comes out clean.

Note: If top browns too quickly, cover with foil during the last 10 minutes. Serves 9-10. For party food, cut into small squares to serve 24 or more.

Lucille Piper
Chautauqua Motet
(1985)

SANDWICH SOUFFLE

16 slices sandwich bread
8 slices cooked chicken breast or sliced ham
8 slices sharp cheese
$^1/_2$ cup chopped pimiento
1 cup chopped green pepper
6 eggs, beaten
3 cups milk
1 tsp. salt
1 tsp. dry mustard
$^1/_2$ cup melted butter
3 cups crushed corn flakes

Remove crusts from bread and place 8 slices on bottom of 9x13" pan. Top each with slice of chicken and slice of cheese. Sprinkle with pimiento and green pepper. Top with remaining slices of bread. Mix eggs, milk, mustard and salt and pour over sandwich. Refrigerate overnight. Before baking, top with crushed cornflakes and melted butter. Bake 1 hour at 350°. Let stand 10 minutes before cutting in squares.

Ruth Morgan   Bonnie Froman
First United . . .   *C.S.E.A.*
Dunkirk   (1988)
(1978)

SHRIMP AND CHEESE CASSEROLE

6 slices of bread
1 lb. cleaned and shelled cocktail shrimp
$^1/_2$ lb. sharp Cheddar cheese
$^1/_4$ lb. melted butter or margarine
$^1/_2$ tsp. dry mustard
3 eggs, beaten
1 pint milk
1 tsp. salt

Break bread into pieces size of a quarter. Break cheese into bite size pieces. Arrange shrimp, bread, cheese in several layers in casserole. Pour melted butter over mixture. Beat eggs. Add mustard and salt to eggs. Then add milk. Mix together and pour over ingredients in casserole. Refrigerate overnight. Bake 1 hour uncovered at 350°. Serves 6.

Mrs. R.A. Jones
Wonderful Cooking
(Date unknown)

HAWAIIAN FONDUE

1 can lobster (or tuna, chicken, turkey, crab or shrimp)
1 cup chopped celery
2 Tbsps. chopped onion
$^1/_2$ cup mayonnaise
2 Tbsps. prepared mustard
4 eggs
2 cups scalded milk
1 lb. American cheese slices (or Velveeta)
1 Tbsp. Worcestershire sauce
Pinch of salt
Dash of Tabasco sauce
$^1/_2$ tsp. paprika
12 slices buttered soft bread (crusts removed)

Mix the first 5 ingredients; check seasoning. It should be sharp, but not hot. Make 6 sandwiches and cut into quarters. Put layer of sandwiches in bottom of a buttered casserole. Cover with a layer of cheese slices and another layer of sandwiches. Top off with cheese. Beat eggs slightly; stir in a spoonful of scalded milk. Combine rest with eggs gradually. Add 2 drops Tabasco sauce and Worcestershire sauce. Pour over the sandwiches and cheese. Store overnight in the refrigerator. Set in a pan of water and bake at 325° for 40 minutes or until top is firm and brown.

J. Cardell
Saint Peter's . . .
(1979)

ARROZ CON JOCOQUI

$^3/_4$ lb. Monterey Jack cheese
3 cups sour cream
$^1/_2$ tsp. salt
2 cans peeled green chiles, chopped
3 cups cooked rice
Salt and pepper
$^1/_2$ cup grated Cheddar cheese

UNBURGERS

1 cup rolled oats (not quick)
$^1/_2$ cup coarsely chopped nuts
$^2/_3$ medium onion, chopped
2 tsps. soy sauce
1 tsp. Savorex or Vegex (from Health Foods Store)
$^1/_2$ tsp. sage
3 eggs

WOWBURGERS

1 cup chopped mushrooms
$^1/_2$ cup chopped onions
2 eggs, beaten
$^1/_2$ cup shredded Mozzarella cheese
1 cup cheese curds or cottage cheese
1 cup shredded Cheddar cheese
$^1/_2$ cup rolled oats
1 cup cooked brown rice
$^1/_2$ cup cracked wheat
$^2/_3$ cup chopped walnuts
Salt, pepper, herbs

Cut Monterey Jack cheese in strips. Thoroughly mix sour cream, salt and chiles. Butter $1^1/_2$ quart casserole well. Season rice with salt and pepper, if necessary. Layer rice, sour cream mixture and cheese strips in that order, until you finish with rice on top. Bake at 350° for about $^1/_2$ hour. During the last minutes of baking sprinkle grated Cheddar cheese over the rice and allow it to melt before removing casserole from oven. Serve with ham, roast pork, broiled chicken or turkey. Serves 6-8.

Carol Preston
Dames in the Kitchen
(1975)

Blend last 6 ingredients. Pour over oats and mix.. Refrigerate $^1/_2$ hour. Form into patties. Fry in oil. Serve on a bun with cheese, sprouts, and a tomato slice. Serves 6.

William Parment
N.Y. Assemblyman
Chautauqua-Allegheny Cookbook
(1990)

Mix everything and make into patties. Broil about 2 minutes each side. Low calorie. Serves 4 to 6.

Phyllis Macer
Cookbook
Westfield
(1986)

BEEF

GOOD BEEF STEW

2 lbs. beef stew meat, cut into 2-inch pieces
$^1/_3$ cup flour
$^1/_4$ cup vegetable oil
$^1/_2$ cup snipped parsley or 2 Tbsps. parsley flakes
1 Tbsp. packed brown sugar
6 potatoes, peeled
1 Tbsp. salt
$^1/_2$ tsp. dried rosemary leaves
$1^1/_2$ cups beef broth
$^1/_4$ cup vinegar
1 (12-oz.) can beer
1 large onion, sliced
1 small clove garlic, crushed

Heat oven to 325°. Coat beef pieces with flour. Brown beef, a few pieces at a time, in oil in a Dutch oven over medium heat; drain. Remove beef from Dutch oven. Stir in broth and vinegar gradually, scraping bottom of pan, until gravy is smooth. Heat to boiling, stirring constantly. Stir in beer, onion, garlic and beef. Add potatoes. Cover and bake until beef and potatoes are tender (about 3 hours). Makes 6 servings.

M. Dykes
"Cookin' From..."
(1987-88)

OLD-FASHIONED BEEF STEW

$^1/_3$ cup flour
2 lbs. stewing beef
4 Tbsps. shortening
1 Tbsp. lemon juice
12 small carrots
8 small white potatoes
salt and pepper to taste
12 small white onions
1 Tbsp. Worcestershire sauce
1 large onion, sliced
2 bay leaves
$^1/_8$ tsp. allspice

Shake beef in flour. Melt shortening in Dutch oven. When fat is hot, add beef and brown until beef is rich, dark color. Add 4 cups hot water, lemon juice, Worcestershire sauce, onion, bay leaves, allspice and salt and pepper. Lower heat and simmer $1^1/_2$ to 2 hours or until meat is tender. Add carrots, onions and potatoes and cook 20-25 minutes. Thicken with flour and water mixture if desired. Serves 8.

Rose Mary Potter McMaster
Kiantone Cookbook
(1989)

BEEF ROULADEN

3 slices bacon, cut in half
$1^1/_2$ lbs. thinly-sliced round steak ($^1/_4$ inch thick)
2 Tbsps. Dijon mustard
3 medium dill pickles, cut in quarters lengthwise
6 medium carrots (about l-lb.) cut in quarters lengthwise
$^1/_4$ cup finely chopped onion
1 can beefy mushroom or golden mushroom soup
$^1/_2$ cup chopped celery
$^1/_2$ cup chopped parsnips
2 Tbsps. chopped parsley

Fry bacon until crisp and crumble. Cut meat into 6 pieces 6 x 4 inches and pound. Spread 1 teaspoon mustard on each. Place 2 pieces pickle and 4 pieces carrot across narrow end. Sprinkle with 2 teaspoons onion and some of the crumbled bacon. Starting at narrow end, roll up. Tuck in ends, fasten with toothpick. Brown roll-ups in bacon fat. Pour off fat. Stir in soup, celery, parsnips and parsley. Cover. Cook over low heat l hour l5 minutes. Serve with mashed potatoes. Garnish with bacon.

Marg Walsh
Culinary Delights
(1988-89)

BOILED DINNER

Boil a piece of beef or pork, same as for boiled corn beef; boil until within three-fourths of an hour of being tender; taste the water and see it is not too salty; add the amount of cabbage you wish to use cut in quarters, and the turnip cut in thick slices or quarters; if beets are used put them in two hours before serving dinner; after adding cabbage and turnip, let boil fifteen minutes; then add pared and whole potatoes, parsnips whole, and if carrots are used, add at the same time as cabbage; when potatoes are done, take up in the old style way if you choose, which is putting everything on a large platter. This is an old style dinner, but good.

Kate Cook
Chautauqua Cook Book
(1882)

CHUCK WAGON PEPPER STEAK

1 round bone arm chuck roast or boneless round roast,
  cut about 2" thick. (3 lbs.)
2 tsps. unseasoned meat tenderizer
2 tsps. instant minced onion
2 tsps. thyme
l tsp. marjoram
l bay leaf, crushed
l cup wine vinegar
$^1/_2$ cup olive oil or salad oil
3 Tbsps. lemon juice
$^1/_4$ cup peppercorns, coarsely crushed
  or 2 Tbsps. bottled cracked pepper

Sprinkle meat evenly on both sides with meat tenderizer (use no salt), pierce deeply all over with a fork, place in a shallow baking pan. Mix instant onion, thyme, marjoram, bay leaf, vinegar, olive oil or salad oil, and lemon juice in small bowl. Place meat in shallow dish, pour over marinade and let stand at room temperature for 1-2 hours, turning meat every half hour to marinate well. When ready to grill, remove meat from marinade, pound half the crushed peppercorns into each side (a wooden mallet makes a handy tool). Grill to rich brown on rack set about 6 inches above hot coals, turn and grill until meat is done as you like it. Time will depend on heat of coals and distance of meat from fire bed, but it should average at least 15 minutes on each side for rare. Cut meat diagonally into $^1/_2$ inch thick slices.

Mrs. Seymour Minsker
What's Cookin' III
(1964-65)

MOLDED COLD MEAT

Remove all fat and gristle from cold meat and chop fine. Make a sauce of one tablespoonful each of sugar, mustard and butter (or salad oil), one teaspoonful of salt, white pepper and half a cup of vinegar; mix well and let it come to a boil. Then beat one egg lightly and stir into the boiling sauce, removing from the fire as soon as the egg is put in. Now add the chopped meat, pack in a mold and place a light weight on top; when cold, slice thin, garnish and serve for tea.

Mrs. H.M. Blood
Brocton Cookbook
(Date unknown)

ESTERHAZY STEAK

Like Swiss steak but more flavorful.

6 carrots
8-12 celery ribs
1 Tbsp. salt
1 tsp. pepper
3 Tbsps. flour
1 Tbsp. paprika
6 capers (bottled)
2 onions, sliced
3 lb. round steak, cut $1/4$ inch thick
3 Tbsps. margarine
6 whole black peppercorns
1 can condensed beef bouillon
1 lemon, thinly sliced

About 3 hours before serving, cut carrots and celery in long thin strips. Cut meat in serving pieces and lay on board and with the rim of a saucer, pound in salt and pepper on both sides. In hot margarine in large skillet, brown meat on both sides. Remove from skillet to a large flat casserole (glass 9"x13" is fine). In margarine left from browning meat, sauté carrots, celery, onions about 15 minutes, stirring occasionally. Remove and place on top of meat. Then stir flour, peppercorns, paprika and bouillon (undiluted) in skillet and pour over meat and vegetables. Add capers and lemon. Cook about l hour at 325°. The liquid should be reduced to about $1/3$. May be served with boiled white rice or buttered wide noodles.

Mildred Szabo
Favorite Recipes
Findley Lake
(1981)

HUNGARIAN GOULASH

2 lbs. stew beef, cut up
2 large onions, sliced
1 clove garlic, chopped
$1/4$ cup shortening
$1^1/_2$ to 2 cups water
1 beef bouillon cube
2 to 3 Tbsps. tomato paste
1 Tbsp. Worcestershire sauce
1 tsp. sugar
1 to 2 Tbsps. paprika
salt and pepper
dash of marjoram

Brown beef cubes in shortening, add sliced onions and garlic and cook until onions are tender; add rest of ingredients and simmer on low until done, about 2 hours. Add water if necessary during cooking. Also, green peppers (sliced) and/or sliced or canned tomatoes may be added. Thicken gravy at the end of cooking time with flour stirred into water or cornstarch-water. mix. Serve over wide noodles or rice. 6 servings.

Gerda Morrissey
Centennial Cook Book
(1987)

MT. KILIMANJARO
(Rice and Curry Dish)
2 lbs. stew beef cubes
2 tsps. curry
1 tsp. salt
4 to 5 small onions
2 Tbsps. shortening
$1^1/_2$ Tbsps. flour
$^3/_4$ cup boiling water
1 beef bouillon cube
$6^1/_2$-oz. can tomato paste
46-oz. can tomato juice
Cooked rice (to serve desired number of people)

Brown beef cubes, curry, salt and onion in shortening. Mix in flour. Add water, bouillon, tomato paste and tomato juice. Simmer for 2 to 3 hours. Cook rice separately. Place your choice of the condiments in separate bowls on the table. Each person creates his own "mountain" by topping his rice with meat sauce and desired condiments. The coconut is the "snow" on top. Condiments: Avocado, almonds, green pepper, cucumber, cheese, peanuts, bacon bits, pineapple, celery, coconut, tomato, raisins, onion, carrots, olives and egg.

Sonia Einfeldt
Culinary Delights
(1988-89)

PEKING ROAST
3 to 5 lbs. beef roast
1 cup vinegar
2 cups black coffee
2 cups water
2 Tbsps. oil

Put meat into a bowl and slowly pour 1 cup vinegar over it. Add enough water to cover roast. Cover with plastic and place in refrigerator for 24 to 48 hours. When meat has marinated long enough, pour off vinegar. Brown in oil in heavy pot or Dutch oven. Pour 2 cups of strong, black coffee over the meat. Add 2 cups water and cover. Cook slowly for about 6 hours on top of stove. Add more water if necessary, but add only a small amount at a time. Do not add salt and pepper until 20 minutes before serving. Make gravy with liquid if desired. This recipe is good for using cheaper cuts of beef.

Leslie Wagner
Centennial Cook Book
(1987)

PAMPERED BEEF FILLETS

6 large fresh mushroom crowns
6 beef fillets, cut 1 inch thick
$^1/_4$ cup chopped green onion
4 tsps. cornstarch
1 cup burgundy
$^1/_2$ cup water
2 Tbsps. butter or margarine
$^1/_2$ cup chopped, fresh mushroom stems and pieces
2 Tbsps. snipped parsley
1 tsp. salt
dash of pepper

For fluted effect on mushrooms, cut "V" shaped pieces out of tops. Set crowns aside. Reserve mushroom pieces for Royal Mushroom Sauce. Heat butter in heavy skillet until golden brown and bubbling. Quickly brown steaks on both sides over high heat, about 1 minute per side. Place fillets on squares of heavy foil on baking sheet. Allow to cool slightly.

Prepare Royal Mushroom Sauce: Add $^1/_2$ cup mushroom stems and pieces and the onions to drippings remaining in skillet after fillets have been browned. Cook vegetables until tender, but not brown. Blend in cornstarch. Add remaining ingredients; cook and stir till thickened and bubbly. Cook 1 minute more.

Spoon 3 Tablespoons sauce over each fillet. Top each with a mushroom crown. Bring corners of foil square up over steak, twist gently and seal. Refrigerate packets. Before baking, open tops of packets slightly. Bake at 450° oven for 14 to 15 minutes for rare, 16 to 18 minutes for medium. If packets aren't refrigerated, bake a few minutes less. Very elegant do-ahead company dinner.

Lesley Mucha
Centennial Cook Book (1987)

SAUCY SHORT RIBS

3 lbs. beef short ribs
all-purpose flour
shortening or fat
salt and pepper
$^1/_2$ cup hot water
4 cups sliced onions
3 Tbsps. all-purpose flour
1 tsp. Worcestershire sauce
$^1/_2$ tsp. Kitchen Bouquet

Heat shortening in Dutch oven. Roll ribs in flour. Brown in hot shortening; spoon off fat. Season. Add water. Cover; simmer in slow oven (325°) until tender, about 2 hours. (Add more water if needed.) Place meat on warm platter; keep hot.

Make onion gravy: Skim fat from short rib stock, reserve 3 tablespoons. Measure stock and add hot water to make 2 cups; set aside. Put reserved fat in skillet. Add sliced onions and cook until tender, but not brown. Remove from heat. Push onions to one side; blend flour into fat. Slowly stir in meat stock. Return to heat; cook and stir until gravy is bubbling all over. Add Worcestershire sauce and Kitchen Bouquet. Season to taste with salt and pepper. Cook slowly about 5 minutes more, stirring now and then. Serve over short ribs. Makes 6 servings.

Barbara Corell
Centennial Cook Book
(1987)

Public Market, Brooklyn Square, Jamestown, ca. 1920.

SAUERBRATEN

3 lbs. top or bottom round roast
1 pint cider vinegar
3-4 bay leaves
1 tsp. black peppercorns
$1/_4$ cup sugar
1 pint water
2 tsps. salt
6 whole cloves
1 medium onion, sliced
1 clove garlic, split

Place meat in a glass, earthenware, or enamel container. Put vinegar, bay leaves, peppercorns, sugar, water, salt and cloves in a saucepan and bring to a boil. Add onion and garlic and pour marinade over meat. Add water, if necessary, to cover meat. Cover container and refrigerate for 3-4 days, turning meat daily. When ready to cook, brown meat in hot fat, then place on rack in a non-iron pot, add 1 cup marinade, the onion, garlic and spices. Cover and simmer 2 hours or until tender. If needed, add more marinade as it cooks. When meat is done, remove it to a hot platter and, to make gravy, thicken the broth with crushed gingersnaps (8-12). Serve with Kartoffel Kloss.

KARTOFFEL KLOSS (Potato Dumplings)
6 medium potatoes
2 eggs
$1^1/_4$ cups flour
2 tsps. salt
bread cubes

Boil potatoes in their jackets. When cooked, remove skins and put potatoes through ricer. Spread on a clean towel to dry out moisture, then place in a bowl and add salt. Make a hollow and break eggs into it. Sift on the flour. Work all this together. If too wet, add more flour. Mold dumpling dough around a few bread cubes which have been fried in fat until crisp. Dumpling should be about the size of a medium potato. Drop into boiling salt water. When dumplings come to the surface of the water, allow to boil, covered, about 10 minutes. When done, the center should be dry; not soggy.

Mrs. M.B. Franks
What's Cooking I
(1954)

STUFFED FLANK STEAK TERIYAKI

1 ($1^1/_4$ lb.) beef flank steak
$^1/_2$ cup soy sauce
$^1/_4$ cup cooking oil
2 Tbsps. molasses
2 tsps. dry mustard
1 tsp. freshly grated ginger root
1 clove garlic, minced
1 cup water
$^1/_2$ cup long grain rice
1 medium carrot, shredded ($^1/_2$ cup)
$^1/_2$ cup sliced water chestnuts
$^1/_4$ cup sliced green onion

Cut pocket in flank steak. Combine soy sauce, oil, molasses, mustard, ginger root and garlic. Place meat in shallow dish; pour marinade into pocket and over meat. Let stand at room temperature 30 minutes, turning meat occasionally. Meanwhile in small saucepan combine water, rice, carrot, water chestnuts and green onion. Bring to boiling. Cover. Reduce heat and simmer 8 minutes. Remove from heat; set aside. Drain meat, reserving marinade. Add $^1/_4$ cup of the reserved marinade to the rice mixture. Spoon rice stuffing into pocket of meat. Secure end with small skewer or wooden picks. Place meat in shallow roasting pan. Cover with foil. Bake in a 350° oven for l hour or till meat is done, brushing occasionally with marinade. Place on serving platter. Garnish with additional green onion. Slice meat diagonally across grain to serve. Makes 4 or 5 servings.

Betty Titus
Finger Lickin'...
(1981)

SLIM-BUT-SAUCY POT ROAST

3 lb. beef arm roast, trimmed of fat
2 tsps. salt
$^1/_8$ tsp. pepper
2 medium onions, sliced thin
1/2 can ($10^3/_4$ oz.) condensed Cheddar cheese soup
8 oz. tomato sauce
4 oz. can mushroom stems and pieces, undrained
$^1/_4$ tsp. oregano
$^1/_4$ tsp. basil

Roast meat, uncovered, in non-stick pan, or add a little oil or water in pan, at 475° just until browned well. Remove from oven. Pour off drippings, lower oven to 325°. Salt and pepper meat. In bowl, mix onions, soup, sauce, mushrooms, oregano, basil. Add to roast. Cover tightly; roast slowly, about $2^1/_2$ hours until tender. To serve, slice meat thinly. Serves 10.

Janice Wilson
Cookbook
Westfield
(1986)

LIVER-HATER'S LIVER

Tom Malinoski, of Forestville, won first prize in a 1982 recipe contest for this recipe. It is his own development, based on the liver-and-onions specialty of Venice, Italy, which he had tasted years earlier.

1. Make decent oil: Smash up a bunch of fresh garlic (about six cloves to a quart of oil) and dump it in a jug with a mixture of peanut/vegetable/olive oil. (I use $^1/_2$ pint peanut and $^1/_2$ pint vegetable oil.) Hide this away for a week or two, then strain out the hunks of garlic so they won't mold. This flavored oil will keep forever if sealed up right.
2. Get some good, fresh calf or baby beef liver—enough to feed your crowd. Liver should be no thicker than $^1/_4$ inch.
3. Mix up a batch of breading for the liver consisting of:
   a) Flour—maybe 2 cups (depends on amount of liver)
   b) Garlic salt—a Tablespoon or more
   c) Black pepper—$^1/_2$ to $^3/_4$ teaspoon
   d) Oregano— $^1/_4$ cup or more
4. Thoroughly smother the meat with breading, using the "Shake-n-Bake" technique.
5. Heat enough oil in a skillet (preferably iron) and FAST-fry the liver to brownish-gold color on both sides. (Liver will probably still be slightly pink on the inside.)
6. In another pan, fry up in real butter and garlic oil a whole batch of onions—as many as you can stand to cut up. Cut in long strips, not dice. Sauté, covered, on medium-high heat and don't let them brown. Add a shot or two of red or white wine to the pan while onions are cooking.
7. In a coverable skillet, put a bit of the garlic oil and about $^1/_8$-inch of red cooking wine and heat it to bubbling. Lay cooked liver pieces into this brew. Smother each piece with the cooked onions. Over the onions put a generous heap of FRESHLY GRATED Parmesan cheese. Grate it so it is shredded, not grated. Cover and simmer until all the cheese melts thoroughly.
8. EAT! Serve with a nice salad dressed with vinegar and garlic oil, pasta with cheese and butter and hot garlic oil ("Spaghetti al Burro"), and a nice wine.

Tom Malinoski in
The Artful Kitchen
(1982)

VEAL

BAKED VEAL WITH SWEET POTATOES

$2^1/_2$ lbs. veal cutlet (one piece about $1^1/_4$ in. thick)
undiluted Pet Milk
$^1/_2$ cup bread crumbs
$^1/_2$ cup flour
salt and pepper
2 Tbsps. shortening
$^1/_2$ cup Pet Milk, diluted with $^1/_2$ cup water
pinch of soda
6 sweet potatoes, peeled

Dredge cutlet in flour. Dip in undiluted Pet Milk, then in bread crumbs, flour and salt and pepper, mixed.

Melt shortening in skillet and brown the breaded veal well on both sides. Place in baking pan and add diluted Pet Milk with pinch of soda added. Surround with sweet potatoes.

Cover and bake in a slow oven, 275°, $1^1/_4$ hours. Serves six.

Mrs. James Gugino
Come Out . . .
(Date unknown)

BREADED VEAL CUTLET

4 (6-oz.) veal cutlets or 1 veal steak
Flour
3 Tbsps. grated Parmesan cheese
1 egg, beaten
1 tsp. minced parsley
$^1/_4$ tsp. grated nutmeg
$^1/_2$ cup milk
6 Tbsps. butter
3 Tbsps. lemon juice
Parsley for garnish
$^1/_2$ tsp. salt
$^1/_4$ tsp. pepper

Wipe meat with damp cloth and pound thin. Dip lightly in flour. Mix cheese, 2 Tablespoons flour, egg, parsley, salt, pepper, nutmeg and milk. Beat smooth. Dip floured cutlets in this batter. Cook over low heat in 4 tablespoons butter until golden and tender. Remove cutlets to warmed serving platter and keep them hot. Heat remaining butter until darkened; add lemon juice. Stir and pour over cutlets; garnish with parsley. Serves 4.

John V. Rizzo
A Cappella Choir . . .
(1986)

FROSTED VEAL LOAF SALAD

$1^1/_2$ Tbsps. unflavored gelatin
$^1/_4$ cup tomato juice
$1^3/_4$ cups tomato juice
1 tsp. grated onion
1 Tbsp. lemon juice
$^1/_8$ cup horseradish
$^1/_2$ cup sour cream
$^1/_4$ cup mayonnaise
2 cups cooked veal (shredded or cut very fine)

FROSTING:
$^1/_2$ tsp. gelatin (unflavored)
3 Tbsps. cold water
$^1/_2$ lb. cottage cheese
$^1/_2$ cup sour cream
$^1/_2$ cup cucumber, finely chopped
Salt and pepper to taste
$^1/_2$ green pepper, chopped
1 Tbsp. parsley, chopped

Soften gelatin in $^1/_4$ cup tomato juice. Bring remaining tomato juice to boiling point. Add onion and lemon juice to tomato juice. Add gelatin to hot mixture and stir until gelatin is dissolved. Chill. Combine horseradish, sour cream and mayonnaise and add to chilled tomato juice mixture. Chill. When slightly thickened add meat and pour into large ring mold. Chill.

Soak gelatin in cold water, then dissolve over hot water. Combine cheese, sour cream, cucumber, green pepper, parsley and seasonings. Add gelatin. Beat thoroughly. Pour on top of congealed mixture in ring mold. Chill until very firm. When ready to serve, unmold on garnished tray or platter. Serves 10-12. Special party buffet.

Mrs. Janice Myers
Post-Journal Cookbook
(1987)

PRESSED VEAL

2 lbs. veal, boiled until tender and seasoned with salt and pepper. Save 1 pint of broth. Put cooked meat through coarse grinder, add 1 Tbsp. or more mixed onion and celery seed to taste. Soak 2 Tbsps. Knox gelatin in cold water and add 1 pint hot broth. Blend with meat. Put half of mixture in bread tin, cover with 3 hard boiled eggs sliced. Add balance of meat. Set on ice. Unmold and serve.

Mrs. John F. Westrom
Norden Club . . .
(1930)

VEAL CACCIATORE

A family recipe for over 100 years.
2 lbs. veal, cut in 1" cubes
$2^1/_2$ cups canned tomatoes
$1^1/_2$ cups cold water
1 cup chopped onions
1 cup chopped celery
1 cup diced green peppers
1 Tbsp. salt
1 Tbsp. sugar
$^1/_2$ tsp. pepper
$^1/_2$ tsp. parsley flakes
pinch garlic powder

Brown veal cubes slightly in saucepan or large skillet with $^1/_3$ cup cooking oil. Add the remaining ingredients to veal and cook over low flame for 2 hours, until veal is tender. If preferred, after veal is browned, bake in large casserole at 350° for $2^1/_2$ hours. Sprinkle with grated Romano cheese and serve with Italian chef salad. Serves 4.

Samuel J. Galati
Galati's Restaurant
Wonderful Cooking . . .
(Date unknown)

VEAL MARSALA

1 clove garlic, sliced thin
$^1/_4$ cup olive oil
$1^1/_2$ to 2 lbs. veal, cut $^1/_2$" thick
$^1/_4$ cup flour
$^3/_4$ tsp. Ac'cent
$^1/_2$ tsp. salt
$^1/_8$ tsp. pepper
$^1/_4$ cup Marsala wine
$^1/_4$ cup water
$^1/_4$ tsp. chopped parsley
$^1/_8$ tsp. salt
$^1/_8$ tsp. pepper

Lightly brown garlic in olive oil in a large, heavy skillet with a tight-fitting cover. Wipe veal with a clean damp cloth and cut into six pieces. Coat veal with a mixture of the flour, Ac'cent, salt and pepper. Add coated veal to the garlic and oil and slowly brown on both sides.

Combine wine, water, parsley, and salt and pepper and slowly add to the browned veal. Cover skillet and simmer for 20 minutes or until veal is tender. If mixture becomes too thick, add a small amount of water. Serves 6.

Mrs. Andrew Scalise
What's Cookin' III
(1964-65)

VEAL PAPRIKA

2 lbs. veal shoulder
2 tsps. salt
$1/_8$ tsp. pepper
4 Tbsps. flour
2 tsps. paprika
2 cloves of garlic cut in two
1 cup hot water
$1/_2$ cup light cream or evaporated milk
4 Tbsps. fat
NOODLES WITH POPPY SEEDS
1 6-oz. package fine noodles
2 quarts boiling water
1 Tbsp. salt
$1/_4$ cup butter
$1/_4$ cup blanched almonds, coarsely chopped
2 tsps. poppy seeds

VEAL SHANKS MILANESE STYLE

(Osso Bucco)
6 veal shanks, about $2^1/_2$" thick
$1/_2$ cup flour
$1/_2$ cup salad oil
1 onion, finely chopped
1 carrot, grated
1 stalk celery, finely chopped
2 cloves garlic, minced
1 tsp. dried marjoram
$1/_2$ cup dry white wine
1 (16-oz.) can tomatoes
1 cup beef bouillon
1 Tbsp. chopped parsley
1 tsp. grated lemon rind

Cut veal in inch-sized pieces; dredge in the flour mixed with seasonings. Heat the garlic with the fat in a frying pan for two minutes. Add the meat and brown lightly; add the water; cover and simmer about 1 hour. Remove the garlic, add the cream or evaporated milk and heat two minutes longer. Serve on noodles with poppy seeds. Serves six.

Cook noodles in boiling salted water until tender, about 15 minutes. Melt 1 Tbsp. butter in frying pan, add almonds and stir over low heat until brown. Add remaining butter, noodles and poppy seeds..

Mrs. Marion Weber
Kiantone Cookbook
(1969)

Dredge veal shanks with flour. Heat oil in large Dutch oven. Brown veal in hot oil; remove. Add onion, carrot, celery, 1 clove garlic and marjoram. Cook over medium heat, stirring constantly, about 3 minutes. Add wine. Cook until wine is reduced by half. Return veal shanks; add tomatoes and bouillon. Cover; simmer 1 to $1^1/_2$ hours, or until veal is tender. Stir in remaining garlic, parsley and lemon rind; cook 1 minute and then serve. Makes 6 servings.

Josie Greco
Here's What's Cookin' ... (1988)

HAM and PORK

BACON ROAST

2 $\frac{1}{2}$ lbs. Canadian bacon in chunk
$\frac{1}{2}$ cup water
2 lemons
1 Tbsp. grated onion
1 Tbsp. dry mustard
1 Tbsp. ginger
1 Tbsp. wine vinegar
1 Tbsp. sherry
$\frac{1}{2}$ tsp. salt
dash cayenne pepper
1$\frac{1}{2}$ cups currant jelly
$\frac{1}{4}$ cup hot water

Place bacon in baking dish. Add $\frac{1}{2}$ cup water, cover and bake at 300° for 2 hours. Cut 1 lemon in strips and put over top of bacon. Grate rind of $\frac{1}{4}$ lemon and squeeze out juice from whole lemon. Mix onion, mustard and ginger in a bowl. Blend in vinegar, sherry, salt, cayenne, lemon juice and rind. Add jelly and $\frac{1}{4}$ cup hot water. Blend and pour over bacon when nearly done. Baste several times. Bake until done.

Mrs. Guy Northrup
Silver Creek's Own . . .
(Date unknown)

BACON AND FRUIT RINGS

Good for Breakfast or Light Dinner. Serve with waffles or pancakes.
1 lb. Bacon
2 oranges
3 red cooking apples, cored
$\frac{1}{4}$ cup honey
$\frac{1}{4}$ cup water
2 Tbsps. packed brown sugar

In large skillet, fry bacon until crisp. Remove from skillet; drain on paper towels. Keep warm in oven. Drain drippings from skillet, reserving 3 Tbsps. Peel oranges and slice into segments. Slice apples into $\frac{1}{2}$-inch rings (do not peel). Brown fruit lightly on both sides in reserved bacon drippings.

Combine honey, water and brown sugar. Pour over fruit in skillet. Cover and simmer just until tender. Arrange fruit and bacon on heated platter. Serves 6.

Woodrow Hollister
Kiantone Cookbook
(1989)

ANNIE'S QUICKIE DINNER
Ham Balls, Spicy Applesauce, Buttered Noodles

HAM BALLS:
4 cups (2 lbs.) ground, cooked ham
1 tsp. minced onion
1 cup crushed/ground seasoned stuffing mix
2 eggs
3 to 4 Tbsps. evaporated milk
dash of pepper
2 Tbsps. salad oil

Combine thoroughly, except salad oil. Shape into balls, lightly brown in oil. Cover pan, reduce heat, cook 10 to 12 minutes until done. Serves 4 to 6.

SPICY APPLESAUCE:
2 cups canned applesauce
juice and grated rind of $1/2$ lemon
$1/3$ cup cinnamon red hots
$1/4$ tsp. nutmeg
dash of salt

In small pan, combine all except lemon rind. Stir over moderate heat until red hots are melted. Cook until very hot and bubbling. May need lid to keep stove clean. Serve hot with ham balls. Sprinkle with lemon rind.

BUTTERED NOODLES:
8 oz. wide noodles
$1/4$ cup heavy cream
2 Tbsps. chopped parsley
2 Tbsps. butter
salt
pepper

Cook noodles as directed, drain. Add other ingredients and toss together until butter melts. Serve with ham balls and applesauce.

Ann E. Weidman
Cookbook
Westfield
(1986)

HAM LOAF I

1½ lbs. ground fresh pork
1½ lbs. ground smoked ham
1 cup soft bread crumbs
1 cup milk
1 egg, beaten

Combine all ingredients and mix well. Form into loaf and bake in a shallow greased pan at 375° for 1¼ to 1½ hours. Baste often while baking, with sauce made of the following ingredients:
½ cup brown sugar
1 tsp. mustard
1½ cup diluted vinegar

Mary S. Lamphear
Chautauqua-Allegheny Cookbook
(1990)

BAKED CROWN OF HAM

3 eggs
¾ cup milk
3 cups soft bread crumbs
1 cup ketchup
4 tsps. Worcestershire sauce
⅓ cup minced onion
⅛ tsp. pepper
2 lbs. ground smoked ham shoulder
2 lbs. ground veal shoulder
½ cup currant jelly
2 Tbsps. fat or salad oil
Parsley, apple wedges

Beat eggs; add milk and crumbs; let stand 10 minutes. Add ketchup, Worcestershire sauce, onion and pepper. Add ham and veal; mix well. Pack in a greased tube pan 10 inches in diameter. Bake in a 350° oven for 2 hours. Unmold in a shallow pan; spread top and sides with jelly. Bake in a 350° oven for 30 minutes. Sauté apple wedges in fat or salad oil. Use to garnish ham. Sprinkle with parsley. Serves 12-16.

Catherine Cleland
Art/Dunkirk
(1960s)

HAM LOAF II

(TO SERVE 50)
5 lbs. ground smoked ham
4 lbs. ground veal
3 green peppers, minced
1 cup chopped celery leaves
$^1/_2$ cup chopped parsley
1 cup minced onion
2 tsps. salt
1 tsp. pepper
8 eggs, beaten
3 (15-oz.) cans evaporated milk
3 cups quick cooking oats

Combine all ingredients and mix well with hands. Shape into 6 loaves and place in shallow baking pans. Bake for $1^1/_2$ hours in a moderate oven (350°). Slice and serve hot. Serve with sauce made with equal parts of prepared mustard and currant jelly, blend together.

Hazel Nixon
Saint Peter's . . .
(1979)

HAM MADIERA

$3^1/_2$ to 4 lbs. ham (boneless, sliced $^1/_2$ inch thick)

3 Tbsps. flour
3 Tbsps. scallions
1 Tbsp. tomato paste
$1^1/_2$ cups heavy cream
large pinch of pepper
1 cup canned beef bouillon
$^1/_2$ cup Madiera or port wine
3 Tbsps. Cognac

Dry ham on paper towel and brown in heavy pan in 2 Tbsps. butter and 1 Tbsp. oil. Pour off all but 2 Tbsps. fat and put ham in casserole.

Make paste of flour and fat already in heavy pan. Add scallions. Cook till scallions are wilted, but not brown. Add bouillon and Madiera. Beat with wire whip until smooth. Add pepper, cream and Cognac. Cook 4 or 5 minutes until sauce coats a spoon lightly. (This can be made ahead and reheated to simmering point. It also freezes well.)

Pour sauce over ham and heat in oven.

Arlene Maier
Dames in the Kitchen
(1975)

HAM STEAK INCREDIBLE

ham steak, 1" thick
maple syrup
$1/4$ cup brown sugar
milk to cover
2 Tbsps. salad-style mustard

Make paste of 2 Tbsps. of mustard and $1/4$ cup brown sugar. Spread on both sides of ham and lay ham slice gently in a pan just big enough. Pour milk into pan until ham is just barely covered. Add $1/2$ cup maple syrup. Bake in oven at 350° for $1^1/2$ hours. Pour off any remaining milk and cut slice into 1-inch cubes. Pour $1/4$ tsp. maple syrup over each cube. Let stand on heated platter before serving.

Dr. Gordon R. Sanctuary
Wonderful Cooking . . .
(Date unknown)

FRENCH PORK CHOPS

6 center cut pork chops, $3/4$ inch thick
2 Tbsps. fat
Sauté chops in fat in electric skillet at 300°.

SAUCE:
1 large onion, chopped
1 Tbsp. fat
2 Tbsps. flour
$1/2$ tsp. salt
$1/8$ tsp. pepper
2 tsps. prepared mustard
1 can bouillon or 2 cups water plus 2 beef bouillon cubes
3 Tbsps. chopped sweet pickles or pickle relish

Cook onions in fat until golden in color; add flour, salt, pepper and mustard. Stir until well blended, add stock and cook 5 minutes, add sweet pickles. Pour over meat and cook at 200° for 50 minutes or more until meat is well done.

Lillian Ball
Cooking with . . .
Dunkirk
(1972)

PORK CHOPS WITH LIMA BEANS

6 loin chops, 1 inch thick
2 onions, sliced
salt and pepper
$^1/_2$ cup water
$^1/_2$ cup milk
1 can cream of celery soup
$^1/_2$ tsp. dried thyme
$^1/_2$ tsp. poultry seasoning
$^1/_2$ tsp. dried oregano
$^1/_2$ tsp. salt
1 Tbsp. flour
1 pkg. frozen Fordhook limas
This makes the most delicious gravy and is our favorite
Sunday dinner.

Brown chops in trimmed fat, sprinkle with salt, pepper. Remove to casserole. Sauté onions in fat and sprinkle over chops. Add 1 Tbsp. flour to fat, then $^1/_2$ cup water and mix. Combine soup, milk, seasonings; add to flour mixture and cook until bubbly. Put thawed limas over chops, pour sauce over all. Cover and bake at 350° for 1 hour. Serves 6.

Alice Deakin
Cookbook
Westfield
(1986)

ROAST PORK POLISH STYLE

4 to 5 lb. pork loin
$1^1/_2$ Tbsps. flour
1 tsp. salt
$^1/_2$ tsp. sugar
1 tsp. dry mustard
$^1/_2$ tsp. sage
$^1/_4$ tsp. pepper

Mix the ingredients and rub thoroughly into the loin. Roast at 325° uncovered from 4 to 5 hours, until tender. Make your gravy as usual using the pan drippings.

Karen Grabowski
Favorite Recipes
Diana Lodge
(1968)

MAPLE BARBECUED RIBS

3 lbs. spareribs
1 cup pure maple syrup
2 Tbsps. chili sauce
2 Tbsps. cider vinegar
1 grind black pepper
$^1/_2$ cup chopped onion
2 tsps. Worcestershire sauce
1 tsp. salt
$^1/_2$ tsp. dry mustard
$^1/_4$ cup brandy

Cut spareribs into serving size pieces and place a single layer in a shallow baking dish. Mix the remaining ingredients and pour over ribs, turning to coat all sides. Bake in preheated 375° oven for $1^1/_2$ to 2 hours. Turn ribs and brush frequently while baking. Ribs are done when meat is very tender. Makes 4 to 6 servings.

Pam Menke
Centennial Cook Book
(1987)

SWEET AND SOUR PORK

1 lb. shoulder pork (for 3; $1^1/_2$ lbs. serves 4)
2 Tbsps. soy sauce
1 Tbsp. cornstarch
1 cup oil
1 medium onion, diced
1 medium cucumber, peeled and diced
1 small can water chestnuts, optional
1 small can bamboo shoots, optional

SWEET-SOUR SAUCE
$^3/_4$ cup sugar
$^1/_4$ cup soy sauce
2 Tbsps. cornstarch
$^1/_3$ cup vinegar
$^2/_3$ cup water

Wash and cube pork. Boil in $^1/_2$ cup cold water until tender (about 20 minutes). Drain and cool. Dredge (cover) pork with mixture of soy sauce and cornstarch. Heat oil very hot. Fry pork until brown. Remove and drain. Sauté vegetables in 2 Tbsps. of the oil for one minute. Add prepared sweet-sour sauce; bring to a boil. Boil for a minute or so, until dark. Add pork and heat thoroughly. Serve with rice (1 cup uncooked rice per pound of meat).

Pat Brininger
Our Favorite . . .
(1970s)

K'AI-OAU-KU

(Barbecued Spareribs)
2 lbs. spareribs in one piece

Marinade:
$1/4$ cup soy sauce
2 Tbsps. honey
2 Tbsps. Hoisin sauce
2 Tbsps. white vinegar
1 Tbsp. Chinese rice wine, or pale dry sherry
1 tsp. finely chopped garlic
1 tsp. sugar
2 Tbsps. chicken stock, fresh or canned
canned plum sauce.

Trim excess fat from the spareribs. Place ribs in a long, shallow dish, large enough to hold them comfortably.

Combine marinade ingredients and stir until they are well mixed. Pour over spareribs and marinate 3 hours (6 if refrigerated). Turn and baste occasionally.

Preheat oven to 375°. To catch drippings and to prevent oven from smoking fill a shallow baking dish with water and place on lowest oven rack. Using S-hooks of 5" lengths or bent wire (coathangers will do) suspend ribs from uppermost rack directly above water. Roast 45 minutes. Raise oven to 450° and roast 15 minutes longer until golden brown. Separate with cleaver or heavy knife. Large ribs should be chopped in half crosswise. Serve hot or cold with plum sauce.

Ann Hallquist
Euclid Avenue . . .
(1980)

CANADIAN BACON STACKUPS

1 cup whole cranberry sauce
2 Tbsps. light corn syrup
1 17 oz. can sweet potatoes, drained
1 Tbsp. butter or margarine, melted
1 Tbsp. brown sugar
$1/4$ tsp. ground ginger
1 lb. unsliced Canadian style bacon

Combine cranberry sauce and corn syrup in a bowl. Beat potatoes, butter, brown sugar and ginger with electric mixer till light and fluffy. Slice bacon into 12 pieces. Arrange 6 slices in baking dish and spread $1/2$ potato mixture equally on each slice. Top with 6 remaining bacon slices and cover with remaining potato mixture. Drizzle with cranberry sauce over stacks. Bake at 350° for 45 minutes, basting once or twice with sauce in dish. Serves 6.

Evelyn Marzullo
Cook Book
Dunkirk
(1978)

LAMB

FASOLIA FRESCA ME ARNI

(String Beans with Lamb)
2 lbs. lamb (leg or shoulder)
$^1/_2$ stick butter (or less)
1 large onion, chopped
1 (15-oz.) can tomatoes
$1^1/_2$ cups water
2 lbs. fresh string beans
salt, to taste
pepper, to taste

Have meat cut into serving pieces. Sauté in butter for 5 minutes in large saucepan, browning on all sides. Add onions and cook for 10 minutes. Add tomatoes, salt and pepper. Cover pan. Bring to boil for 7 minutes. Add water and reduce heat and cook for $^1/_2$ hour.

In the meantime clean and wash string beans. Break in half, add to meat and continue cooking for $1^1/_2$ hours or until done. Serve as main dish. Serves 4 to 6.

Mrs. Catherine Petra
recipe from Greece
Jamestown's International . . .
(1960s)

SPRING LAMBURGERS

1 lb. ground lean lamb
$^1/_2$ cup fine bread crumbs
$^1/_3$ cup grated carrot
1 Tbsp. grated onion
1 Tbsp. chopped parsley
1 tsp. salt
dash of pepper
1 slightly beaten egg
4 pineapple slices
melted butter

Combine all ingredients, except pineapple and butter. Form in four $^3/_4$ inch thick loosely packed patties. Place patties on broiler rack. Broil 4 to 5 inches from heat for 7 to 8 minutes, or until browned. Turn patties, place pineapple along side and brush with butter. Broil 5 to 6 minutes more until meat is done. Serves 4.

Marion Hiller
Cookbook
Westfield
(1986)

KIBEE

1 lb. lean ground lamb or beef
2 cups cracked wheat (bulgur)
1 medium onion, ground
salt and pepper to taste
cinnamon to taste
$^1/_2$ cup cold water

FILLING:
clarified butter
1 Tbsp. butter
cinnamon to taste
salt and pepper to taste
2 large onions
$^1/_4$ cup pine nuts (optional)

Grease a 10 x 14" baking pan with clarified butter. Mix lamb or beef, bulgur, onion, salt, pepper, and cinnamon. Dip hand in water and spread half of raw kibee smoothly over bottom of pan.

For filling, simmer onions in 2-4 Tbsps. clarified butter. Add cinnamon, salt, and pepper and mix. Brown pine nuts in additional Tbsp. of butter and add to onions. Spread this filling evenly over the layer of kibee in the pan. Cover filling with remaining kibee and smooth surface well. Score in triangles with a knife. Loosen edges from tray with spatula. Pour one cup clarified butter over top. Bake in 400° oven for one hour until browned. Serves 8 to 10.

Mary Sam Catalano
Treasured Recipes
(1988)

OSSO BUCCO A LA C.I.A.O.
BRAISED LAMB SHANKS

2 pounds lamb shanks, cut into $1^1/_2$ inch sections
Salt and pepper
Oil for sautéeing
Flour for dredging
1 cup sliced onions
1 cup sliced fennel bulbs
1 Tbsp. chopped garlic
1 cup red wine
2 cups chopped tomatoes
3 cups light stock
2 Tbsps. chopped fresh oregano
$^1/_4$ cup pitted Kalamata olives
2 ounces Feta cheese, crumbled

Preheat oven to 400°. Highly season the lamb shanks on both sides with salt and pepper. Heat $^1/_2$ cup oil in a large Dutch oven. Dredge the shanks in the flour, shake off any excess flour. Sear the shanks on both sides until golden brown. Add the onions, fennel, and garlic. Cook for 4 minutes, moving everything around to ensure it's all cooking. Add the wine, tomatoes and stock. Bring to a boil, cover and place in the oven.

Cook for $1^1/_2$ hours or until the meat is so tender it falls from the bone. Adjust the seasonings. Remove from the Dutch oven and place on a platter. Top with chopped oregano, olives, and feta. Serves 4.

No name given
C.I.A.O. Italian Traditions Cookbook
(1980s)

POULTRY

PRESSED CHICKEN

After a chicken has been prepared for cooking, place in kettle and put on enough cold water to cover, skim as the scum rises; let boil until the chicken is tender enough to drop from the bones; skim out; if water has not boiled away to the amount of one tea cup, boil it so; free chicken from bone, skin and gristle, pick fine with the hands; season with salt, pepper and butter the size of a small egg, unless chicken is very rich, then do not use as much; stir in the cooking liquid (reduced), and mix well; pour into a square, deep baking tin, and with a spoon press down well. Lay on the chicken a piece of cloth, then a light board, and a very light weight, and set in a cold place.

Kate Cook
Chautauqua Cook Book
(1882)

PRESSED CHICKEN

Take one or two chickens, boil in a small quantity of water with a little salt and when thoroughly done take all the meat from the bones, removing the skin and keeping the light meat separate from the dark; chop and season to taste with salt and pepper; put in a pan a layer of light and a layer of dark meat till all is used; add the liquor it was boiled in which should be about one teacupful; then cover and put on a heavy weight. When cold cut in slices.

Philergian . . .
(1888)

Remove pin feathers from a foul with a strawberry huller.
Cook Book, Jamestown (1920s)
TIP

BRENT'S FAVORITE CHICKEN

6 boneless chicken breasts
1 tsp. oregano
2 Tbsps. Parmesan cheese
salt and pepper to taste
$^1/_2$ cup bread crumbs
1 tsp. basil
$^1/_2$ tsp. garlic salt
$^1/_4$ lb. butter or margarine

SAUCE:
$^1/_4$ cup fresh parsley
$^1/_4$ cup green onions
$^1/_4$ cup white wine

Mix bread crumbs, cheese, and seasonings together. Melt butter and dip breasts in melted butter and cover with bread crumbs mixture. Bake at 350° for 55 minutes. Remove from oven and cover with remaining melted butter to which you add parsley, green onion, and wine. Put back in oven for another 5 minutes and serve.

Eileen Catalano
Treasured Recipes
(1988)

Originally in WCA Cookbook, this casserole appeared often. It's a favorite.

NO PEEK CHICKEN CASSEROLE

1 can mushroom soup
1 pint fresh, sliced mushrooms
1 can celery soup
1 cup water
parsley flakes
dash curry
1 envelope Lipton's onion soup mix
6 large half chicken breasts,
    boned or 6 to 8 pieces chicken (legs, thighs, breasts)
$1^1/_3$ cup Uncle Ben's Long Grain & Wild Rice,
    with seasoning

Mix rice, canned soups, water, parsley and curry in well-buttered casserole. Sprinkle on sliced mushrooms. Lay chicken on top. Sprinkle onion soup mix over chicken. Seal tightly with heavy duty foil and bake at 350° for $2^1/_4$ hours and Don't Peek! Slivered, toasted almonds may be sprinkled over the top just before serving. This is a never-fail casserole when you have guests and want to take the work out of cooking. It should be served with a green vegetable, tossed salad and dessert. Serves 5-6.

Mrs. Howard Johnson
100 Years of Cooking . . .
(1986)

CHICKEN CON QUESO

3 lbs. chicken breasts
salt and pepper
2 cans (13-oz.) chicken broth
1 medium chopped onion
1 cup sliced celery
2 chopped carrots
$^1/_3$ cup butter
$^1/_2$ cup flour
1 cup heavy cream
1 cup shredded Monterey Jack cheese (4 oz.)

TOPPING:
2 cups Bisquick
$^1/_2$ cup milk
3-oz. cream cheese
2 Tbsps. milk
1 Tbsp. parsley
1 Tbsp. chives

Wash chicken, dry, and sprinkle with salt and pepper. Place pieces in large kettle with cover. Add chicken broth, onion, celery, and carrots. Cover. Heat to boiling and simmer 45 minutes (until chicken is tender). Remove chicken and vegetables to 2-quart casserole dish. Reserve 2 cups of broth for sauce. Melt butter in saucepan over low heat, stir in flour. Gradually add chicken broth and cream. Add Jack cheese and stir until cheese is melted. Pour over chicken and vegetables in casserole and stir. (Refrigerate if making early in day, then heat slowly while making topping.)

Combine Bisquick mix and milk in bowl. Remove to lightly floured surface and knead dough a few times until it forms a smooth ball. Roll out to an 8" square. Mash cream cheese and milk in a small bowl until fluffy, stir in parsley and chives. Spread cream cheese mixture over dough. Roll up jelly roll fashion. With a sharp knife, cut roll into 8 slices. Place slices cut side up, side by side on top of casserole. Bake at 400° for 25 minutes or until crust is lightly browned.

Carol Mahany
Our Culinary Favorites
(1984)

TIP *If a chicken is rubbed inside and out with a cut lemon before it is cooked, it will make the meat white, juicy and tender.*
Cook Book, Jamestown (1920s)

CHICKEN PICCATA

4 whole chicken breasts, skinned,
    boned and halved (8 pieces)
$1/_2$ cup flour
$1^1/_2$ tsps. salt
$1/_4$ tsp. freshly ground pepper
paprika
$1/_4$ cup butter
1 Tbsp. olive oil
2 to 4 Tbsps. dry Madeira or water
3 Tbsps. fresh lemon juice
lemon slices
3 to 4 Tbsps. capers (optional)
$1/_4$ cup minced fresh parsley

Place chicken breasts between two sheets of waxed paper and pound them until thin (about $1/_4$ inch). Combine flour, salt, pepper and paprika in a bag. Add breasts and coat well; shake off excess. Heat butter and olive oil in large skillet until bubbling. Sauté chicken breasts, a few at a time, 2 to 3 minutes on each side. Do Not Overcook. Drain on paper towel and keep warm. Drain off all but 2 Tbsps. of butter and oil. Stir Madeira or water into drippings, scraping bottom of skillet to loosen any browned bits. Return chicken to skillet, interspersing with lemon slices and heat until sauce thickens. Add capers; sprinkle with minced parsley. Serve immediately with fettucini and cooked broccoli. Serves 4 - 8.

Rachel Borzelleri
Cooking by Degrees
(1985)

SKILLET CHICKEN BREASTS PARMIGIANA

2 Tbsps. vegetable oil
3 large cloves garlic
4 skinned, boned chicken breast halves
$3/_4$ tsp. salt
$1/_4$ tsp. pepper
2 medium yellow summer squash, sliced thin
$1^1/_2$ cups cooked fresh or frozen green beans
$1/_4$ tsp. oregano
4 slices mozzarella cheese
$2/_3$ cup spaghetti sauce

Heat oil in large heavy skillet over medium heat. Add garlic and cook until golden; discard garlic. Add chicken; cook about 3 minutes, sprinkle with $1/_4$ tsp. salt and pepper and remove from skillet. Add squash and green beans to skillet, sprinkle oregano and remaining salt and pepper in vegetables. Cook 5 minutes. Push to sides of pan and place chicken in center of pan. Top each piece of chicken with slice of cheese, then spoon on sauce. Cover and cook 7 minutes, until cheese is melted and sauce is hot. Serves 4.

Laurie Volpe
Here's What's Cookin' . . .
(1988)

SATÉ AYAM

(Chicken Saté, Indonesian)
3 whole chicken breasts (2 1/2 lbs. in all)

MARINADE:
2 Tbsps. butter or margarine, melted
1 clove garlic, finely chopped
$^1/_2$ tsp. ginger or 1/4 inch slice of fresh ginger root
2 Tbsps. soy sauce
$^1/_2$ tsp. salt

PEANUT SAUCE:
1 Tbsp. salad oil
$^1/_2$ clove garlic, finely chopped
2 Tbsps. coarsely chopped green onion
1 Tbsp. soy sauce
$^1/_2$ tsp. paprika
$^1/_2$ tsp. shrimp or anchovy paste
$^1/_4$ tsp. salt
$^1/_2$ tsp. chili powder
$^1/_2$ cup chunk-style peanut butter
1 Tbsp. light brown sugar
1 Tbsp. lime or lemon juice
$^3/_4$ cup coconut water (liquid poured out of coconut)

GARNISH:
2 Tbsps. salad oil
2 Tbsps. sliced green onion

Skin and bone chicken breasts; then cut chicken into strips, 1 inch wide and $1^1/_2$ inches long. On each of 6 skewers thread about 5 chicken strips. Make marinade by combining butter, garlic, ginger, soy sauce and salt in flat glass baking dish. Use to coat chicken on skewers. Let chicken stand in marinade 30 minutes, turning several times.

Meanwhile make peanut sauce. In hot oil in small saucepan, sauté garlic and onion until golden, stirring. Add rest of sauce ingredients; cook over medium heat, stirring until sauce is thickened and hot. Keep warm. Broil chicken satés on rack in broiler pan 4 inches from heat for 15 minutes, turning several times.

Meanwhile in small skillet, combine 1 Tbsp. brown sugar and 1 Tbsp. soy sauce. Stir over low heat, just until sugar is melted and set aside. Make garnish: In hot oil in small skillet, sauté onion just until golden brown and crisp. Drain on paper towels. To serve: Arrange satés on platter. Pour peanut sauce over chicken; then drizzle soy sauce mixture over top and garnish with fried onion. Makes 8 servings.

Dorothy Maché
Centennial Cookbook
(1987)

SHERRIED CHICKEN BREASTS

4 whole chicken breasts, skinned and boned, cut in half
$1/4$ to $1/2$ cup margarine
$1/2$ cup sliced mushrooms
3 scallions, chopped
$1/4$ cup dry sherry
$1/2$ cup chicken broth
$1/2$ cup grated mozzarella cheese
3 Tbsps. grated Parmesan cheese

Sauté chicken breasts in large skillet using 2 Tbsps. of the margarine, adding more margarine if necessary. Cook chicken 15 minutes, over low heat. Remove chicken from skillet. Place in a single layer in a greased baking dish. Melt 2 more tablespoons of the margarine in the same skillet. Sauté mushrooms and scallions until mushrooms are lightly colored. Spoon mushrooms and scallions over chicken, reserving pan drippings. Add sherry and broth to drippings. Blend well, scraping pan. Simmer 2 to 3 minutes. Pour sauce over chicken. Sprinkle with mozzarella and Parmesan. (Can be refrigerated until baking time.) Bake uncovered at 350° for 20 minutes. 4 to 6 servings.

Mary Ann Domenico
Centennial Cook Book
(1987)

BARBECUED CHICKEN

(Cornell University tested recipe)
1 cup cooking oil
2 cups cider vinegar
2 Tbsps. salt
1 tsp. poultry seasoning
1 tsp. pepper
1 egg
10 broiler halves

Beat egg; add oil and beat again. Add remaining ingredients and stir. Place broiler halves over fire. Turn every 5 to 10 minutes, basting with sauce. Baste lightly at first. Increase as cooking time goes on. Chicken will be ready in 45 to 80 minutes, depending on heat of fire. Makes 10 servings.

Lucille Keech
Cookbook
Westfield
(1986)

HERBED CHICKEN

3 to 3$^1/_2$ lbs. chicken pieces
$^1/_2$ tsp. thyme
$^1/_2$ tsp. marjoram
$^3/_4$ to 1 cup flour
fat or oil
$^1/_2$ tsp. rosemary
1 Tbsp. parsley
$^1/_2$ tsp. salt
$^1/_4$ tsp. pepper
$^3/_4$ cup water

Sprinkle chicken with thyme and marjoram and let stand 1 hour. Roll chicken in flour and brown on all sides. Place in baking dish. Sprinkle browned chicken with rosemary, parsley, salt and pepper. Pour water into frying pan. Mix well and pour over chicken. Bake at 375° for 40 to 45 minutes. Makes 4 or 5 servings.

Virginia Savage
What's Cooking V
(1980)

CHICKEN A L'ORANGE

The oranges give both color and flavor.
1 frying chicken, cut up
salt and pepper
$^1/_4$ cup flour
$^1/_4$ cup vegetable shortening or oil
1 cup orange juice
$^1/_2$ cup chili sauce
$^1/_4$ cup chopped green pepper
1 tsp. prepared mustard
$^1/_2$ to 1 tsp. garlic salt
2 Tbsps. soy sauce
1 Tbsp. molasses
3 medium oranges, peeled and sliced in half cartwheels

Wash and dry chicken pieces and season with salt and pepper. Dredge with flour. Heat shortening in skillet; add chicken and brown lightly on all sides. Remove chicken to 3 quart casserole. Drain fat from skillet. Add remaining ingredients, except orange slices, and simmer 2 or 3 minutes. Pour sauce over chicken in casserole. Cover and bake in a moderate oven (350°) 50 to 60 minutes, or until chicken is tender. Just before serving, add orange slices. Serves 4.

Faith Hall
What's Cooking VI
(1966)

CHICKEN CURRY ON RICE

1 chicken
2 Tbsps. butter
2 Tbsps. bacon drippings
3 Tbsps. flour
2 Tbsps. curry powder
2 cups chicken stock, fat removed
salt and cayenne
1 Tbsp. chopped celery
1 Tbsp. chopped onion

Boil chicken in 3 quarts water with a little celery, onion, salt and pepper. Bone, skin, cut meat into $1^{1}/_{2}$-inch cubes. Slightly brown flour in butter and drippings. Add curry, brown a little more. Add stock, make a good gravy. Season to taste. Put chicken meat in double boiler, add onion, celery and pour gravy over all. Keep hot 1 to 2 hours. Serve over rice. Serves 8. Condiments for 12 to 14 servings (2 fowl, 2 pounds rice): 1 pound bacon, fried crisp, chopped fine; 4 hard-boiled eggs, mashed through a potato ricer; 3 small green peppers, shredded fine; 1 dozen chopped walnuts; sliced onion rings; 1 pound chutney. Note: From a Filipino Navy steward.

Dr. Kent Brown
Cookbook
Westfield
(1986)

CHICKEN CHAUTAUQUA

Pour hot tap water over the contents of a $2^{1}/_{2}$-ounce jar of dried (chipped) beef. Allow to stand about 10 minutes. (Soaking removes excess salt and rehydrates the beef.) Lightly squeeze the excess water from the meat and line a baking dish with it. Since it's wet, it will stick to the sides of a straight-sided dish so you can make a pretty scalloped edge with the beef if you're artistic.

Next, wrap pieces of a cut-up chicken with thin slices of ham or half-slices of uncooked bacon. Put the chicken in the lined dish.

In a bowl, stir together 1 can of cream of chicken soup, a cup of sour cream and a couple of tablespoons of sherry. Pour over all and cover closely.

Bake 2 hours at 300° - no hotter or sauce will "split". Remove cover and bake an additional 45 minutes. Serve with rice.

Elaine Laughlin
Goodbye Dining Hall . . .
(1982)

CHICKEN CACCIATORE

2 (2$^1/_2$ - 3 lb.) chickens, cut up for frying
6 Tbsps. fat or salad oil
1 cup minced onion
$^3/_4$ cup minced green pepper
4 cloves garlic, minced
$^1/_2$ tsp. oregano
1 bay leaf
1 (6-oz.) can tomato paste
1 (15-oz.) can tomato puree
$^1/_2$ cup Chianti wine (or vinegar)
3$^3/_4$ tsps. salt
$^1/_2$ tsp. pepper
$^1/_2$ tsp. thyme
dash of cayenne
1 (29-oz.) can tomatoes

Heat fat in iron skillet or Dutch oven, brown chicken. Add onion, green pepper and garlic. Brown lightly. Add other ingredients; cover tightly and simmer 45 minutes. Serve with rice.

Mrs. William Dickson
What's Cooking I
Jamestown
(1954)

GARLIC-ROASTED CHICKEN AND POTATOES

4 Tbsps. butter or margarine
6 chicken legs
6 medium potatoes
24 garlic cloves, unpeeled
1 tsp. salt
$^1/_4$ cup maple syrup

In large roasting pan (17$^1/_4$ x 11$^1/_4$ inches) in a 400° oven, melt butter. Remove. Cut chicken legs apart at joints. Cut potatoes in bite-sized chunks. Place chicken, potato, and garlic in roasting pan. Sprinkle with salt. Turn to coat with melted butter. Arrange chicken skin-side up. Bake 40 minutes. Baste occasionally with drippings. Brush chicken with maple syrup. Spoon drippings over potatoes occasionally. Bake 20 minutes longer or until tender.

Emily Graham
Culinary Delights
(1988-89)

SPICY OVEN-FRIED CHICKEN

$^1/_3$ cup yellow corn meal
$^1/_3$ cup flour
1 tsp. salt
$^1/_2$ tsp. cayenne
$^1/_2$ tsp. leaf oregano, crumbled
$^1/_2$ cup milk
1 broiler-fryer, about $3^1/_2$ lbs. cut up
6 Tbsps. ($^3/_4$ stick) butter or margarine, melted

Combine corn meal, flour, salt, cayenne and oregano on waxed paper. Pour milk into pie plate. Dip chicken pieces into milk, then roll in corn meal mixture, coating thoroughly. Place in a jellyroll pan in single layer. Drizzle butter over. Bake at 375° for 40 minutes or until chicken is fork-tender.

Marion Hiller
Cookbook
Westfield
(1986)

HUNGARIAN CHICKEN PAPRIKA

4 lbs. chicken (16 pieces)
4 rounded Tbsps. shortening
3 tsps. sweet paprika
2 tsps. salt
1 large onion, diced
1 large green pepper, diced (optional)
1 cup water
1 pint sour cream
1 Tbsp. cornstarch

Season chicken with salt and paprika, let stand for $^1/_2$ hour. In Dutch oven, melt shortening and sauté onion until golden. Add peppers, paprika and 2 Tbsps. water. Stew for 5 to 10 minutes. Add chicken, salt and water. Stew, covered, until chicken is tender, turning once. If necessary, add water to retain level. Before serving, spoon off several ladles of juice into a saucepan. Add sour cream gradually until smooth gravy forms, return to Dutch oven and bring to boil. If thicker gravy is desired, add cornstarch. Serve with dumplings. Serves 5.

Julianne M. Panty
"Someone's in . . ."
(1980s)

CHICKEN RING

2 fowls, cooked tender (about 4 lbs. each)
4 cups soft bread crumbs
2 cups cooked rice
2 tsps salt
1 tsp. paprika
$^1/_2$ cup chopped pimiento
8 well-beaten eggs
$^1/_2$ cup butter or chicken fat
$1^1/_2$ quarts milk or stock (half and half may be used.
   Use less salt if stock is used.)

Remove meat from bones and cut into uniform pieces. Combine all ingredients in order given and mix well. Pack in 2 generous sized, buttered ring molds. Bake at 325° 45-60 minutes. Allow to stand 10 minutes or longer in warm place for easy removal. Turn onto large platters and fill with mushroom sauce made as follows:

MUSHROOM SAUCE
$^1/_2$ cup butter or margarine
1 lb. fresh mushrooms
$^1/_2$ cup flour
1 quart chicken stock
4 beaten egg yolks
$^1/_2$ cup cream
$^1/_2$ tsp. salt
$^1/_4$ tsp. paprika
1 Tbsp. chopped parsley
1 Tbsp. lemon juice

Melt 4 Tbsps butter in frying pan, add mushrooms. Cook gently 5 minutes. Do not brown. Place remaining butter in upper part of double boiler, add flour, and stir to smooth paste. Stir in gradually hot broth, cook until thick and creamy. Add egg yolks beaten with cream, seasonings. Add mushrooms, parsley, lemon juice. Serve hot. Serves 20.

Marion Mead
To the Town's Taste
(1964)

TIP

PICNIC MEAL FOR 100 PEOPLE
20 chickens   *2 hams*
9 dozen deviled eggs   *9 dozen pimiento cheese sandwiches*
7 quarts pickles   *20 pies*
7 cakes   *1 lb. tea*
5 gallons potato salad   *2 lbs. coffee*

Cook Book, Dunkirk (1978)

MAPLE CHICKEN

$2^1/_2$ - 3 lbs. chicken, cut-up
$^1/_4$ cup melted butter
$^1/_2$ tsp. salt
dash of pepper
$^1/_2$ cup maple syrup
$^1/_2$ tsp. grated lemon rind
$^1/_2$ cup chopped almonds (optional)
2 tsps. lemon juice

Place chicken pieces in shallow baking pan. Mix remaining ingredients and pour evenly over chicken. Bake uncovered about 1 hour at 325°, basting occasionally.

Maple Syrup . . .
(1983)

MOROCCAN-STYLE CHICKEN

1 lemon
1 frying chicken
salt and freshly ground pepper
$^1/_4$ cup butter
2 Tbsps. olive oil
2 shallots or scallions, finely chopped
$^1/_2$ tsp. finely minced garlic
$^3/_4$ cup chicken stock
1 tsp. dried oregano
$^1/_4$ cup chopped parsley

With a swivel-blade paring knife pare away half of the lemon rind and cut it into very thin strips. Reserve. Squeeze the lemon and reserve the juice. Sprinkle chicken parts with salt and pepper. Heat the butter and oil in a skillet. Brown chicken pieces on all sides and transfer to a warm plate. Add shallots and garlic to skillet. Cook, stirring until golden. Add $^1/_4$ cup of stock and stir to dissolve all brown particles. Cook until liquid is almost evaporated. Reduce the remaining stock to one-third cup. Return chicken to skillet and sprinkle with the parsley, oregano, lemon rind, juice and reduced stock. Cover and cook slowly for about 30 minutes or until chicken is tender. Serve immediately.

Jean Haynes
Down Home . . .
(1989)

SCANDINAVIAN "PEPPER ROOT" CHICKEN

Pepper Root (horseradish) is a favorite in Scandanavia. This recipe won Third Prize in the National Chicken Cooking Contest in 1968. I was awarded 4 major appliances and 7 minor appliances as prizes in this contest.

8 chicken drumsticks
Basting sauce:
1 cup oil
3 Tbsps. tomato ketchup
3 tsps. instant horseradish
$1^1/_2$ tsps. salt
1 egg

Mix oil, ketchup, salt and egg in blender or beat well. Dip drumsticks in sauce. Place over a charcoal fire which was started about $^1/_2$ hour previously. Turn drumsticks frequently. Cook until almost done (40-50 minutes). Add horseradish to remainder of basting sauce. Baste drumsticks frequently and generously and continue cooking til golden brown and tender. Remove from grill. Place foil covers on end of each drumstick and place on serving platter with bone end toward the outside. Accompaniment could be saffron rice and mixed vegetables, raw or cooked. Serves 4.

Ragnar Carlson
Wonderful Cooking
(Date unknown)

TERIYAKI CHICKEN WITH RED PEPPER

Put chicken parts in a plastic bag. (Use wings, drumsticks, thighs or whole cut-up chicken.)

Combine and shake in a covered jar and pour over the chicken:
$^1/_4$ cup soy sauce
3 Tbsps. each oil and honey
3 mashed garlic cloves
$^1/_4$ cup sherry or whiskey
2 Tbsps. sesame seeds
$^1/_2$ tsp. dry red pepper flakes

Squeeze out air, close the bag and refrigerate all day. Remove from the bag, arrange on a baking sheet, pour the sauce over the top and bake uncovered at 350° about an hour.

Elaine Laughlin
Goodbye Dining Hall . . .
(1982)

SPANISH CHICKEN AND RICE

1 fryer
fat or oil
1 onion
2 cloves garlic
1 bay leaf
1 pinch saffron
1 cup rice
1 stalk celery, chopped
2 pimientos, chopped
1 green pepper, chopped
2 Tbsps. salt
1 (15-oz.) can tomatoes or tomato sauce
1$^1/_2$ quarts water
1 (15-oz.) can small green peas

Cut chicken in quarters, brown and set aside. Sauté onion, celery, garlic and green peppers. Add tomatoes, or sauce, and water to large pan with sautéed ingredients. Boil for 5 minutes. Add bay leaf, salt, rice and saffron. Add chicken. Stir thoroughly, cook slowly until chicken is done.

Garnish with peas and pimientos. Note: Rice may be partly cooked separately, drained and then added to chicken-vegetable mixture until completely cooked. Total cooking time is about 1 to 1$^1/_2$ hours. Serves four.

Rosemarie Brown
Art/Brocton
(1960s)

CHICKEN SUPREME

(or Chicken Divan)
1 (5-lb.) chicken
2 tsps. salt
2 cups white sauce
$^1/_4$ tsp. nutmeg
$^1/_2$ cup mayonnaise
$^1/_2$ cup cream, whipped
3 Tbsps. sherry
1 tsp. Worcestershire sauce
1 cup Parmesan cheese, grated
1 bunch broccoli or asparagus or 3 frozen packages

Place chicken in large kettle. Add salt and about 5 cups water. Boil. Lower heat and simmer until tender, about 3 hours. Let cool in broth. When cooled, remove skin, slice breast and leg meat.

Prepare white sauce, adding nutmeg, mayonnaise, whipped cream, sherry and Worcestershire. Boil 15 to 20 minutes.

Cook and drain vegetable and place on deep oven-proof platter. Arrange chicken over and cover with sauce. Sprinkle generously with cheese. Place in broiler 5 inches below flame until brown and bubbly. Serve immediately on same platter. Serves 4 to 6.

Mrs. James D. Furlong
Home Cooking . . .
(Date unknown)

HOT CHINESE CHICKEN SALAD

3 broiler-fryer chicken thighs, skinned, boned and
   cut into 1" chunks (I boil chicken 50 minutes,
   cool, then it is easier to skin and debone)
$1/_4$ cup cornstarch
$1/_4$ cup mazola corn oil
$1/_8$ tsp. garlic powder
1 large ripe tomato cut into chunks (optional)
1 can water chestnuts (drained and sliced)
1 can mushrooms (sautéed in butter)
1 bunch green onions, coarsely chopped
1 cup diagonally sliced celery, sautéed in butter
1 tsp. Ac´cent
$1/_4$ cup soy sauce
2 cups finely shredded iceberg lettuce or cabbage
   (optional)

Roll chicken in cornstarch. Heat oil in fry pan or wok
over high heat. Add chicken chunks and quickly brown.
Sprinkle with garlic powder. Add tomato, water chest-
nuts, mushrooms, onions and celery. Stir. Sprinkle with
Ac´cent. Add soy sauce. Stir. Cover, reduce heat to
simmer, and cook 5 minutes.
   Lightly toss chicken mixture with lettuce or cabbage.
Serve with hot plain rice, or rice pilaf. Serves 4-5.

JoAnn Reid
Euclid Ave . . .
(1980)

UPSIDEDOWN CHICKEN

3 cups chicken stock
1 cup finely cut celery
1 small onion, minced
1 bay leaf
2 Tbsps. shortening
4 Tbsps. flour
1/2 tsp. salt
dash pepper, paprika
3 cups diced, cooked chicken
1/4 cup sliced, stuffed olives

CORN BREAD MIXTURE
1 tsp. salt
1 beaten egg
3/4 cup thick sour milk
1/2 cup flour sifted
3/4 cup corn meal
1/2 tsp. soda
1/2 tsp. baking powder

   Simmer stock, celery, onion and bay leaf, 5 minutes.
Remove leaf. Melt shortening in deep 9-inch oven-proof
skillet. Add flour, salt, pepper and paprika. Blend. Add
stock, stirring constantly. Cook until thickened. Add
chicken and olives.
   Sift dry ingredients. Cut in shortening. Combine egg
and milk, stir into corn meal mixture. Pour cornmeal
mixture over sauced chicken in skillet. Bake in 425° oven
for 35-40 minutes. Turn over on platter, serve. Serves 6.

Lou Corrough
To the Town's Taste
(1964)

SAVORY SOUTHERN CHICKEN PIE

8 oz. mild pork sausage (bulk)
4 Tbsps. margarine
$^1/_3$ cup flour
$^1/_4$ tsp. salt
$^1/_8$ tsp. pepper
1 ($13^3/_4$-oz.) can chicken broth
$^2/_3$ cup milk
2 cups cubed, cooked chicken
1 (10-oz.) package frozen peas

PASTRY:
1 cup flour
1 tsp. celery seed
$^1/_2$ tsp. salt
$^1/_2$ tsp. paprika
$^1/_3$ cup shortening
2 Tbsps. water

Brown sausage. Drain. Pour off fat. Melt margarine. Blend in flour, salt, pepper. Stir in broth and milk. Cook and stir until thick. Cook 1 minute. Add chicken, sausage and peas. Heat through . Pour chicken and sausage in casserole. Place pastry on top. Bake at 450° degrees for 25-30 minutes. Serves 6.

PASTRY: Mix flour, celery seed, salt and paprika. Cut in shortening with two knives or a pastry cutter until mixture forms small "peas" of dough. Quickly stir in water to moisten. Form into a ball and roll out to size to fit casserole.

Pat Schrantz
Favorite Hometown . . .
(Date unknown)

SCALLOPED CHICKEN

(from Henneker Tea room at West Portland around 1930.)
3 to 4 lbs. chicken
onion
celery tops
$^1/_2$ loaf Pepperidge Farm white bread
$^1/_4$ loaf corn bread
1 tsp. poultry seasoning or sage
$^1/_8$ lb. butter

Cook chicken with onion and celery tops and water to cover. Cut cooked chicken into good-sized pieces. Cover flat casserole with chicken. Thicken broth to consistency of heavy cream. Pour on chicken. Mix breads, dried out and cubed, 1 onion, chopped fine, poultry seasoning, butter. Place on top of chicken and gravy. Bake 300° for 1 hour. Take out. With 2-tong fork, push bread into gravy. Bake 1 hour more at 250°. Serves 6.

Fanny Swain
Cookbook
Westfield
(1986)

Nu-Way Market, 115 East Fourth, Jamestown, 1940s.

BRAISED CORNISH GAME HEN WITH GRAPES

6 Cornish game hens (or small wild game)
flour
salt and pepper
$1/4$ cup butter or margarine
$1^1/_4$ cups chicken broth
1 tsp. chopped parsley
$1/_8$ tsp. thyme
1 bay leaf
1 tsp. slivered orange rind
dash of pepper
1 cup halved white grapes
6 slices buttered toast

Coat hens lightly with combined flour, salt and pepper. Brown in butter or margarine in large skillet; remove. Combine chicken broth, parsley, thyme, bay leaf and pepper; pour into skillet. Cover and simmer 10 minutes; remove bay leaf. Add browned birds; cover and simmer 15 minutes. Add orange rind and grapes, simmer 5 minutes longer or until birds are tender. Place a bird on each slice of buttered toast. Serve with sauce. May be garnished with more grapes and orange slices if desired. Serves 6.

Mrs. William E. Chalecke
Wonderful Cooking
(Date unknown) . . .

TURKEY CASSEROLE

5 Tbsps. sifted flour
1 tsp. salt
$1/_4$ tsp. onion salt
$1/_4$ cup butter, melted
$2^1/_2$ cups milk or light cream
$1^1/_2$ cups Minute Rice
$1^1/_2$ cups turkey or chicken broth
$1/_2$ cup grated American cheese
$1^1/_2$ cups cooked asparagus
2 cups or 6 slices turkey
2 Tbsps. toasted almonds

Stir flour, half of salt, onion salt into butter. Stir in milk. Cook over hot water, stirring occasionally until thickened. Pour rice into 2 quart shallow baking dish (right from box). Combine broth and remaining salt and pour over rice. Sprinkle half of cheese over rice. Top with asparagus; then turkey. Pour cream sauce over turkey. Sprinkle with remaining cheese. Bake at 375° for about 20 minutes. Top with almonds.

Sharing Our Best
(1987)

GAME and GROUND MEAT DISHES

HUNTERS' STEW

1$\frac{1}{2}$ lbs. boneless venison, cut into 1 inch cubes
1 tsp. salt
$\frac{1}{2}$ tsp. pepper
3 Tbsps. oil
2 onions, sliced
3 stalks celery, chopped
4 potatoes, cubed
4 carrots, sliced
2 cans mushrooms, drained
3 Tbsps. soy sauce
$\frac{1}{2}$ tsp. ginger
Water

Season meat with salt and pepper. Coat with flour and brown in oil in Dutch oven. Arrange onions, celery, potatoes, carrots and mushrooms around meat. Add soy sauce, ginger and enough water to cover. Cover; bring to a boil and reduce heat, simmering 1 hour or longer, until meat and vegetables are tender. If desired, stew may be thickened with 1 Tbsp. cornstarch mixed with 1 Tbsp. water.

Nancy Mangine
Finger Lickin' . . .
(1981)

ROAST VENISON

Venison loin roast (about 4 lbs.)
$\frac{1}{4}$ tsp. marjoram
$\frac{1}{4}$ tsp. thyme
2 tsps. salt
$\frac{1}{2}$ tsp. pepper
$\frac{1}{4}$ - $\frac{1}{2}$ cup flour
strips of bacon
1$\frac{1}{2}$ cup water
$\frac{1}{4}$ cup dry wine
4 Tbsps. beef or bacon fat
3 or 4 walnuts in shells

Mix salt, pepper, marjoram, thyme and flour. Rub this mixture well into the meat; sear roast on all sides in the beef fat in a heavy pan. Place in roasting pan, add the water and wine and the walnuts in shells; cover roast with strips of bacon. Cover pan tightly and roast at 325° for about 3 hours, turning roast often.

Mrs. Alfred A. Grant
Wonderful Cooking
(Date unknown)

VENISON STEAKS OR CHOPS

A venison dinner is an important occasion. All it needs is the addition of a fine, robust burgundy for accompaniment.

Cut steaks $^3/_4$ inch thick
   and place them in the following mixture:
1 onion sliced
4 sprigs parsley
4 peppercorns
3 Tbsps. salad oil
1 cup white wine
1 carrot sliced
$^1/_8$ tsp. thyme
1 tsp. salt

   The meat should stand in this solution in a cool place for three days. The steaks should be turned and rubbed in this brine from time to time. Broil the steaks about 7 minutes to a side. Serve with puree of boiled chestnuts and this sauce poivrade:
8 peppercorns, crushed
$^1/_2$ cup vinegar
2 Tbsps. red currant jelly
1 cup thickened gravy made with stock from venison bones and trimmings

   First mix together peppercorns and vinegar and cook until reduced to about $^1/_4$ cup. Then add thickened gravy and boil slowly $^1/_2$ hour. Add currant jelly and strain. Serves 6.
                    Henri Rousseau
                    Moon Brook Country Club
                    Wonderful Cooking . . .
                    (Date unknown)

EMPANADAS

$^3/_4$ lb. ground beef
1 small onion, diced
2 tsps. chili powder
1 (8-oz.) can tomato sauce
2 oz. chopped hot peppers
1 tsp. sugar
1 tsp. salt
1 cup flour
$^1/_2$ cup yellow corn meal
$^1/_2$ cup shredded Cheddar cheese
$^1/_2$ cup shortening

Cook beef and onion until meat is brown and drain off fat. Stir in chili powder, tomato sauce, peppers, sugar and $^1/_2$ teaspoon salt. Heat to boiling, reduce heat and simmer 15 minutes, uncovered. Stir occasionally. Meanwhile, in medium bowl, stir flour, corn meal and $^1/_2$ teaspoon salt. Cut cheese and shortening into flour mixture to resemble coarse crumbs. Sprinkle 5 or 6-tablespoons cold water into mixture until pastry is just moist enough to hold together. Shape into ball. Roll out pastry on floured surface, about $^1/_8$ inch thick. Using a 5" round plate, cut out 8 circles of pastry. Preheat oven to 400°. Spoon filling of meat onto half of a circle of pastry. Brush edges with water and fold dough over. With fork, firmly press edges together to seal. Place on ungreased cookie sheet. Bake for 15 minutes or until golden brown.

Gale VerHague
Family Favorites
(1989-90)

HUNGARIAN CABBAGE ROLLS

Swedes call them Koldolmar and Poles call them Golabki. Under any name they are delicious.
1 large head cabbage
1 lb. ground meat or meat loaf mix
$^1/_2$ cup chopped onion
1 egg
$1^1/_2$ tsp. salt
$^1/_4$ tsp. pepper
1 Tbsp. paprika
1 can, $2^1/_2$ cups, tomato juice
1 cup sour cream
1 cup raw rice, rinsed
3 cups water
$2^1/_2$ cups sauerkraut

Core and cover cabbage in boiling water, head down in Dutch oven. Turn off heat when cabbage is wilted. Remove and peel off leaves, leaving leaves whole. Trim heavy vein down to make leaves lie flat. Sauté meat in pan until lightly browned. Add onion, rice and $^1/_2$ cup water (turn off heat). Add seasonings. Mix well and, in center of each cabbage leaf, place a heaping tablespoon of this mixture. Fold sides of each leaf, then roll up. Place each leaf folded side down in Dutch oven (large cooking pot). Spread sauerkraut over rolls. Add tomato juice and $2^1/_2$ cups water. Bring to boil. Reduce to simmer, cooking $1^1/_2$ hours. Place rolls on serving platter. Mix a little of the juice with sour cream and pour over rolls. Makes 8 servings. (Any remaining pieces of cabbage can be added to the pot while cooking.)

Toothpicks may be inserted into each leaf to hold in place.

Howard E. Ford
A Cappella Choir . . . (1986)

STUFFED CABBAGE A LA MEIER

1 large head cabbage, preferably savoy
2 lbs. ground beef (round or chuck)
1 egg
1 slice white bread soaked in 1 cup warm milk
3 large onions chopped and sautéed in butter until golden
1 cup cooked rice
3 tsps. salt
$1/_4$ tsp. ground nutmeg
fresh ground pepper
$1/_2$ pint heavy cream
1 bunch fresh dill

Chop onions and sauté in butter over low heat. Set aside. Soak bread in milk. Heat cream and add the finely cut dill.

Put meat in large bowl and add rice, onions, bread in milk, egg, salt, nutmeg and pepper. Work thoroughly with wooden spoon till fluffy and pink.

Boil cabbage in large pot for 15 minutes. Drain and let cold water run over cabbage. Peel off leaves. Cut out the coarsest part of the stem about one inch. Put a large spoonful of meat on the leaf and fold. Begin with the stem part, then the left and right sides and close with the tip of the leaf. Line them up in a buttered baking pan.

Cook in pre-heated 450° oven for 20 minutes. Lower heat to 350° and baste with one-third of cream with dill. Cook for another 40 minutes, basting two more times. When cooked, grind fresh pepper over cabbage and let sit for 5 minutes before serving.

Johanna Meier
Chautauqua Celebrity . . . (1980)

SPAGHETTI PIE

6 oz. spaghetti
2 Tbsps.. butter or margarine
$1/_3$ cup grated Parmesan cheese
2 well-beaten eggs
1 lb. ground beef or bulk Italian sausage
    ($1/_2$ and $1/_2$ is good)
$1/_2$ cup chopped onion
$1/_4$ cup chopped green pepper
1 (8-oz.) can tomatoes, cut up
1 (6-oz.) can tomato paste
1 tsp. sugar
1 tsp. dried oregano, crushed
$1/_4$ tsp. salt
$1/_4$ tsp. garlic salt
1 cup (8-oz.) cottage cheese, drained
$1/_2$ cup (2-oz.) mozzarella cheese, shredded

Cook spaghetti using package directions, drain (should have $3^1/_4$ cups). Stir in butter. Stir in Parmesan cheese and eggs. Form spaghetti mixture into a "crust" in a buttered 10" pie plate. In a skillet cook meat, onion and green pepper until vegetables are tender and meat is browned. Drain off excess fat. Stir in undrained tomatoes, tomato paste, sugar, oregano, salt and garlic salt. Spread cottage cheese over bottom of spaghetti crust. Fill "pie" with tomato mixture. Cover with foil and chill in refrigerator 2 - 24 hours.* Bake, covered, 350° for 60 minutes. Uncover, sprinkle with mozzarella cheese. Bake 5 minutes longer or until cheese melts. Makes 6 servings. *May be frozen. Bake frozen pie, covered, at 350° for 2 hours. Uncover, sprinkle with cheese, bake 5 minutes more.

Pat Spencer
Euclid Avenue . . . (1980)

SWEDISH-AMERICAN KOLDOLMAR

$^3/_4$ lb. pork and $1^1/_4$ lbs. beef (ground together)
1 large head cabbage
1 Tbsp. sugar
salt to taste
$^1/_4$ lb. butter
1 Tbsp. minced onion
$^1/_2$ cup Minute Rice
$1^1/_2$ cans beef bouillon
$^1/_2$ tsp. salt

Parboil cabbage in water to cover, salted to taste and sweetened with sugar, until leaves are slightly tender. Cook Minute Rice according to directions on box, using equal parts of water and bouillon. Mix together thoroughly meat, onion, $^1/_2$ tsp. salt, cooked rice and $^1/_2$ cup bouillon. Place 1 Tablespoonful of meat mixture in each cabbage leaf, roll tightly and place in roaster; cover with bits of butter, the balance of the bouillon and $^1/_2$ cup of the water in which cabbage has been boiled.

Bake $2^1/_2$ to 3 hours in 350° oven. Serves 18-20

Mrs. Fred B. Clarke
Wonderful Cooking . . .
(Date unknown)

CAVATINI

1 lb. lean ground beef
1 lb. bulk Italian sausage
1 stick pepperoni, chopped
1 green pepper, chopped
2 cups sliced mushrooms
2 lb. mozzarella cheese, grated
1 large onion, chopped
1 gallon spaghetti sauce (your recipe or store jars)
$1^1/_2$ lbs. cooked macaroni (mixed: small spirals, shells, elbows, cartwheels, etc.)

Brown beef, sausage, pepperoni, pepper, mushrooms and onion separately, starting with meats. Mix in large bowl. In lasagne pans, make layers of macaroni, sauce, meat, then cheese until all ingredients are used. Bake at 350° for 45 minutes. The cheese layer should be golden. Serves 12.

Carol G. Boltz
Down Home . . .
(1989)

HUNGARIAN STUFFED GREEN PEPPERS

(Toltott Paprika)
Base:
3 Tbsps. sweet butter
4 Tbsps. flour
$^1/_4$ cup cold water

$1^1/_2$ lbs. lean ground beef
1 lb. ground pork
$^1/_2$ lb. ground veal
1 cup (8-oz.) rice - cooked not too soft
10 medium size green peppers
48 oz. tomato juice
2 Tbsps. margarine or butter
1 small onion, cut into small pieces
2 cloves garlic, pressed
2 tsps. salt, or according to taste
pinch of ground black pepper
1 egg
1 tsp. dry basil leaves
2 bay leaves
$^1/_4$ cup sugar, or according to taste
$^3/_4$ cup water
fresh dill

Cook flour in butter over low flame until light brown (about 10-15 minutes), stirring often. When finished, add water and stir until base becomes smooth and of uniform texture. Then put aside while preparing green peppers.

In a bowl, mix well ground meat with salt, black pepper, basil leaves, onion, egg, garlic, $^1/_4$ cup of cold water, melted butter or margarine. Add cooked rice, and mix well again.

Cut out tops of green peppers (holes not too large), and core out insides. Wash peppers in hot water, and rinse them in cold water.

Stuff green peppers with meat mixture, and place them standing up (holes at top) in a wide pot, covered by the tomato juice, and $^1/_2$ cup of cold water. Add $^1/_2$ tsp. salt, bay leaves, fresh dill. Cook over medium flame until tomato juice begins to boil. Then cover pot and continue cooking over low flame (about 45 minutes).

With a sieve, strain the BASE prepared at the beginning, into the tomato juice, that has been cooking for 45 minutes. On low flame, continue cooking for about 15 minutes longer until sauce has thickened to desired consistency.

Green peppers in tomato sauce can be frozen, and reheated when needed.

Claudette Sorel
Chautauqua Celebrity . . .
(1980)

GERMAN-STYLE MEATBALLS

$1^1/_2$ lbs. lean ground round
2 eggs, beaten
2 Tbsps. fine dry bread crumbs
2 Tbsps. instant minced onions
1 Tbsp. lemon juice
2 Tbsps. dried parsley flakes
$1^1/_2$ tsps. salt
$^1/_4$ tsp. pepper
3 envelopes or 3 tsps. instant beef broth
3 cups boiling water
3 Tbsps. flour
$^1/_4$ cup cold water
1 tsp. Worcestershire sauce
3 Tbsps. hamburger relish

Lightly combine ground beef, eggs, bread crumbs, onion, parsley, salt, pepper, lemon juice in large bowl. Shape into 24 meat balls.

Dissolve instant beef broth in water in large saucepan. Bring to boil, add meatballs. Bring to boil again, lower heat, cover, simmer 15 minutes.

Remove meatballs to serving dish, keep warm, skim fat off.

Mix flour, cold water to paste. Stir into simmering broth. Add Worcestershire sauce and relish. Heat till thickened, and cook 3 minutes. Pour over meat balls.

Marj Tietz
Adventures in Food
(1977)

OVEN PORCUPINES

1 lb. ground beef
$^1/_2$ cup uncooked regular rice
$^1/_2$ cup chopped onion
1 tsp. salt
$^1/_2$ tsp. celery salt
$^1/_8$ tsp. garlic powder
$^1/_8$ tsp. pepper
1 can tomato sauce (15-oz.)
1 cup water
2 tsps. Worcestershire sauce

Heat oven to 350°. Mix meat, rice, $^1/_2$ cup water, onion, salt, celery salt, garlic powder, and pepper. Shape into balls. Place meatballs in ungreased baking dish. Stir together remaining ingredients, and pour over meatballs.

Cover with aluminum foil and bake 45 minutes. Uncover and bake 15 minutes longer. Serves 4-6.

Onda Keppel
Favorite Recipes
Findley Lake
(1981)

SWEDISH MEATBALLS

(Kottbullar)
2-3 lbs. ground beef (meatloaf mix may be used)
4 slices bread, crumbled
3/4 cup milk
1 small onion, chopped finely
$1^1/_2$ tsps. salt
$^1/_4$ tsp. pepper
$^1/_4$ tsp. nutmeg
dash allspice
3 eggs, lightly beaten

4 Tbsps. margarine
1 cup light cream
1 can condensed beef broth
2 Tbsps. flour

Combine first group of ingredients. Form small meatballs. Brown in margarine. Remove meatballs from skillet with slotted spoon and put in baking dish.

Lower heat under skillet. Add flour to drippings and stir until smooth. Add beef broth and cream. Let bubble for a minute or so. Pour over meatballs.

Bake, covered, for about 30 minutes at 350°. If gravy looks pale, a bit of Gravy Master may be added.

Ruth Mohney
Adventures in Food
(1977)

MEAT LOAF

2 lbs. chopped beef
$^1/_2$ lb. sausage
6 crushed crackers or
4 Shredded Wheat biscuits
1 tsp. salt
2 heaping tsps. poultry seasoning
1 egg beaten and diluted with
1 cup milk
1 can tomatoes (about 15-oz.)
1 small onion, chopped fine

Mix well and turn into oblong pan. Place a few slices of bacon on top and bake at 350° for $1^1/_2$ to 2 hours.

Lola D. Raymond
Cook Book
Cassadaga
(1950)

MEAT LOAF

GLAZE:
$^1/_2$ cup ketchup
3 Tbsps. brown sugar
1 Tbsp. mustard

MEATLOAF:
2 lbs. ground beef
$^3/_4$ cup oatmeal
$^1/_2$ cup ketchup
$^1/_4$ cup milk
2 eggs
1 Tbsp. horseradish
2 tsps. salt
$^1/_4$ tsp. pepper

Combine all ingredients for glaze, set aside.

In a large bowl combine ground beef and oatmeal, set aside. In blender combine remaining meatloaf ingredients. Cover, blend until smooth, mix with ground beef. Preheat oven to 375°. Spoon $^1/_2$ glaze on loaf. Bake 45 minutes. Spoon remaining glaze on top of loaf and bake for 10 minutes more.

Kathie Holly
Treasured Recipes
(1988)

POLPETTONE

(Italian Meatloaf)

Spread your ground meat on a floured board so that it will not stick. Season with very little salt and some pepper. Cover the meat with thin slices of ham, and cover the ham with a thin Italian omelet. Roll into a loaf, oil and flour it lightly. Brown in a little butter and cook gently in a covered pan on a small fire. When the meat is almost done, add half a glass of white wine, and when this has evaporated, a little diluted tomato paste or tomato juice. Cooled and sliced thin, the Polpettone will look very attractive.

Miss Sarah Paterniti
recipe from Italy
Jamestown's International . . .
(1960s)

MIDNIGHT SUN CHIP LOAVES

This recipe won Second Place in a Men's National Cooking Championship contest with a prize of a week for two at the Sands Hotel in Las Vegas and $750.00.

Ground together:

2 lbs. lean beef

$^1/_2$ lb. pork

$^1/_2$ lb. veal

Mixed with:

1 cup crushed potato chips

1$^1/_2$ tsps. salt

$^1/_4$ tsp. pepper

$^1/_4$ tsp. cloves

$^1/_2$ tsp. allspice

$^1/_4$ tsp. garlic salt

$^1/_4$ tsp. ginger

2 eggs, slightly beaten

1 cup instant mashed potatoes

   (mixed according to directions on box)

$^1/_4$ cup light Karo syrup

1 (4-oz.) can mushrooms (add liquid too)

$^1/_2$ cup milk

Garnish with:

2 peach halves

pineapple tidbits

parsley

Preheat oven to 350°. Place ground meat in a large mixing bowl. Add spices to potato chip crumbs and mix. Add to meat, also adding eggs, potatoes, Karo, milk and mushrooms. Mix well. Divide mixture in half. Make 2 loaves and place in baking pan. Bake at 350° for one hour. Remove from oven and place a peach half on each loaf (round side up to resemble sun and make sun rays from pineapple tidbits).

Brush fruit with Karo syrup and return to oven for 45 minutes. Place on platter and garnish with parsley. Serves 8.

Ragnar Carlson
Wonderful Cooking . . .
(Date unknown)

A maxim, too, that must not be forgot,
Whatever be your dinner, serve it hot.
Your fine ragouts like epigrams require
A little salt - but to be full of fire.
   Ladies' Guild
   Grace Episcopal Church
   The Parish Cookbook, 3rd Edition
   Randolph, 1937

FISH AND SEAFOOD

BOUILLABAISSE

(Fish Stew)
3 onions
3 tomatoes
Bouquet of parsley, thyme, bay leaf, and fennel
2 slices of lemon with peel
1 carrot, chopped
$^1/_2$ cup canned pimiento, cut in small pieces
1 garlic clove, bruised
4 Tbsps. olive oil
3 lbs. fresh or frozen fish (flounder, sole, haddock,
  perch—a combination of 2 or more)
2 lobsters or 6 lobster tails, cooked
1 cup shrimp or crabmeat
water
$^1/_2$ tsp. saffron
salt and pepper
Toast made of French bread

Cook carrot, onions, and garlic in olive oil, until golden brown. Add fish cut into 3 inch squares, tomatoes, herb bouquet and water. Simmer 20 minutes. Add shellfish and lobster tails with shells. Add pimiento and saffron. Season with salt, pepper and lemon. Heat through. Put toast in soup plate, add bouillabaisse and sprinkle with parsley.

Miss Julia Gorman
Recipe from France
Jamestown's International . . .
(1960s)

SALMON CHEESE PIE

1 (1-lb.) can salmon
$^1/_4$ cup green onion
$^1/_4$ cup green pepper
2 eggs
2 Tbsps. parsley
1 pie shell (unbaked)
2 Tbsps. butter
1 Tbsp. flour
$^1/_2$ tsp. celery salt
1 cup cottage cheese
2 Tbsps. Parmesan cheese

CREAMED PEA SAUCE:
3 Tbsps. butter
$^1/_2$ cup liquid from peas
2 Tbsps. flour
salt and pepper to taste
1 cup cooked peas
1 cup milk
2 or 3 green onions

Drain and flake salmon, no skin or bones, reserving liquid. Sauté onions and green pepper in butter. Blend in flour and celery salt. Add salmon liquid stirring until thickened. Stir in salmon. Turn into unbaked pie shell. With beater, beat eggs, cottage cheese, Parmesan cheese and parsley until blended. Spoon over salmon. Bake at 375° 25 to 30 minutes. Serve with creamed pea sauce.

SAUCE: Sauté onion in butter. Blend in flour. Add milk and liquid from peas. When thick, add peas. Serve with Salmon Cheese Pie.

Dorothy Johnson
Culinary Delights
(1988-89)

WHITE WINE COURT BOUILLON

(For cooking fish.)
1 quart dry white wine
1 quart water
2 small carrots, thinly sliced
2 medium onions, thinly sliced
12 peppercorns, bruised
2 large bay leaves
2 whole cloves
1 Tbsp. salt
1 large sprig thyme

Put all in kettle. Bring to rapid boil and simmer for 25 to 30 minutes. Rub the court bouillon through a fine sieve.

Father Phillip Lord
Favorite Recipes from
our Best Cooks
(1978)

CRAB MEAT AU GRATIN

$1/_2$ cup butter
$2/_3$ cup flour
2 tsps. salt
$2^2/_3$ cups milk
2 cans ($6^1/_2$-oz.) crab meat drained
4 cups chopped celery
$1/_2$ cup chopped green pepper
2 pimientos, drained and chopped
2 Tbsps. grated onion
$1/_3$ cup slivered blanched almonds, toasted
4 hard-cooked eggs, chopped
1 cup shredded sharp cheddar cheese
1 Tbsp. butter
$2^1/_2$ cups (about 3 slices) bread cubes–double amount
   to cover entire surface

Heat butter in a saucepan. Add a mixture of the flour and salt; blend well. Heat until mixture bubbles, stirring constantly. Remove from heat and add milk gradually, stirring until blended.

Return to heat and cook rapidly, stirring constantly until mixture thickens. Cook 1 to 2 minutes longer.

Remove and discard bony tissue from crab meat and separate into pieces. Mix crab meat, celery, green pepper, pimientos, onions, almonds, and hard-cooked eggs into sauce. Turn mixture into a shallow 2 quart casserole. Sprinkle with shredded cheese.

Heat 1 Tbsp. butter in a skillet. Add bread cubes and toss until coated. Spoon onto top of casserole. Heat in a 350 degree oven 35 minutes. If desired, garnish with slices of hard-cooked eggs. Serves 8 to 10.

Mrs. Dorothy Morgan
Kiantone Cookbook
(1969)

LOBSTER THERMIDOR

1 lobster, freshly boiled
3 mushrooms, sliced
$1/_4$ cup butter
1 dash paprika
1 Tbsp. minced parsley
$1/_2$ cup sherry wine
$1^1/_2$ cups cream sauce (page 285)
2 Tbsps. grated Parmesan cheese
$1/_8$ tsp. mustard

Cut lobster in half lengthwise, remove meat from shell and cut into small pieces. Sauté with mushrooms in butter about 5 minutes, then add paprika, mustard, parsley, sherry and 1 cup cream sauce and mix will. Return mixture to lobster shell and cover with remaining $1/_2$ cup cream sauce. Sprinkle with Parmesan cheese and bake at 450 degrees about 10 minutes.

Mrs. Howard Dow
What's Cooking I
(1954)

WHOLE BAKED FISH IN FILBERT SAUCE

3 lbs. fish (pike, white fish, trout)
juice of $1/_2$ lemon
6 Tbsps. melted butter
$1/_2$ cup dry milk
pinch of nutmeg
salt and pepper
one pound filberts, finely chopped
$1/_2$ cup sherry
$1/_2$ cup water
$1/_2$ cup dry bread crumbs
1 cup grated sharp cheese

Brush fish with lemon juice; sprinkle lightly with salt and pepper and let stand one hour. Wipe fish, place in baking pan. Brush inside and out with part of melted butter. Combine nuts, dry milk and nutmeg. Add wine and water and mix well. Blend in cheese thoroughly and season to taste with salt and pepper. Place some nut mixture in the fish and pour the remainder over it. Mix remaining melted butter with crumbs and sprinkle over fish. Bake at 350 degrees 30 to 40 minutes, until fish is tender. Makes 4 to 6 servings.

Pauline Valone
Recipe Roundup
(1954)

MOCK LOBSTER

1 lb. boneless, skinless haddock, frozen,
   cut up into 1 inch pieces.
Bring to a boil:
1 quart water
1 tsp. salt
2 tsps. sugar
2 Tbsps. vinegar

Add frozen haddock to this boiling mixture. Cook until fish floats to top of pan. Dip in melted butter just like lobster tail.
Note: This recipe appeared in several county cookbooks.

Sandra Zenns
Cookbook
Mayville
(1981)

LIGHT AND CRISPY FISH FILLETS

Oil for deep-frying
1 cup pancake mix
1/3 cup club soda
1 lb. frozen fish fillets (not breaded), thawed
$^1/_2$ cup buttermilk

Heat oil in deep fat fryer or 3-quart saucepan. In a medium bowl, stir together $^1/_2$ cup pancake mix and club soda. Dip fillets in buttermilk, then roll in the remaining $^1/_2$ cup pancake mix and then into the mixture of soda and pancake mix. Deep-fry, turning once until deep brown (3 or 4 minutes). Serves 4.

Bob Hofgren
A Cappella Choir...
(1986)

HALIBUT STEAK

$2^1/_2$ lb. Halibut steak, 1" thick
3 Tbsps. butter
4 Tbsps. flour
$^1/_8$ tsp. each salt and pepper
$^1/_4$ tsp. nutmeg
$1^1/_2$ cup milk
$^3/_4$ cup grated American cheese
paprika

Wipe fish; remove skin and bones. Place sections back together in greased dish. Sprinkle salt and pepper on it. Melt butter in a saucepan. Add flour, salt, pepper and nutmeg. Stir until smooth. Add milk and cheese. Pour over fish, add paprika. Bake at 325° for 45 minutes. Serves 4-6.

Hazel and Margaret Johnson
100 Years of Cooking
(1986)

FISH AU GRATIN WITH A DIFFERENCE

1 lb. fresh or frozen fish (if you want a deluxe version
   add a bag of shrimp, but this really is not necessary)
salt
1-2 yellow onions
$^1/_2$ cup chopped parsley or 3 Tbsps. chopped dill mixed
   with 3 Tbsps. grated horseradish

SAUCE:
$^1/_2$ cup mayonnaise
2 tsps. mustard (French is best)
$^1/_2$ cup milk
breadcrumbs

Rinse the fish quickly or cut the frozen fish in inch-thick slices or thaw to separate the filets. (Add shrimp.) Place in greased pan, salt. Peel, chop and fry onion. Cover fish with onion and chopped parsley (or dill/horseradish mixed). Stir and mix the mustard, mayo and milk and spread over fish. Put some breadcrumbs on top and bake for about 25 minutes at 475°. Serve with rice and a tossed salad. Surprisingly good!

Eva Ollen
100 Years of Cooking
(1986)

BOB'S WALLEYE FOIL-BAKED ON GRILL

Walleye fillets (patted dry)
lemon pepper and parsley
lemon juice and paprika
sliced tomato (optional)
butter or margarine
sweet onion or fresh green onion

Lightly coat fillets with butter. Sprinkle with lemon pepper and place 2 fillets on foil sheet large enough to fold and cover fish tightly. Add sliced onion and tomato, and sprinkle with 1/2 tsp. lemon juice and paprika. Wrap foil tightly and place foil packets on grill over medium-high heat. Turn once, cooking approximately 5 minutes on each side. This will vary with the thickness of the fillets.

Garnish with parsley and serve on foil. Sprinkle with more paprika, if desired. Each packet serves 1 or 2, depending on size of fillets.

Bob Genthner
Chautauqua-Allegheny Cookbook
(1990)

MEDITERRANEAN BAKED FISH

1 large onion, sliced thinly
2 Tbsps. chopped pimiento
2 lbs. sole or haddock
1 tsp. salt
$1/4$ tsp. pepper
$1/4$ tsp. mace
$1/8$ tsp. cayenne pepper
3 large tomatoes, peeled and cut into thick slices
1 cup fresh sliced mushrooms
$1/4$ cup water
2 Tbsps. lemon juice
1 cup fine bread crumbs (dry)
$1/4$ cup melted butter
$1/4$ cup minced green onion

Grease a shallow baking dish (13x9x2 inches). Sprinkle separated onion slices and pimiento over bottom of the dish. Lay the fish on top. Combine salt, pepper, mace, cayenne pepper; sprinkle over the fish with the green onion. Lay the tomato slices on top and sprinkle with mushrooms. Pour in water and lemon juice. Sprinkle crumbs over the top and drizzle on the butter. Bake for 15 minutes at 350° or until the fish flakes easily with a fork. Serves 6.

Mary Shopland
Saint Peter's . . .
(1979)

ESCALLOPED MUSKELLUNGE

This was the recipe served to President Theodore Roosevelt when he breakfasted at Chautauqua Institution.   Breakfast prepared by Mrs. Alice P. Norton and the Chautauqua School of Domestic Science.

1 Muskellunge (cut in fillets one-inch thick)
salt and pepper
melted butter
Bechamel Sauce, makes 3 cups
3 cups of hot milk or cream
$4^{1}/_{2}$ Tbsps. flour
$3/4$ cup butter
salt and white pepper
dash of nutmeg

Broil muskellunge until flaky, place on large heated platter, pour over Bechamel Sauce, sprinkled with chopped parsley.

Bechamel Sauce, follow directions for making white sauce (page 285).

Athenaeum Hotel
Chautauqua Celebrity . . .
(1980)

HOLLENDEN HALIBUT

Arrange 6 thin slices of fat salt pork, $2^1/_2$ inches square, in a dripping pan. Cover with 1 small onion thinly sliced, a bit of bay leaf.

Wipe a two pound piece of halibut and place over pork and onion. Mask with 3 Tbsps. butter, creamed and mixed with 3 Tbsps. flour. Cover with 3/4 cup buttered cracker crumbs and arrange thin strips of fat salt pork over crumbs. Cover with buttered paper and bake 50 minutes in a moderate oven, removing paper during the last fifteen minutes of the cooking to brown crumbs. Remove to hot serving dish and garnish with slices of lemon cut in fancy shapes, sprinkled with finely chopped parsley and paprika. Serve with white sauce.

Irene B. Clark
Victory Cook Book
(1940s)

FISH TASTY

1 pint of flaked fish or crab meat, measured after flaking; 2 ounces of dry, fine bread crumbs, 3 hard boiled eggs chopped very fine, 1 sweet green pepper chopped fine, 1 Tbsp. parsley chopped fine, 3 ounces of butter, $^1/_2$ pint of sweet milk or cream, salt and cayenne pepper to taste. Have everything ready, then melt the butter in a heavy frying pan, then add the bread crumbs; mix well; then the cream and mix again; then the chopped eggs and pepper; stir some more; then the fish or crab meat, parsley and seasonings; stir constantly and let it simmer 3 minutes, and if you like wine add 3 Tbsps. of cooking sherry; if not, use 3 more Tbsps. of cream instead, and let it boil up again; serve very hot upon squares of buttered toast with salty crackers as an accompaniment.

Mrs. Ralph C. Sheldon
Needlework . . .
(1910)

SHREDDED WHEAT OYSTER, MEAT OR VEGETABLE PATTIES

Cut oblong cavity in top of biscuit, remove top carefully and all inside shreds, forming a shell. Sprinkle with salt and pepper, put small pieces of butter in bottom, and fill the shell with drained, picked and washed oysters. Season top of biscuit over oysters, then bits of butter on top. Place in a covered pan and bake in a moderate oven. Pour oyster liquor or cream sauce over it. Shellfish, vegetables, or meats may also be used.

An English Cookbook
(1911)

A Day's Catch from Chautauqua Lake, ca. 1915.

SALMON LOAF

1 can (1 lb.) salmon
$^1/_4$ cup ($^1/_2$ stick) butter
2 Tbsps. chopped parsley
1 Tbsp. grated onion
1 Tbsp. lemon juice
3 eggs, separated
$^1/_4$ cup milk
1 cup coarsely crumbled crackers (12)
$^1/_2$ tsp. salt
$^1/_8$ tsp. pepper
$^1/_2$ tsp. Worcestershire sauce

Grease a 9x5x3-inch loaf pan; line bottom and ends with strip of waxed paper, leaving 1 inch overhang; grease paper. Preheat oven to 350°.

Drain salmon liquid into medium saucepan. Stir in butter and milk. Heat until butter melts. Stir in crackers; let stand 5 minutes.

Flake salmon, remove large bones, skin. Fold into crumb mixture with parsley, onion, lemon juice, Worcestershire sauce, salt, pepper and egg yolks.

Beat egg whites with mixer until soft peaks form. Fold into salmon mixture. Pour into pan.

Set in shallow baking pan. Place on oven shelf; pour 1 inch boiling water in shallow pan. Set loaf pan gently in water. Bake at 350° 40 minutes. Remove; let stand 5 minutes. Peel off paper, slice, serve. Approx. 6 servings.

Marj Tietz
Cook Book
Silver Creek
(1977-78)

CLASSIC FRENCH CREAMED SCALLOPS

(Microwave)
3 Tbsps. butter
1 (4-oz.) jar sliced mushrooms, drained
2 green onions, sliced
$^1/_4$ cup chopped celery

2 Tbsps. flour
$^1/_2$ tsp. salt
$^1/_4$ tsp. thyme
1 Tbsp. pimiento, chopped
$^1/_3$ cup white wine
1 lb. raw scallops

In 2 quart casserole place butter, mushrooms, onions and celery. Microwave at High 2 to 3 minutes, stirring after 1 minute.

Stir in flour, salt, thyme and pimiento well, then wine and scallops, stirring again. Microwave at high 5 to 6 minutes, stirring after 3 minutes until thickened.

Jim Corell
Centennial Cook Book
(1987)

COQUILLE ST. JACQUES (SCALLOPS)

3/4 lb. scallops
$^1/_2$ cup clam juice
$^1/_4$ cup light rum
$^1/_4$ cup water
1 sprig parsley
2 Tbsps. chopped onion
$^1/_2$ bay leaf
dash of pepper
pinch of thyme
$^1/_4$ tsp. sugar
$^1/_4$ lb. sliced mushrooms
3 Tbsps. butter
1 Tbsp. lemon juice
1 Tbsp. flour
$^3/_4$ cup light cream
$^1/_4$ cup buttered bread crumbs
$^1/_2$ tsp. salt
$^1/_4$-$^1/_2$ cup grated Parmesan, Swiss, or Cheddar cheese

In saucepan, combine clam juice, rum, water, parsley, onion, bay leaf, thyme , salt and pepper and sugar. Bring to a boil. Add scallops, lower heat and simmer until tender (5-7 minutes). Remove scallops from pan, strain broth and reserve. Sauté mushrooms in 1 tablespoon butter, add lemon juice and set aside. Melt remaining 2 tablespoons butter in a pan and add flour. Gradually stir in $^3/_4$ cup of reserved broth and $^3/_4$ cup light cream. Cook until smooth and thickened. Add scallops and mushrooms. Turn into a greased baking dish, top with crumbs and sprinkle with cheese. Bake at 400° for 10 minutes.

Gail and Jean Bloomquist
Favorite Recipes
Findley Lake (1981)

SEAFOOD CASSEROLE

$^1/_2$ cup butter
$^1/_2$ cup chopped green pepper
$^1/_2$ cup chopped onions
$^1/_2$ cup chopped celery
$^1/_2$ cup sauterne
$^2/_3$ cup flour
$^1/_2$ tsp. salt
$^1/_2$ tsp. garlic salt
$^1/_2$ cup grated Cheddar cheese
$^1/_4$ tsp. paprika
$^1/_{16}$ tsp. cayenne
2 cups milk
1 (7 $^3/_4$-oz.) can crabmeat, drained
1 ($9^1/_2$-oz.) can tiny shrimp, drained
1 (4-oz.) can mushroom stems, drained
1 (5-oz.) can water chestnuts, drained
2 Tbsps. melted butter
$^1/_2$ cup fine bread crumbs

Melt butter in 2-quart saucepan. Add green pepper, onion and celery. Sauté until tender. Add sauterne. Stir in flour, salt, garlic salt, paprika and cayenne. Add milk, stirring constantly. When smooth add crabmeat, shrimp, mushroom stems and water chestnuts. Grease 2-quart casserole. Pour mixture in dish. Top with melted butter, Cheddar cheese and bread crumbs. Bake at 350° for 15 to 25 minutes.

Laura R. Wilson
A Cappella Choir . . .
(1986)

SHRIMP & CASHEW STIR-FRY

For 4 servings you will need:
1 lb. medium-sized uncooked shrimp
$1/3$ cup dry roasted cashews
3 Tbsps. peanut oil or salad oil
1 medium onion, slivered
$1/2$ cup thinly sliced celery
6-oz. mushrooms, sliced
1 clove garlic, minced or pressed
1 tsp. cornstarch
2 Tbsps. soy sauce
$1/4$ cup chicken broth or water
2 cups shredded fresh spinach (leaves only)
$1/4$ lb. pea pods (optional), ends and strings removed
salt
cooked brown rice

Shell and devein shrimp and set aside. Stir cashews in heated oil in a large frying pan until they give off a nutlike aroma and begin to brown. Remove with a slotted spoon and reserve. To same oil add onion and celery. Cook, stirring occasionally over medium-high heat until onions are transparent, about 3 minutes. Add mushrooms and cook until they begin to brown. Mix in garlic and shrimp, stirring until shrimp turns pink. Mix cornstarch smoothly with soy sauce and chicken broth. To shrimp mixture add spinach and peas (if used). Stir 30 seconds. Mix in cornstarch mixture, stirring just until thickened. Taste. Add salt if needed. Sprinkle with reserved cashews. Serve shrimp over brown rice.

Linda Valone Davis
Home Town Recipes
Dunkirk
(1989)

FILLETS WITH DANISH MUSTARD SAUCE

2 cups water
2-3 onions, sliced
1 bay leaf
6 sprigs fresh dill
2 whole allspice
2 peppercorns
2 tsp. salt
1 lemon slice
2 - 2 1/2 lb. flounder or haddock fillets

Combine the first 8 ingredients in saucepan; simmer 15 minutes. Strain and keep hot in pan. Spread fillets on a tray and cut in serving-size pieces. Sprinkle with salt; place a fresh dill sprig on each; roll the fish and fasten with toothpicks. Put fish in skillet. Pour hot liquid over fish. Simmer, covered, 15 minutes. Occasionally spoon liquid over fish. Drain fish; arrange on platter; pour sauce (below) over fish. Serves 6.

DANISH MUSTARD SAUCE:
3 Tbsps. butter
2 tsps. dry mustard
1/2 tsp. salt
1/4 tsp. sugar
1 Tbsp. cold butter
3 Tbsps. flour
2 cups fish stock, milk, or clam juice
2 tsps. grated horseradish

Melt butter, stir in flour, then mustard and stir for 2 minutes. Add fish stock gradually, stirring all the while. Add salt and sugar. Let cook 5-8 minutes. Stir as it cooks. Stir in cold butter just as you take it from heat. Beat and add horseradish. Serve at once. For a more yellow sauce, beat in 1 egg yolk just before adding cold butter.

Mrs. Bessie Cheney
Chautauqua C. Home Bureau
Kiantone Cookbook   (1989)

TUNA FISH, CABBAGE AND CHEESE CASSEROLE

1 quart shredded cabbage
1 cup boiling water
1$^1/_2$ Tbsps. butter or margarine
2 Tbsps. flour
1 cup evaporated milk
$^1/_2$ tsp. salt
$^1/_2$ cup grated American cheese
1 (7-oz.) can tuna fish
$^1/_2$ cup soft bread crumbs

Cook the cabbage for 10 minutes in the water; do not drain. Melt butter in double-boiler, add flour and blend. Add the milk, salt and cheese and cook over hot water until smooth and thickened, stirring often. Combine this sauce with cabbage and water, and pour over the tuna fish arranged in casserole. Top with bread crumbs. Bake in a pan of hot water in 350° oven for 45 minutes. Serves 2 or 3. Double this recipe using 1 12-oz. can of tuna fish to serve 6.

Jeannette Hartlieb
Cook Book
Cassadaga
(1950)

HOT TUNA DELAHANTY

2 (7-oz.) cans tuna
3 large tomatoes
3 hard-boiled eggs
2 Tbsps. flour
2 Tbsps. butter
$^1/_2$ dill pickle, chopped
1$^1/_4$ cups milk
$^3/_4$ cup mayonnaise
$^1/_2$ cup cream
1 Tbsp. catsup
2 tsps. salt
$^1/_4$ tsp. pepper

Drain tuna. Peel tomatoes, cut in eighths and remove seeds, then cut eighths in half and drain. Cut eggs in eighths, lengthwise. Melt butter in top of double boiler over boiling water. Add flour and cook until smooth. Add milk gradually and stir until thickened. Pour in cream, cover and cook slowly for 10 minutes, stirring often. Mix mayonnaise, catsup, dill pickles and seasonings, then add to the sauce. Add the tuna, tomatoes and eggs. Heat through well. Serve with baked potatoes, toast or melba toast. Serves 4.

U.S. Rep. Amo Houghton
Chautauqua-Allegheny Cookbook
(1990)

SALADS

There wasn't a lot of discussion of what we now regard as salads in the early Chautauqua County cookbooks. What Kate Cook had to say about them related to chicken salad and ham salad, both of which seem to have been served on lettuce as cold luncheon dishes.

Recipes for chicken salad appeared in nearly every cookbook we looked at, for an obvious reason: chicken salad is still easy to make, delicious, and a welcome food for most of us especially in summer. Some of the best recipes have been included here.

By the 1930s molded "salads" made on a Jell-o "base" were on everyone's table. Jell-o, under that brand name, hit the mainstream in the early 1900s, and by 1906 had reached the $1,000,000 mark in sales. As much as with any other product in any other company, the growing popularity of Jell-o and its use in molded salads was orchestrated by the manufacturer. To this day the periodic Jell-o recipe books are favorites, although Jell-o salads have lost favor. Here, though, you'll find all those old familiars: "Perfection Salad" (lemon Jell-o with cabbage, carrots, celery, etc.), the black cherry-olive combinations, the pineapple-cheese, ginger ale salad, holiday ribbon salad, and so on.

In the 1960s and 1970s layered salads came into vogue and they are represented here, as are the pasta salads which followed and which are still very popular.

Here also are seafood salads, another variety that never goes out of style.

And of course, there are cole slaws. Kate Cook knew about cole slaw; again, not a single cookbook went cole slaw-less, unless it was a book containing only cookie or dessert recipes.

No salad worth its place on the table would be there without its dressing. So here, too, are some favored salad dressings. There is one for blue cheese dressing, which has a special place in Western New York cuisine because it was the house dressing of one of the long-lived restaurants (The Vineyard in Dunkirk) and because it was anointed to be the flavor-accompaniment to the now-famous Buffalo Chicken Wings.

Yet perhaps the most famous dressing is one that earned national fame in the 1950s when it appeared in the old *Ford Times* magazine. In Chautauqua County, for some reason, it was called variously, "French Dressing," "Parisian Dressing," or "Persian Dressing." It will be recognized by the presence of a can of tomato soup in the ingredient list. Again, it appeared in the majority of the cookbooks consulted.

When you look at the salad chapter here, you will surely be impressed, as we were, at the variety of salad possibilities, and why salads are still very much a part of our eating pattern.

AVOCADO-ORANGE SALAD

DRESSING:
$^1/_2$ cup vinegar
2 tsps. orange peel
$^1/_2$ cup orange juice
juice of large lemon
$^1/_4$ cup sugar
$^1/_2$ tsp. dry mustard
$^1/_2$ tsp. salt
1 cup salad oil

3 large sliced oranges
2 sweet (medium size) onions, sliced
2 large avocados, sliced
2 heads romaine
1 head leaf lettuce
1 head iceberg lettuce

Make dressing of dressing ingredients. Pour over oranges, avocados and onions. Chill for several hours. Break lettuces and add just before serving. Toss well. Serves 12.

Erna Dawley
Dames in the Kitchen
(1975)

FROZEN COLE SLAW

1 medium head of cabbage, shredded
1 tsp. salt
1 cup white vinegar
1 shredded carrot
$^1/_4$ cup water
1 tsp. whole mustard seed
1 tsp. celery seed
 2 cups sugar

Mix salt with cabbage. Let stand 1 hour. Squeeze out excess moisture. Add shredded carrot. Make the dressing with remaining ingredients and boil 1 minute. Cool. Pour over cabbage mixture. Put in tight container and freeze. Thaw and serve when needed.

Bertha Jones Wilkes
Centennial Cook Book
(1987)

CAULIFLOWER-LIMA BEAN SALAD

1 small head cauliflower
1 cup dry lima beans, cooked and drained
1 red onion
$^1/_2$ lb. Swiss cheese

DRESSING
$^3/_4$ cup safflower oil
$^1/_4$ cup wine vinegar
1 tsp. salt
1 tsp. pepper
1 clove garlic, minced

Cook cauliflower florets until barely tender. Drain and add lima beans, and thinly sliced onion. Cut up cheese in 1 inch cubes and add. Mix all ingredients with dressing.

Shake all salad dressing ingredients together. Serves 4-6.

Sarah Warmbrodt
First United . . .
Dunkirk
(1978)

CUCUMBER SALAD

2 Tbsps. cider vinegar
1 Tbsp. Tarragon vinegar
1 Tbsp. chopped chives
1 tsp. each salt, sugar, mustard seed
$^1/_2$ tsp. paprika
$^1/_4$ tsp. black pepper
1 cup sour cream
1 medium onion cut in thin strips
2 cucumbers pared and sliced thin

Mix together lightly to serve 4.

Joann Pane
Cooking by Degrees
(1985)

GRUYERE, CELERY AND WALNUT SALAD

3 ribs celery, cut into 2-inch julienne strips
$^1/_2$ lb. Gruyere, cut into 2-inch julienne strips
$^1/_2$ cup coarsely chopped walnuts, toasted lightly
1 tsp. minced shallot
1 scallion, sliced thin
2 Tbsps. Dijon mustard
$1^1/_2$ tsps. lemon juice
$^1/_3$ cup heavy cream
1 Tbsp. minced parsley

Slice celery and Gruyere and put in medium bowl. Add walnuts. Mix remaining ingredients in small bowl; add to celery mixture and stir to coat evenly. Chill. Serves 6.

Claire Davis
Soup and Salad . . .
(1989)

DIANNE SALAD

1 bunch Romaine lettuce
6 slices crisp bacon
1 small red onion, thinly sliced
1 avocado
Croutons
Grated Romano cheese

DRESSING:
1 cup salad oil
$^1/_2$ cup white vinegar
$^1/_3$ cup sugar
1 tsp. salt
1 small onion, minced
1 tsp. paprika
1 egg white

Combine lettuce, bacon and onion. Sprinkle with grated Romano cheese. Add wedges of avocado and croutons. Toss with Dianne dressing.

Use medium speed on blender to mix dessing ingredients. Serves 6.

Ruth Swisshelm
Cooking by Degrees
(1985)

EXOTIC SALAD
1 large head lettuce
1 cup sweet peas
1 cup diced sweet apples
1 cup Miracle Whip salad dressing
$1^{1}/_{2}$ cups shredded cheese (Cheddar)
1 cup crushed pineapple (drained)
$^{1}/_{2}$ cup mandarin oranges (drained)
$^{3}/_{4}$ cup sweet coconut shreds
$^{1}/_{2}$ cup walnuts (chop), optional

Shred or chop lettuce into large bowl. Add peas, apples, pineapple and mandarin oranges. Add Miracle Whip. Mix thoroughly. Toast coconut in oven 5 minutes or so. Add coconut and nuts and mix together. Top with shredded cheese. Serves 4 to 6.

Pu Chau
A Cappella Choir ...
(1986)

ORANGE AND CASHEW SALAD
(With Lime French Dressing)
4 to 6 cups lettuce pieces
2 medium oranges, peeled and sliced
$^{1}/_{2}$ small red onion, sliced
$^{1}/_{2}$ small white onion, sliced
$^{1}/_{3}$ cup coarsely chopped cashew nuts
Dressing:
1 cup oil
1 clove garlic, split
1 tsp. salt
$^{3}/_{4}$ tsp. sugar
$^{1}/_{8}$ tsp. pepper
$^{1}/_{3}$ cup lime juice

Toss together lettuce, oranges, onions and nuts in bowl. Combine all but lime juice in jar, cover and let stand at least 1 hour in refrigerator. Remove garlic, add lime juice and shake. Pour over salad . Serves 6.

Jean Spaulding
Soup and Salad
(1989) . . .

PENNSYLVANIA DUTCH SALAD

5 slices bacon, cooked and crumbled
1 beaten egg
$1/3$ cup minced onion
2 Tbsps. sugar
$1/2$ tsp. salt
$1/3$ cup vinegar
2 Tbsps. water
1 bunch leaf lettuce

Remove bacon from frying pan. To bacon grease add all ingredients except lettuce. Heat just to boiling. Add bacon and pour over lettuce. Serves 4.

Johanna Sobszak
Art/Dunkirk
(1960s)

MARINATED VEGETABLE SALAD

1 package (10-oz.) frozen broccoli spears
1 package (10-oz.) frozen cauliflower
1 jar (6-oz.) marinated artichoke hearts, drained
7 oz. carrots, sliced, cooked until tender
1 large green pepper, seeded, cut into strips
1 medium red onion, sliced into rings
1 cup fresh parsley, minced
$1/3$ cup lemon juice
1 can (1 pound) black olives, drained
4 oz. Blue cheese (crumbled)
1 tsp. salt
1 tsp. sugar
1 tsp. oregano
1 tsp. basil
$1/2$ tsp. mustard
$1/4$ tsp. pepper
$2/3$ cup salad oil

Thaw broccoli spears and cauliflower, but do not cook. Cut into 1 inch chunks. Place in large bowl. Add drained artichoke hearts (quartered), carrots, green pepper, red onion, and parsley.

Mix lemon juice, salt, sugar, oregano, basil , mustard and pepper in a small bowl; whisk in oil (slowly drizzling into bowl) until smooth. Pour dressing over vegetables. Chill, covered, turning occasionally until flavors blend, at least 4 hours and preferably overnight., Stir in olives and Blue cheese just before serving. Serves 6-8.

Mary Ellen Kimble
Chautauqua Motet ...
(1985)

PEA SALAD

1 box frozen peas, defrosted, left raw, drained well
1 lb. shredded Cheddar cheese
$^1/_2$ cup chopped green onions
$^1/_2$ cup celery
2 hard boiled eggs (optional)
Dressing:
2 Tbsps. Dijon mustard
$1^1/_2$ Tbsps. vinegar
1 cup Hellmann's mayonnaise
1 drop Tabasco

Combine the dressing, add peas, cheese, onions, celery and eggs to dressing and mix well. Refrigerate until time to serve. Serves 6.

Pat Windsor
Here's What's Cookin' ...
(1988)

SAUERKRAUT SALAD

$^1/_2$ cup shredded celery, cut fine
1 large can sauerkraut (juice included)
1 fresh green pepper, shredded or cut thin
1 small jar pimiento, cut in small pieces
$^1/_2$ cup cooking oil
$^1/_2$ cup vinegar (white or brown)
$1^1/_4$ cups sugar (check for taste and add more)
$^1/_4$ tsp. allspice powder (optional)
$^1/_2$ tsp. celery seed
$^1/_2$ tsp. mustard seed
$^1/_4$ tsp. turmeric

Bring vinegar, oil, sugar, allspice, celery seed, mustard seed and turmeric to a rolling boil and pour over sauerkraut, celery, pimiento and green pepper in glass container. Let stand at least overnight in refrigerator but it's better after 2 days. Stays good at least 2 weeks, covered , in refrigerator. Recipe may be doubled in a large-mouthed gallon jar, covered and refrigerated. Goes over very well at parties and picnics.

Mrs. Florence Ludwiszewski
Sharing Our Best
(1987)

LAYERED PARTY VEGETABLE SALAD

1 small head lettuce, shredded
$^2/_3$ cup chopped green onions
$^2/_3$ cup chopped celery
1 green pepper, thinly sliced
1 (5 oz.) can water chestnuts, drained, sliced
1 (10 oz.) package frozen green peas
Parmesan Mayonnaise (recipe follows)
1 Tbsp. mixed salad herbs
2 medium tomatoes, sliced
3 hard-cooked eggs, sliced
$^1/_3$ cup shredded Cheddar cheese
6 slices bacon, cooked crisp and crumbled (optional)

PARMESAN MAYONNAISE:
1 egg
$^1/_3$ cup Parmesan cheese
2 Tbsps. cider vinegar
$^1/_2$ tsp. each salt and pepper
$^1/_2$ tsp. prepared mustard
1 cup salad oil

In large, clear, glass salad bowl, layer first the lettuce evenly. Top with onion, celery, green pepper, water chestnuts and then unthawed green peas, making an even layer of each ingredient. Spread Parmesan Mayonnaise evenly over top. Sprinkle with herbs. Cover and refrigerate overnight. The next day, layer top of salad with sliced eggs, sliced tomatoes, cheese and bacon, if used.

Put egg, Parmesan cheese, vinegar, salt, pepper and mustard in blender container or work bowl of food processor fitted with steel blade. Turn motor on. Very slowly add oil, blending until an emulsified mayonnaise forms. Makes about $1^1/_2$ cups. Serves 8.

Pat Schultz
Westfield Jayncees . . .
(1983)

Note: If using a raw egg worries you, simply use commercial mayonnaise for the salad and add the Parmesan cheese and dry mustard to it before dressing salad.

GLORIFIED ONIONS

5 or 6 medium sweet onions, sliced
$^1/_2$ cup vinegar
1 cup sugar
2 cups water
$^1/_2$ cup mayonnaise
1 tsp. celery salt (optional)

Slice onions and soak slices in refrigerator for 2 to 4 hours in mixture of vinegar, sugar and water. Drain well, then toss onion slices with mayonnaise and, if desired, celery salt.

Margaret Bigler
Warm Your Heart . . .
(1987)

ONE-DISH SALAD MEAL

1 lb. small shell macaroni
1 cup frozen peas
1 can salmon or 2 cans tuna fish
1 cup diced celery
1 cup diced dill pickle
$1^1/_2$ cups mayonnaise plus 2 Tbsps. lemon juice
 or $1^1/_2$ cups Miracle Whip
$^1/_2$ large head of lettuce
1 Tbsp. diced onion if desired

Early in the day boil macaroni according to package directions. Rinse with cool water, drain well, place in large bowl. Flake salmon or tuna into another large bowl. Add celery, frozen peas, dill pickle and dressing. Mix well. Add to macaroni and chill well. If desired add onion, also. Just before serving add chopped lettuce. This keeps lettuce crisp and crunchy. Serve with crackers or garlic bread.

Annivera J. Mighelis
Culinary Delights
(1988-89)

MACARONI SALAD

1 lb. spiral macaroni
$^7/_8$ cup vegetable oil
1 cup vinegar
$2^3/_4$ cup sugar
1 tsp. garlic powder
1 tsp. dill weed
2 tsps. prepared mustard
1 diced onion
1 diced green pepper
1 diced tomato
1 cup pitted black olives, sliced
1 grated carrot
1 cup chick peas

Boil macaroni, al dente, rinse with cold water. Combine oil, sugar, vinegar, garlic and dill weed and mustard in a large bowl. Stir to dissolve sugar, add remaining ingredients. Add salt and pepper to taste. Serves 12.

Joanna Erskine
Cooking with . . .
(1987)

RICE SALAD RING

3 cups cold cooked rice
1 cup sour cream
$^1/_2$ cup mayonnaise
1 Tbsp. lemon juice
3 green onions, minced
1 small green pepper, finely chopped
3 cloves garlic, minced or pressed
1 tsp. salt
$^1/_4$ tsp. pepper
Garnish with cherry tomatoes, rolled ham slices
    and lettuce, if desired

Break up cold rice with fork to separate. Stir together the sour cream, mayonnaise, lemon juice, onions, green pepper and garlic. Add salt and pepper. Fold sour cream mixture into rice until well blended. Pack into 1-quart ring mold. Cover with plastic wrap and refrigerate for later serving. To serve, unmold onto platter and fill center with garnish, if desired.

Emily Graham
Culinary Delights
(1988-89)

CHICKEN SALAD

Prepare a chicken the same as for fricasseeing. Boil until chicken will drop from the bone; when it begins to get tender, salt well; before quite cold pick from bones, free the meat from skin and gristle, and pick into small shreds; do not chop. Take twice the amount of celery that you have of chicken, cut it about three-fourths of an inch in length, shred very fine, and put in some ice water. Boil hard four eggs; when cold, shell and slice them. For dressing, put one-half pint of not very sharp vinegar into a saucepan, and put on stove, with butter the size of an egg; beat two eggs with one tablespoon mustard, one even teaspoon black pepper, one tablespoon sugar, a scant teaspoon salt; beat these thoroughly together and pour slowly into the hot vinegar, stirring constantly; take care not to let it boil, as it will curdle. If you have salad oil, stir one tablespoon of it in with the mustard; if you have not the salad oil, use two tablespoons of the oil from the chicken. This may be prepared the day before using. Pour the dressing over the chicken, mixing thoroughly; just before serving add celery, which should be very crisp. In place of the celery, nice crisp lettuce, or finely shaved white cabbage may be used. Either makes a nice salad. If either cabbage or lettuce is used, use celery salt for flavoring (or celery seed). When pouring the dressing on the salad, and, adding the celery, mix lightly with a silver fork, but mix well. Place in a dish and form a mound; garnish the top with the sliced boiled eggs and garnish the edges of the dish with the fine leaves of the celery; set in a cold place until needed. The liquor in which the chicken has been boiled will make a nice soup by adding noodles.

Kate Cook
Chautauqua Cook Book
(1882)

GERMAN POTATO SALAD

3 lbs. potatoes, boiled with peelings on day before
1 lb. bacon, browned lightly
1 cup celery with leaves, chopped
$^3/_4$ cup onions, chopped
$^1/_2$ doz. hard boiled eggs, sliced
6 Tbsps. flour
$^3/_4$ cup vinegar
3 cups water
$^3/_4$ cup sugar
2 Tbsps. salt

Add to diced potatoes, chopped celery, chopped onions, hard-boiled eggs, and browned bacon. Make dressing by adding flour to $^1/_2$ the bacon fat and mix, then add vinegar, water, sugar, salt. Boil until thick, pour over potatoes, mix well. Can be served hot or cold.

Dora Barbknecht
Adventures in Food
(1977)

OLD-FASHIONED POTATO SALAD

4 cups diced, cooked potatoes
$1^1/_2$ cups sliced celery
$^1/_2$ cup cut-up scallions
$^1/_4$ cup sliced radishes
2 Tbsps. snipped parsley
1 cup mayonnaise
1 Tbsp. prepared mustard
$^1/_8$ tsp. pepper
$^1/_2$ tsp. celery seeds
$1^1/_2$ to 2 tsps. salt

Several hours ahead or day before combine all ingredients and refrigerate. Serve on lettuce garnished with tomato or hard-boiled egg wedges, sliced olives, grated carrots or pickles. May taste salty at first, but that disappears as flavors blend. Serves 6.

Bernice Bouchard
Dames in the Kitchen
(1975)

POTATO SALAD

Boil 8 medium-sized potatoes and cut in $^1/_4$-inch cubes; add 2 cups cucumbers cut in $^1/_4$-inch cubes, 1 cup shredded almonds, 2 Tbsps. red and green peppers chopped fine, 1 small onion chopped fine. Serve with mayonnaise.

Mrs. William Bates
Sweets and Meats II
(1917)

JERRY BELL'S BEST-EVER CHICKEN SALAD SUPREME

3 cups diced, cooked chicken (white meat)
1 cup pineapple chunks, packed in own juice, drained, halved
1 tsp. freeze-dried chives
1 tsp. Lawry's seasoned salt
1 tsp. celery seed
2 tsp. dried parsley
1 cup Hellmann's mayonnaise
1 cup finely diced celery
1 small can water chestnuts, sliced
$\frac{1}{2}$ cup sliced almonds, toasted a light brown
paprika for garnish (optional)

Blend first 6 ingredients. Add mayonnaise and stir well. Add celery, water chestnuts and almonds. Blend well and refrigerate for several hours. This is very necessary to completely blend the flavors. Makes 6 generous servings.

Thyra Grey Howard
Favorite Recipes . . .
Findley Lake
(1981)

TABBOULEH

1 beef bouillon cube
1 cup boiling water
1 cup bulgur wheat
$\frac{1}{4}$ - $\frac{1}{3}$ cup lemon juice
$\frac{1}{4}$ cup vegetable oil
$\frac{1}{4}$ tsp. salt
$\frac{1}{2}$ tsp. finely minced garlic
$\frac{1}{2}$ tsp. oregano
$\frac{1}{4}$ tsp. black pepper
$1\frac{1}{2}$ cups minced fresh parsley
1 cup diced green pepper
1 cup diced, peeled carrots
$\frac{1}{4}$ cup sliced green onions
1 can (20 oz.) chick peas, drained
3 lemon slices, halved
tomato wedges for garnish

Thoroughly dissolve bouillon cube in 1 cup boiling water. Pour over bulgur, cover, let stand 30 minutes; bulgur will absorb water and swell. Place lemon juice, oil, salt, garlic, oregano and pepper in small screw-top jar. Put the parsley, green pepper, carrots, onions, chick peas and soaked bulgur into a large bowl. Shake dressing vigorously to thoroughly blend; pour over vegetable mixture and bulgur; toss gently to mix. Put in large bowl and garnish with lemon slices and tomato wedges. May be served at once or chilled for several hours. Makes 4 servings.

Thyra Grey Howard
Favorite Recipes . . .
Findley Lake
(1981)

SHRIMP AND CHICKEN SALAD SUPREME

2 cooked chicken breasts
1 lb. cooked shrimp, diced
$^1/_2$ dozen hard-boiled eggs
2 cups celery
(your measurement) French dressing
2 cups mayonnaise
4 Tbsps. chili sauce
2 Tbsps. chopped chives
salt to your taste
1 cup whipped cream

Remove skin and bones from chicken breasts; cut into strips. Combine chicken, shrimp, chopped egg whites and celery in a small amount of French dressing; set aside to marinate for one hour. Mash egg yolks, add mayo, chili sauce, chives and salt; mix well. Fold in whipped cream; let dressing chill thoroughly. Combine shrimp mixture and dressing. Toss lightly; serve on lettuce. Serves 8-10

Joann Williams
100 Years of Coooking . . .
(1986)

POLYNESIAN SHRIMP BOWL

1 (15$^1/_2$-oz.) can pineapple chunks, drained
2 tsps. cornstarch
1$^1/_2$ tsps. curry powder
$^1/_4$ tsp. salt
2 tsps. lemon juice
$^1/_2$ cup sliced water chestnuts
2 cups medium noodles, cooked and drained
2 (4$^1/_2$-oz.) cans shrimp, rinsed and drained
$^1/_4$ cup chopped green pepper
$^1/_3$ cup salad dressing
$^1/_3$ cup sour cream

Drain pineapple, saving juice. Cook pineapple juice, cornstarch, curry powder and salt until thick and bubbly. Stir in lemon juice; cool. Blend curry mixture, salad dressing (or mayonnaise) and sour cream. Fold into remaining ingredients. Chill thoroughly. Makes 6 servings.

Charlotte Anderson
Soup and Salad . . .
(1989)

SPRING TUNA SALAD
(Quantity recipe)

36 servings:
$^3/_4$ cup finely chopped scallions
$1^1/_2$ cups chopped, pitted ripe olives
$4^1/_2$ quarts broken crisp salad greens
1 quart chopped celery
1 Tbsp. salt
1 Tbsp. Ac'cent
8 ($12^1/_2$ oz) cans chunk tuna in oil, drained
$^3/_4$ cup chili sauce
$^3/_4$ cup French dressing
$^3/_4$ cup mayonnaise
9 hard-cooked eggs, sliced

4 servings:
2 Tbsps. finely chopped scallions
3 Tbsps. chopped, pitted ripe olives
2 cups broken crisp salad greens
$^1/_2$ cup chopped celery
$^1/_8$ tsp. salt
$^1/_8$ tsp. Ac'cent
2 ($6^1/_2$ oz) cans chunk tuna in oil, drained
$1^1/_2$ Tbsps. chili sauce
$1^1/_2$ Tbsps. French dressing
$1^1/_2$ Tbsps. mayonnaise
1 hard-cooked egg, sliced

Sprinkle scallions, olives over greens and celery. Add salt, Ac'cent. Add tuna. Blend chili sauce and French dressing into mayonnaise. Toss lightly with tuna mixture. Chill. Portion salad into lettuce cups. Garnish with sliced eggs.

Martha Laughlin
Cookbook
Westfield (1986)

WINTER FRUIT SALAD
1 (20-oz.) can pineapple chunks
2 (11 oz.) cans mandarin oranges, drained
$1^1/_2$ cups seedless red or green grapes (halved if large)
3 kiwi, peeled, halved lengthwise and sliced
$^1/_2$ cup orange juice
$^1/_4$ cup honey
1 Tbsp. lemon juice

Drain pineapple, reserving juice. In a large bowl, combine drained pineapple chunks, mandarin orange sections, grapes and kiwi slices.

Add water, if necessary, to pineapple juice to make 1 cup liquid. Combine pineapple juice mixture, orange juice, honey, and lemon juice. Pour over fruit. Cover and chill until serving. Serves 6.

Becky Jones
Food for . . .
(1987)

STUFFED TOMATOES

4 medium size tomatoes
1 cup crab meat
salt and cayennne pepper
$^1/_4$ cup chopped pickles
$^1/_2$ cup chopped celery
$^1/_2$ cup mayonnaise
1 hard-cooked egg, chopped
chopped parsley

Peel tomatoes and scoop out center of each leaving perfect shells. Sprinkle with salt and cayenne pepper. Turn upside down and chill in refrigerator.
Mix crab meat with pickles, celery, diced tomato pulp and mayonnaise to moisten. Season. Stuff mixture into tomatoes; top with mayonnaise. Sprinkle a little paprika on top. Mix chopped egg and parsley together and decorate around tomatoes. Serves 4.

Milly Boyd
Soup and Salad . . .
(1989)

MOLDED SALMON SALAD

2 cups red salmon
$^1/_2$ tsp. salt
$1^1/_2$ Tbsps. sugar
$^1/_2$ Tbsp. flour
1 tsp. dry mustard
dash of cayenne pepper
2 egg yolks
$1^1/_2$ Tbsps. butter, melted
$^3/_4$ cup milk
$^1/_4$ cup vinegar
$^3/_4$ Tbsp. gelatin
2 Tbsps. cold water

Flake the salmon. Mix dry ingredients together. Add egg yolks, butter, milk and vinegar; cook in the top of a double boiler, stirring constantly, until mixture thickens. Soak gelatin in cold water 5 minutes and pour hot mixture over it. Add salmon and stir until gelatin dissolves. Fill individual molds and chill. Serve with Cucumber Sauce. Serves 8.

CUCUMBER SAUCE:
$^1/_2$ cup heavy cream
$^1/_4$ tsp. salt
few grains white pepper
2 Tbsps. vinegar
$^1/_2$ cup cucumber, diced, drained and chilled

Beat heavy cream to stiff peaks. Add salt and white pepper. Gradually add vinegar. Just before serving, add cucumber.

Verna Jackson
Soup and Salad. . .
(1989)

FROZEN FRUIT SALAD

A delicious, pretty salad to have in the freezer for
   holiday entertaining

4 (1 lb. 4 oz.) cans crushed pineapple

2 (1 lb.) cans sliced peaches

2 cups fresh white grapes, halved or 2 (1 lb. 4 oz.) cans

$1^1/_2$ cups maraschino cherries, cut in eighths

$^1/_2$ lb. (30) marshmallows, quartered

2 tsps. crystallized ginger, finely chopped

1 envelope (1 Tbsp.) unflavored gelatin

$^1/_4$ cup cold water

1 cup orange juice

$^1/_4$ cup lemon juice

$2^1/_2$ cups sugar

$^1/_2$ tsp. salt

2 cups coarsely chopped pecans

3 cups mayonnaise

2 qts. heavy cream, whipped or 10 packages dessert
   topping mix, or 1 quart heavy cream and 5 packages
   dessert topping mix

Drain fruit; save $1^1/_2$ cups pineapple juice. Cut peaches in $^1/_2$" cubes. Combine fruit, marshmallows and ginger. Soften gelatin in cold water.

Heat pineapple juice to boiling. Add gelatin; stir to dissolve. Add orange and lemon juice, sugar and salt; stir to dissolve. Chill. When mixture starts to thicken, add fruit mixture and nuts. Fold in whipped cream and mayonnaise. Spoon into quart freezer cartons. Cover and freeze. Makes 9 quarts.

To serve, remove from freezer and thaw enough to slip out of carton. Cut in 1" slices. Serve salad on lettuce; garnish with cherries. For dessert, top with whipped cream. Each quart makes 6 to 8 servings.

Mrs. Pauline Dennison
Kiantone Cookbook
(1969)

ADDITIONS AND GARNISHES FOR SALADS

Sliced hard-cooked eggs	*Cubed celery*
Radishes	*Onions - pickled, grated or pearl onions*
Chopped green or ripe olives	*Tomatoes, sliced and dipped in finely chopped parsley or chives*
Nut meats	*Capers*
Pimiento	*Dwarf tomatoes stuffed with cottage cheese*
Green pepper	*Fresh herbs - sprigs or chopped*
Sardines	*Mint leaves*
Anchovies	*Cooked beets, cut into shapes or sticks*
Slivered cheeses	*Lemon slices with pinked edges and dipped in chopped parsley*
Julienned Ham	*Raw cauliflower*
Chicken	*Grated carrots*

Soup and Salad . . . (1989)

24-HOUR SALAD

2 beaten eggs
4 Tbsps. sugar
2 Tbsps. vinegar
pinch of salt
1 Tbsp. butter
$^1/_2$ cup cream or 1 cup Cool Whip
1 cup chunk pineapple
1 cup pears
1 cup peaches
1 banana
marshmallows
cherries or grapes

Put eggs, sugar, vinegar and salt in double boiler. Cook until thick and add 1 Tbsp. butter. Cool. Whip 1/2 cup cream (you may substitute 1 cup Cool Whip) and fold into egg mixture. Add listed fruits or any fruits you may have. Chill 24 hours, then serve.

Millie Longhouse
Finger Lickin' . . .
(1981)

SUMMER FRUIT BOWL

1 medium watermelon
1 medium cantaloupe
6 large plums
4 large nectarines
1 lb. seedless green grapes

SAUCE:
2 cups water
$1^1/_2$ cups sugar
3 Tbsps. lime juice
$^3/_4$ cup mint leaves (fresh) or 1 Tbsp. dried mint

Cut all fruit into bite-size pieces. Put all fruit in large bowl.

Over medium heat, cook water, sugar, and lime juice for 15 minutes. Stir in mint and cool in refrigerator. Strain out mint leaves and pour over fruit.

Joyce Blakeslee
Food for. . .
(1987)

MOLDED SALADS

APRICOT NECTAR SALAD

4 cups apricot nectar
1 large box (6 oz.) lemon Jell-o
1 can (16 oz.) crushed pineapple,
   drained, reserving juice
1 package (8 oz.) cream cheese
$1/_2$ cup celery, chopped
$1/_3$ cup walnuts, chopped

Heat the apricot nectar and add lemon Jell-o and pineapple. Pour half of the mixture in a 9 x 12 pan. When set solidly, spread with softened cream cheese thinned with reserved pineapple juice. Cover cream cheese with celery and nuts. Add remaining Jell-o and set. Serves 12.

Jean Badger
Chautauqua Motet . . .
(1985)

SHERRY CHERRY SALAD

1 (16 oz.) can light or dark sweet cherries
1 (3 oz.) package cherry flavored gelatin
1 cup boiling water
$1/_2$ cup cherry syrup
$1/_2$ cup sherry wine
2 Tbsps. chopped nut meats

Drain and pit cherries, reserving syrup and 12 cherries for dressing.

Dissolve gelatin in boiling water. Add cherry syrup and sherry wine. Refrigerate until partially set. Fold in cherries and nut meats. Turn into oiled 1 quart heart-shaped mold. Chill until set. Serve with cherry cream dressing.

CHERRY CREAM DRESSING:
12 canned sweet cherries, diced
1 Tbsp. cherry syrup
1 tsp. lemon juice
$1^1/_2$ tsps. sugar
$1/_2$ cup dairy sour cream

Fold cherries, cherry syrup, lemon juice and sugar into dairy sour cream. Refrigerate until serving.

Martha Fay
Kiantone Cookbook
(1989)

AVOCADO PEAR SALAD

1 package lime Jell-o
1 cup boiling water
2 Tbsps. mayonnaise
1 tsp. onion juice
1 Tbsp. green pepper, cut fine
2 Tbsps. lemon juice
$^1/_3$ cup celery, cut up fine
1 cup chopped avocado (1 pear)
$^1/_2$ cup whipped cream

Dissolve Jell-o in boiling water, add mayonnaise, onion juice, green pepper, lemon juice and celery. Cool. Add the avocado and the whipped cream. Pour into a mold. Chill in the refrigerator until ready to serve. Serve on lettuce leaf.

Clementine Hayes
Art/Dunkirk
(1960s)

CRANBERRY MOLD

1 (3 oz.) package wild cherry gelatin dessert
1 scant cup sugar
dash of salt
1 (8 oz.) can crushed pineapple with juice
1 cup raw cranberries, chopped or ground*
1 cup chopped celery
1 navel orange, ground with peel on*
$^1/_2$ cup pecans, coarsely chopped
1 Tbsp. freshly squeezed lemon juice or more to taste

SAUCE:
1 cup mayonnaise
1 cup sour cream
Combine both ingredients.

Oil an 8-inch ring mold and set aside. Dissolve the gelatin in 1 cup boiling water and stir until all the granules disappear. Add the sugar and salt; then add the pineapple with its juice, cranberries, celery, ground orange, pecans and lemon juice. Pour the mixture into the prepared mold and refrigerate until set. Unmold and serve with the sauce on a bed of lettuce or watercress. Makes 12 servings.

Note: Use food processor or food grinder.

Barb Henry
Soup and Salad . . .
(1989)

ZIPPY CUCUMBER SALAD
2 (3 oz.) packages lemon Jell-o
2 Tbsps. unflavored gelatin
2 cups boiling water
$1/_2$ cup cold water
1 tsp. salt
$1/_4$ cup vinegar
2 Tbsps. grated onion
$1/_4$ cup horseradish
2 cups grated, unpeeled cucumber

DRESSING:
$1/_2$ cup mayonnaise
1 tsp. horseradish
1 cup sour cream
$1/_2$ tsp. salt
1 tsp. dry mustard

Mix, pour into a mold and chill until set. Serve with dressing on the side.

Use small amount of green coloring in both salad and dressing.

Charlotte Guest
Cookbook
Westfield
(1986)

OLIVE WREATH MOLD
1 No. 2 can ($2^1/_2$ cups) crushed pineapple
1 (3 oz.) package lime Jell-o
$1/_2$ cup grated American cheese
$1/_2$ cup chopped pimiento
$1/_2$ cup finely chopped celery
$2/_3$ cup chopped walnuts
$1/_4$ tsp. salt
1 cup heavy cream, whipped
Small stuffed olives
Sliced curly endive

Drain pineapple. Heat syrup to a boil. Add to Jell-o and stir. Cool. When Jell-o begins to thicken, add pineapple, cheese, pimiento, celery, nuts, salt. Fold in whipped cream.

Place row of olives in bottom of a 9" ring mold. Pour Jell-o mixture into mold and chill until firm. Arrange endive on platter. Unmold salad on top. Serves 8-10.

Mrs. George F. Kessler
Wonderful Cooking . . .
(Date unknown)

VEGETABLE SALAD

2 packages lemon Jell-o
2 cups hot water
1 cup cold water
1 cup mayonnaise
4 Tbsps. vinegar
1 tsp. salt
3 cups finely shredded cabbage
1 cup sliced radishes
1 cup finely sliced celery
4 Tbsps. finely cut green pepper
2 Tbsps. diced onion
$^1/_2$ cup sliced green olives

Dissolve Jell-o in hot water. Add cold water, mayonnaise, vinegar, salt. Let cool, then beat until fluffy. Add vegetables and olives. Chill until firm. Serves 12.

Caroline Betts
Cookbook
Westfield
(1986)

DINING AT CHAUTAUQUA

The Breakfast was given in honor of Theodore Roosevelt. The menu was planned and prepared by the Chautauqua School of Domestic Science. It was served in Higgins Hall to about 125 guests on August 12, 1905.

Rocky Ford Melon

Escalloped Muskellunge   Broiled Chicken
Creamed Potatoes   Timbales of Green Peas
Raspberry Short Cake and Whipped Cream
Coffee
Rolls, Boston Brown Bread   Southern Beaten Biscuit
Stuffed Prunes

Luncheon was to honor Eleanor Roosevelt, at the Arthur Bestor home at 1 Root Avenue for about 12 guests.

Salmon Mousse with Cucumber Sauce   Sliced Tomatoes
Hot Biscuits   Stawberry Shortcake   Iced Tea

SALAD DRESSINGS

AUNT ANITA'S SALAD DRESSING

$1/_2$ cup sugar
pinch of salt
1 Tbsp. onion juice
4 Tbsps. vinegar
1 cup Mazola oil
1 level tsp. dry mustard
$1/_2$ tsp. celery salt
$1/_2$ tsp. celery seed
1 Tbsp. paprika

Mix all, adding oil slowly, beating all the time.

Dr. Kent Brown
Cookbook
Westfield
(1986)

CELERY SEED CREAM DRESSING

$1/_4$ cup sugar
1 Tbsp. flour
$1/_2$ tsp. dry mustard
$1/_2$ tsp. salt
$1/_2$ tsp. black pepper
$1^1/_4$ cups lemon-lime carbonated beverage
    (room temperature)
4 egg yolks, slightly beaten
2 Tbsps. butter
$1/_2$ cup chilled whipping cream
$1/_2$ tsp. dry mustard
2 tsps. confectioners' sugar
2 tsps. celery seed

Mix together first 5 ingredients in top of a double boiler. Add 1 cup of the carbonated beverage, gradually blending in. Set over direct heat. Stirring gently and consistently, bring mixture to boiling. Cook 1 to 2 minutes longer. Add and stir in remaining $1/_4$ cup carbonated beverage. Vigorously stir about 3 Tbsps. of the hot mixture into the beaten egg yolks, immediately blend into mixture in top of double boiler. Set over simmering water and cook 3 to 5 minutes, stirring slowly to keep mixture cooking evenly. Remove from heat and stir in the butter. Cool; chill thoroughly. Before serving, using a chilled bowl and beater, beat whipping cream until it is of medium consistency (piles softly). With final few strokes, blend in a mixture of the dry mustard and confectioners' sugar. Blend whipped-cream mixture and celery seed into salad dressing. Use on chicken salad. About $2^1/_4$ cups dressing. Note: Dressing may be stored covered in refrigerator for several weeks.

The Parish Cook Book (1937)

BLUE CHEESE DRESSING

1 small onion, cut up
1 cup mayonnaise
$^1/_3$ cup salad oil
$^1/_4$ cup catsup
2 Tbsps. sugar
dash of pepper
2 Tbsps. vinegar
1 tsp. prepared mustard
$^1/_2$ tsp. salt
$^1/_2$ tsp. paprika
$^1/_4$ tsp. celery seed
1 cup crumbled blue cheese (4 oz.)

Put all ingredients, except blue cheese, in blender container. Cover and blend until smooth. Remove dressing from blender; stir in blue cheese. Cover; chill. Serve over your favorite tossed salad. Makes $2^1/_2$ cups salad dressing.

Carol Lamphear
Soup and Salad . . .
(1989)

BLUE CHEESE DRESSING II

1 small pkg. blue cheese (use enough for your taste)
$^1/_2$ pint sour cream
$^1/_2$ cup cottage cheese
$^1/_4$ tsp. garlic powder
juice of $^1/_2$ lemon
$^1/_4$ tsp. Worcestershire sauce
dash of hot pepper sauce (optional)
1 pint mayonnaise
$^5/_8$ tsp. salt

Mix the above together and refrigerate.

Mary Teemley
Butter 'n Love II . . .
(1987)

Milk maid, ca. 1915.

IRONSTONE DRESSING

Suggestions for serving: This dressing is excellent for any crispy green salad. Also use for topping for baked potatoes. Good for shrimp or crabmeat cocktails. Ladle over any open-face or club sandwich, especially chicken or bacon.

Origin: In 1947, while fishing in Canada in the French River district, a Scottish chef concocted this recipe for our fishing group, and it has become a Jamestown favorite.

$1/4$ cup margarine
$1/4$ cup flour
1 Tbsp. salt
$1/2$ tsp. white pepper
2 cups milk
$1/2$ lb. sharp cheddar cheese, grated
$1/2$ cup salad oil
$1/2$ cup cider vinegar
1 tsp. Worcestershire sauce

In medium saucepan slowly heat margarine until melted, remove from heat. Add flour, salt, pepper, Worcestershire sauce. Stir until smooth. Add milk, a small portion at a time. Bring to boiling over medium heat, stirring continually. Reduce heat and simmer. Stirring continually, add the $1/2$ lb. of grated cheddar cheese while simmering and continue to simmer til cheese is completely melted. Remove and cool. When the cheese sauce has cooled, add alternately portions of oil and vinegar stirring continuously. To add zest, your choice of 1 squashed clove of garlic or 1 Tbsp. horseradish. Place in glass container and chill. Shake before using. Makes one quart.

Thomas P. Ciancio
Ironstone Restaurant
Wonderful Cooking . . .
(Date unknown)

AVOCADO FRUIT DRESSING

1 large ripe avocado
$1/2$ cup orange juice
$1/2$ tsp. salt
1 Tbsp. lemon juice
1 tsp. honey

Peel avocado, remove stone, mash avocado. Beat smooth. Gradually add remaining ingredients. Beat thoroughly. Chill. Makes 1 cup. Serve over citrus or fruit salad.

Ruth Brady
Cookbook
Brocton   (1974)

OLD-FASHIONED COOKED DRESSING

2 tsps. flour
2 tsps. sugar
1 tsp. dry mustard
$^3/_4$ tsp. salt
1 Tbsp. corn oil
1 large egg
4 Tbsps. cider vinegar
$^1/_2$ cup light cream or half and half

In top of double boiler, stir together flour, sugar, mustard and salt. Stir in oil to blend. Beat the egg with 2 Tbsps. of vinegar; gradually stir into flour mixture. Cook over hot water, stirring constantly until thickened (about 5 minutes). Cool. Gradually stir the remaining 2 Tbsps. of vinegar into the cream or milk. Gradually beat into cooked mixture. Refrigerate, tightly covered. Mixture will thicken after chilling. Good for potato salad as well as other vegetable salads.

Lucille Piper
Chautauqua Motet . . .
(1985)

PARISIAN (OR PERSIAN) DRESSING

1 can tomato soup
1 cup sugar
$^2/_3$ cup vinegar
2 cups salad oil
4 tsps. salt
2 tsps. paprika
3 tsps. dry mustard
2 tsps. pepper
4 tsps. onion juice
2 Tbsps. Worcestershire sauce

Mix thoroughly dry ingredients; stir in onion juice and Worcestershire sauce, then salad oil. Add soup and vinegar together and beat well with rotary beater. Makes a big quart of dressing. If you like garlic, cut one clove twice and place in dressing for two hours, then remove. Store in refrigerator.

Mrs. Horace Chadbourne
From Allen Park . . .
(1960s)

VEGETABLES

Today, we know that simple steamed vegetables are both nutritious and delicious. However, in the hundred years that we covered in our cookbook search, there was not a single recipe for steamed vegetables.

In Kate Cook's time, most of the vegetables we know and use were available, but always boiled, fried or perhaps roasted along with meat. They were used in cream sauce and served on toast or in patty shells, or they might be made into croquettes (as with one recipe suggestion for "old" peas).

Until about 1950, vegetables were either fresh or canned (often home-canned), and people ate them on a seasonal cycle — asparagus in the early spring, peas and beans in summer, tomatoes, peppers, squash in the fall, and nothing but root vegetables (turnips, parsnips, potatoes) in the winter. Nutrition must have been hard to manage under those conditions, though those home-canned vegetables and fruits served Chautauqua eaters well throughout the winter.

As you'll notice in the recipes here, after World War II frozen vegetables became very popular in Chautauqua County, as in the rest of America. It was also in the 1950s that use of canned soups in saucing up casseroles became so favored, and vegetable casseroles were part of that. We have tried not to use too many canned soup concoctions in this book, but have included a few in cases where we know the recipe to be particularly popular and particularly good.

Another point: it is no wonder that cooks who feel it their duty to provide a healthful vegetable choice at every meal get tired of plain, boiled or steamed vegetables night after night. Especially for company meals, a more glamorous vegetable medley is popular. Therefore, the majority of the recipes in this chapter are that kind of elaboration or enhancement, if you will: an interesting combination of vegetables, seasonings and, probably, a sauce, and usually baked. The method has two advantages: it can be done ahead — all except the baking; and the mixing and baking results in a nice flavor-blend that pleases all.

ASPARAGUS ON TOAST

Wash the asparagus and cut off the tough ends. Soak in cold water $^1/_2$ hour. Now tie it in small bundles and put into kettle of boiling water, and boil 20 minutes; add 1 teaspoonful of salt and boil 10 minutes longer. While the asparagus is cooking, boil 2 eggs hard. Toast squares of bread; butter while hot, and lay on a hot platter. Carefully drain the asparagus and lay it on toast, heads all one way. Put 1 tablespoonful of butter to melt, adding 1 Tablespoonful of flour; mix until smooth; add $^1/_2$ pint water in which asparagus was boiled; stir constantly until it boils. Season with salt and pepper to taste, and pour over the asparagus and sliced eggs. If liked, a little vinegar may be added to the sauce, and is a great improvement.

Mrs. C.M. Rathbun
The Fredonia Cook Book
(1899)

ASPARAGUS SWISS

2 Tbsps. butter
3 Tbsps. flour
1$^1/_2$ cups milk
3 bouillon cubes
dash of pepper
2 Tbsps. chopped onion
$^2/_3$ cup bread crumbs mixed with melted butter
$^1/_2$ cup coarse-grated sharp cheese
1 diced hard-cooked egg
3 Tbsps. chopped pimiento
2 Tbsps. chopped celery
1 large can asparagus, green tips,
   or cooked fresh asparagus

Make first five ingredients into a sauce. Butter a shallow baking dish. Place a layer of asparagus in dish, then onion, grated cheese, diced egg, pimiento, celery and some sauce. Continue in layers, ending with sauce. Top with buttered crumbs. Bake 20 minutes at 350°. Serves 5-6.

Inez Petrie
Dames in the Kitchen
(1975)

BEETS AND APPLESAUCE

Cook, drain and peel 6 medium beets. Mash with potato masher, or put through ricer. Add 1 cup fresh or canned applesauce and heat. Add butter, and season. Serves 4.

Mabel LaFrance
Good Cooking
(1950s)

BEETS IN SHERRY

This recipe is added for the time when only carrots stare you in the face at the green grocer's and you're sick of CARROTS VICHY. Get one large can of whole beets instead. Drain and save a bit of the juice. Put the beets into a frying pan with $1/16$ lb. of butter. Gently roll the beets until well covered with melted butter. When they are thoroughly hot, turn down the flame. Add 1 Tbsp. of beet juice and 3 Tbsps. of good sherry. Cover. Cook 1 minute and serve. (Almost as good with sliced beets if you can't find whole ones and of course good with diced cooked fresh ones.) Serves 4.

Editor's Request
Wonderful Cooking . . .
(Date unknown)

POLISH GRATED BEETS

2 bunches large beets
6 Tbsps. vinegar
2 Tbsps. sugar
3 slices bacon
salt to taste

Wash beets, put in cooking kettle, cover with cold water. Let boil for $1/2$ hour. Then drain and cool. Peel beets and grate. Mix with vinegar and sugar. Cut bacon in $1/2$" pieces and fry until light brown. Add beets with seasonings to bacon and fry for 5 minutes. Serve hot. Serves 6-8.

Mrs. Richard Ramsauer
From Allen Park . . .
(1960s)

GERMAN GREEN BEANS

4 cups green beans, 1" length
4 strips bacon
2 Tbsps. bacon fat
$1^1/_2$ Tbsps. flour
2 tsps. sugar
2 Tbsps. vinegar
2 Tbsps. chopped onion
$^1/_4$ tsp. dill seeds
1 tsp. salt
$^1/_4$ tsp. pepper
2 cups cooked, diced potatoes

Cook beans in salted water till tender. Drain, reserving juice. Cook bacon until crisp; drain, reserving fat. Put 2 Tbsps. fat back in skillet. Blend in flour and sugar. Add vinegar and 1 cup bean liquid (add water if necessary to make 1 cup). Cook, stirring constantly until mixture is thickened and comes to a boil. Add onion, dill seeds, salt and pepper. Combine beans and potatoes in saucepan. Add sauce and heat just till vegetables are heated, stirring occasionally. Serve at once in serving dish, topped with crumbled bacon. Serves 6.

Mrs. Janet Brooks
Home Cooking
Forestville
(1960s)

GREEN BEANS SWISS

2 Tbsps. butter
2 Tbsps. flour
1 tsp. salt
4 cups (2-10 oz. packages) frozen green beans, cooked
$^1/_4$ tsp. pepper
1 tsp. sugar
$^1/_2$ tsp. grated onion
1 cup sour cream
$^1/_2$ lb. Swiss cheese, shredded
2 cups cornflakes, crushed
2 Tbsps. butter

Melt 2 Tbsps. butter; stir in flour, salt, pepper, sugar and onion. Add sour cream. Toss with cooked green beans and pour into 2 qt. casserole. Sprinkle with shredded cheese. Melt remaining butter, mix with cornflakes and sprinkle on top of cheese. Bake at 400° 20 minutes. Serves 6.

Barbara Sweet
100 Years of Cooking . . .
(1986)

BROCCOLI CASSEROLE

2 packages frozen chopped broccoli, cooked and drained
1 can cream of mushroom soup, undiluted
$^1/_2$ cup mayonnaise
$^1/_2$ cup grated sharp cheese
$^1/_4$ cup slivered almonds
1 cup cheese crackers, crushed
1 Tbsp. lemon juice
2 oz. chopped pimiento

Put broccoli in buttered 2-quart casserole. Mix soup, mayonnaise, lemon juice and cheese. Mix with broccoli. Top with pimiento, crackers and nuts. Bake at 350° for 20 minutes. Serves 6-8.

Peggy (Olson) Schnars
A Cappella Choir...
(1986)

BROCCOLI-CHEESE CASSEROLE

1 (10 oz.) box frozen broccoli, cooked and drained
1 cup milk
1 cup crushed crackers (Ritz are best!)
1 cup cubed longhorn cheddar cheese
1 (2 oz.) jar pimientos
$^1/_4$ cup margarine (melted)
2 eggs, beaten well

Mix all ingredients together adding broccoli last. Bake at 350° in covered casserole dish for 1 hour. Uncover last 20 minutes until golden brown. Serves 4-6.

Lynne (Freeman) Leinenbach
Favorite Recipes
Mayville
(1982)

TO REMOVE BUGS FROM VEGETABLES
Salted water is said to induce worms and bugs to come from their hiding places in vegetables and float upon the water.
Needlework Cook Book (1907)

TIP

CREAMED BRUSSELS SPROUTS AND CELERY

Remove wilted leaves from 1 qt. Brussel sprouts and soak sprouts in cold water 15 minutes. Drain, put in saucepan, and cook in boiling water 20 min. or until tender. Drain. Cut washed celery in small pieces, $1\frac{1}{2}$ cups. Melt 2 Tbsps. of butter, add celery and cook 2 min., then add 3 Tbsps. flour and pour on gradually $1\frac{1}{2}$ cups of scalded milk. Bring to boiling point, add sprouts, season with salt and pepper. Serve as soon as sprouts are reheated. Serves 6.

Cook Book, Second Edition
Jamestown
(1920s)

SAUCY BRUSSELS SPROUTS

2 pints fresh Brussels sprouts
$\frac{1}{2}$ cup chopped onion
2 Tbsps. butter or margarine
1 Tbsp. flour
1 Tbsp. brown sugar
1 tsp. salt
$\frac{1}{2}$ tsp. dry mustard
$\frac{1}{2}$ cup milk
1 cup sour cream
1 Tbsp. snipped parsley

Wash and trim sprouts. Cut any large sprouts in half. In saucepan cook sprouts, covered, in a small amount of boiling salted water for 10-15 minutes or till tender; drain. Meanwhile in a medium saucepan, cook onion in butter or margarine till tender but not brown. Stir in flour, brown sugar, salt and dry mustard till blended. Stir in milk. Cook and stir till mixture thickens and bubbles; blend in sour cream. Add sprouts and stir gently to combine. Cook till heated through but do *not* boil. 6-8 servings.

Lotte Morse
Dames in the Kitchen
(1975)

ROD KAAL

(Red Cabbage)
1 medium red cabbage
$^1/_2$ cup butter
2 apples
1 cup currant jelly
2 to 3 Tbsps. vinegar
pinch of salt

The outside leaves and stalk should be removed and the cabbage cut very fine. Slice but do not peel the apples. Put all the ingredients in a kettle. Steam for about two hours. To serve, add more vinegar or currant jelly.

This is traditionally served with goose, duck or pork roast for Christmas dinner. Serves 6

Mrs. Otto B.A. Svendsen
recipe from Denmark
Jamestown's International . . .
(1960s)

BAKED CAJUN CABBAGE

1 large cabbage head
1 cup chopped onions
1 cup chopped celery
1 cup chopped bell peppers

CHEESE SAUCE:
$1^1/_2$ cups milk
$^1/_2$ cup margarine or butter
4 Tbsps. flour
$^1/_2$ lb. Cheddar cheese, shredded
1 tsp. cayenne pepper to taste
Topping:
1 cup chopped green onions
$^1/_4$ cup seasoned Italian bread crumbs

Cut cabbage into small bite-size chunks and boil about 10 minutes until tender crisp. Drain and set aside.

In saucepan combine the butter and flour, blending well over low heat; add onions, celery, peppers and seasoning. Add milk and blend well over low heat until creamy. Add cheese and stir until smooth. Place cabbage in a 2-quart casserole, top with cheese sauce. Sprinkle onions and bread crumbs over the top. Bake 30 minutes at 350°. Serves 6 people.

Esther Travis
Down Home . . .
(1989)

FRIED CABBAGE AND SPAETZLES

1 large head of cabbage, shredded or sliced thin
1 stick of butter or margarine
1 small onion, sliced thin

SPAETZLES:
4 eggs
$1/_2$ cup milk
$1/_2$ cup water
$2^1/_2$ cups flour, unsifted
1 tsp. salt
pepper, to taste

Shred or slice cabbage, then brown in butter or margarine. Also add onions, then salt and pepper. Add Spaetzels and continue to brown until hot and serve.

Beat eggs until foamy, add milk and water, flour and salt. Mix together until completely mixed. Drop by teaspoons or use spaetzle maker (kitchen specialty store) into salted, boiling water. When pieces float to top, take out and rinse under cold water. Add these to fried cabbage. Serves 8.

Kim Tuccio
What's Cooking . . .
(1988)

SAUERKRAUT AND SPLIT PEAS

1 cup green split peas (dried)
1 qt. sauerkraut
salt and pepper
1 chopped onion
4 Tbsps. butter
2 Tbsps. flour
1 cup cold water

Soak washed peas overnight. Cook in water to cover until tender, about 1 hour. Add more water if necessary. Rinse sauerkraut, cover with water, add salt and pepper and cook for 1 hour. Sauté onion in butter, add flour, and stir in cold water and mix until smooth. Add to sauerkraut and peas. Season to taste. (Yellow peas or lima beans may also be used.) Serves 6.

Mrs. Stephen Kaleta
Sharing Our Best
(1987)

CARROT RING

1¹/₂ cups cooked carrots, mashed
¹/₂ cup soft bread crumbs
3 well-beaten egg yolks
¹/₂ cup Pet milk diluted with ¹/₂ cup liquid from carrots
1 tsp. grated onion
1 tsp. salt
pepper
paprika
3 egg whites, beaten

Mix all ingredients, except egg whites, then fold in the stiffly beaten egg whites. Turn into greased ring mold and set in pan of water. Bake at 350° for 1 hour. Unmold and serve with peas, or your choice of vegetable, in the center. Serves 6.

Lonora Forgrave
Cook Book, Second Edition
Jamestown
(1920s)

CARROT CASSEROLE

1 lb. carrots
¹/₄ cup carrot liquid
2 Tbsps. grated onion
³/₄ tsp. horseradish
¹/₂ cup mayonnaise
¹/₂ tsp. salt
¹/₂ tsp. pepper
¹/₂ cup seasoned bread crumbs
¹/₄ cup melted butter

Scrape or peel carrots and slice into ¹/₄" slices. Cook in salted water until crisp-tender. Drain. Save ¹/₄ cup cooking liquid. Mix onions, horseradish, mayonnaise, salt, pepper and liquid. Combine with carrots in buttered casserole. Sprinkle the buttered bread crumbs over the carrots. Bake at 375° for 15-20 minutes or until bubbly. Serves 6.

Lois Franz
Finger Lickin' . . .
(1981)

COPPER PENNIES

2 lbs. peeled, sliced carrots
1 medium green pepper
1 medium onion
1 can tomato soup, undiluted
$1/2$ cup vegetable oil
$2/3$ cup sugar
$3/4$ cup cider vinegar
1 tsp. dry mustard
$1/2$ tsp. salt
$1/2$ tsp. pepper
1 tsp. Worcestershire sauce

Cook carrots in boiling water until tender but not mushy. Drain. Cut onion into thin rings, cut pepper into rings, discarding seeds. Combine onion and pepper with cooked carrots in heatproof bowl. Combine all remaining ingredients in separate saucepan. Slowly bring to a simmer over medium heat. Remove from heat and pour over carrots, onion and pepper. Cover and refrigerate overnight. Serve cold. Will keep for 2 to 3 weeks in refrigerator. Serves 8.

Florence Ludwiszewski
Sharing Our Best
(1987)

CAULIFLOWER-WALNUT CASSEROLE

1 medium cauliflower, broken into flowerets
1 cup sour cream
1 cup shredded Cheddar cheese
1 Tbsp. flour
2 tsps. chicken-seasoned stock base
1 tsp. dry mustard
$1/3$ cup coarsely chopped walnuts
$1/4$ cup fine dry bread crumbs
1 Tbsp. butter, melted
1 tsp. marjoram, crumbled
$1/2$ tsp. onion salt

Cook cauliflower until just tender and drain. Heat oven to 400°. Mix sour cream, cheese, flour, stock base and mustard. Place cauliflower in baking dish, approximately 10"x6"x1$3/4$". Spoon cheese mixture over cauliflower. Mix walnuts, bread crumbs, butter, marjoram and onion salt. Sprinkle over sauced cauliflower. Bake at 350° until hot and bubbly, 15 to 20 minutes. Serves 8.

Berry-Good . . .
(1977)

CREAMED CAULIFLOWER

Wash and cook the whole cauliflower in salted water. Drain. Break the cauliflower into pieces in a baking dish, add 2 hard-boiled eggs, chopped fine. Pour over this a white sauce as follows: One cup milk, 1 Tbsp. butter, 2 Tbsps. flour or enough to thicken. Cook. Pour the sauce over cauliflower and grate cheese over the top and set in oven to brown. Serve in baking dish garnished as desired. Serves 8.

Mrs. Harry McMaster
Sweets and Meats II
(1917)

EXTRA SPECIAL CAULIFLOWER

1 medium head cauliflower
$1/_2$ lb. mushrooms, sliced
$1/_4$ cup diced green pepper
$1/_3$ cup margarine
$1/_4$ cup flour
2 cups milk
1 tsp. salt
6 slices pimiento cheese
dash of paprika

Separate cauliflower and cook in salted, boiling water until just tender. Drain. Brown mushrooms and pepper lightly in margarine. Blend in flour and gradually add milk, stirring constantly until thick. Add salt. Place $1/_2$ of cauliflower in a casserole. Cover with $1/_2$ the cheese, then $1/_2$ the sauce. Repeat with additional cauliflower, cheese and sauce. Bake at 350° for 15 minutes. Serves 8.

Robert Anderson
A Cappella Choir . . .
Jamestown
(1986)

CELERY CASSEROLE

3 cups diced celery
$1/4$ cup slivered almonds
$1/2$ cup sliced water chestnuts
1 can (4 oz.) sliced mushrooms (drained)
$1/4$ cup plus 1 Tbsp. butter or margarine
3 Tbsps. all-purpose flour
1 cup chicken broth
$3/4$ cup half-and-half
$1/2$ cup (2 oz.) grated Parmesan cheese
$1/2$ cup soft bread crumbs
3 Tbsps. butter or margarine, melted
parsley sprigs

Cook celery in small amount of boiling water until tender (about 5 min.) and drain; combine celery, almonds, water chestnuts, and mushrooms. Mix well and pour into a greased 12"x8"x2" baking dish.

Melt $1/4$ cup plus 1 Tbsp. butter in a heavy saucepan over low heat; blend in flour. Cook 1 minute, stirring constantly. Gradually add chicken broth and half-and-half. Cook over medium heat, stirring constantly until thickened and bubbly. Pour sauce over celery mixture.

Combine cheese and bread crumbs; sprinkle over casserole. Drizzle melted butter over top. Bake at 350° for 25 minutes. Garnish with parsley. Serves 8.

Marion Hiller
"Someone's in . . ."
(1980s)

CORN-GREEN BEAN CASSEROLE

1 (16-oz.) can cut green beans, drained
1 can whole kernel corn, drained
$1/2$ cup chopped celery
$1/2$ cup sour cream
$1/2$ cup shredded Cheddar cheese
butter
$1/2$ cup chopped onion
$1/4$ cup chopped green pepper
1 can cream of mushroom soup
1 cup Cheezit crackers, crushed

Mix green beans, corn, celery, onion, green pepper, sour cream, and mushroom soup and place in a greased baking dish. Combine cheese and cracker crumbs and sprinkle over top. Dot with butter. Bake at 350° for 45 minutes. Serves 6-8.

Caroline Munson
Chautauqua-Allegheny Cookbook
(1990)

CORN SCALLOP

1 cup cream-style corn
1 cup whole kernel corn
2 eggs
$^2/_3$ cup evaporated milk
$^1/_4$ cup butter
3 Tbsps. minced fresh onion
$^1/_2$ tsp. salt
$^1/_4$ tsp. pepper
2 cups crushed saltine crackers
1 (12 oz.) package Swiss cheese, grated

Drain liquid from whole corn but save the juice. Beat eggs in bowl, stir in corn, $^1/_4$ cup corn juice, cream corn, milk, melted butter, onion, salt and pepper. Fold in crackers and Swiss cheese. Pour into greased baking dish. Bake at 325° for 1 hour. Serves 6.

Stella Hojna
Sharing Our Best
(1987)

NEVER-FAIL CORN ON THE COB

Place husked corn in large cooking pot, cover with cold water. Add 1 Tbsp. each lemon juice and sugar for every gallon of water. Bring to boil, uncovered. Boil for 2 minutes. Remove from heat, cover. Let stand at least 15 minutes, but it will still be hot and crunchy if left up to an hour.

Marion Hiller
Cookbook
Westfield
(1986)

ROASTED CORN ON THE COB

6 ears corn
$^1/_3$ cup butter
2 Tbsps. mustard
2 Tbsps. horseradish
1 tsp. Worcestershire sauce
1 tsp. lemon pepper

Melt butter and mix in next four ingredients. Brush onto husked corn ears. Wrap in aluminum foil and grill over medium fire turning every 15 minutes for 1 to $1^1/_2$ hours. Serves 6.

Mary Tota
What's Cooking . . .
(1988)

SCALLOPED CORN

$^1/_2$ green pepper, chopped
$^1/_2$ onion, finely chopped
2 Tbsps. butter
2 Tbsps. flour
1 tsp. salt
$^1/_4$ tsp. paprika
$^1/_4$ tsp. mustard
few grains cayenne
$1^1/_2$ cups milk
$^1/_2$ cup dried bread crumbs
1 Tbsp. butter
2 cans canned or 1 package frozen corn
1 egg, beaten
$^1/_2$ cup buttered cracker crumbs

Cook pepper, onion and butter 5 minutes, stirring constantly. Add flour mixed with seasonings and stir until well blended. Add milk gradually, blend, and bring to boiling point.

Brown bread crumbs in 1 Tbsp. butter. Add corn and eggs. Turn into greased baking dish. Cover corn mixture with crumbs and bake in hot oven, 400°, about 20 minutes. Serves 6.

Mrs. Irene Kimball
Kennedy's Favorite Recipes
(1950)

CUCUMBER RAGOUT

Pare and cut some nice cucumbers in half-inch crosswise slices. Slice equal amounts of firm tomatoes and medium-sized white onions. Flour and fry together the cucumbers and onions, using a little salt pork fat or butter. When brown, lay in the tomatoes, add 1 Tbsp. of flour rubbed to a paste with a little extra fat. Stir in $^1/_2$ pint of water (or weak stock if on hand). When smoothly thickened, add a teaspoonful of salt, pepper to taste and simmer, covered for 1 hour. Just before serving, add 1 Tbsp. of walnut catsup.

Florence Windsor
Needlework . . .
(1907)

SAUTÉED CUCUMBERS

Few people cook cucumbers, but these are perhaps the most delicious of all cooked vegetables.

8 med. cucumbers, peeled
salt to one's taste
1 tsp. chopped chives
1 tsp. granulated sugar
3 Tbsps. butter

Cut cucumbers in half lengthwise. Use a spoon to remove seeds. Slice cucumber halves into 1" pieces. Cover with boiling water, for about 5 minutes. Heat butter in large skillet. Drain cukes thoroughly and sauté in the melted butter or margarine, until nicely golden on all sides. Sprinkle sugar over pieces as they cook. When all pieces are sautéed, transfer the cukes to a serving dish, season with salt and sprinkle with chopped chives. Serves 8.

Evelyn Margullo
Cook Book
Dunkirk
(1978)

CUCUMBER/TOMATO COMBO

Melt $^1/_4$ cup butter
Add 1 Tbsp. sugar
$^1/_2$ tsp. salt
2 large cucumbers, peeled and cut into 2" chunks
1 medium onion, chopped
2 tomatoes, cut into wedges
Simmer 5 to 10 minutes.
Add $^1/_2$ cup water
1 tsp. lemon juice
$^1/_4$ tsp. dill weed

Cook 10 to 12 minutes.
Stir in $^1/_2$ cup sour cream.
Serve warm. Serves 6.

Freddie Korzenski
Our Culinary Favorites
(1984)

EGGPLANT PYRAMIDS

6 ($^1/_2$") slices peeled eggplant
flour
salt, optional
basil
oil
oregano
6 Tbsps. butter or margarine
6 thick slices tomatoes, $^1/_4$" to $^1/_2$"
6 slices sharp cheese or Velveeta

Dip eggplant in flour, season with salt, basil, oregano. Sauté each side in butter for 5 minutes or until slices just begin to soften. Place on broiler pan, top with a slice of tomato. Pour a little oil on them, season with basil, oregano. Broil 5 minutes. Put a slice of cheese on each, and broil until it melts. Serves 3 to 6.

Janice Wilson
Cookbook
Westfield
(1986)

MOTHER'S STUFFED EGGPLANT

2 med. eggplants
2 eggs, slightly beaten
1$^1/_2$ cups coarse cracker crumbs
3 Tbsps. butter
$^3/_4$ cup chopped salted peanuts
$^1/_4$ tsp. oregano
$^1/_4$ tsp. basil
freshly ground pepper and salt to taste
3 Tbsps. Parmesan cheese, grated

Wash eggplant, cut in half lengthwise. Remove pulp, leaving $^1/_4$ inch shell; set shells aside. Cut pulp in cubes and cook 6 minutes. Drain well and add cracker crumbs, eggs, butter, peanuts and seasonings. Stuff shells with mixture and place in flat baking dish with $^1/_2$" water in bottom. Cover with foil and bake at 350° for 30 minutes. Remove foil, add cheese and bake an additional ten minutes. Serve on platter and garnish with parsley.

Ruth F. Steese
Cooking by Degrees
(1985)

Sheridan Grange booth, Chautauqua County Fair, Mrs. A.M. Geiger, ca. 1950.

MARY TANGELO'S CURRIED LENTILS

1 lb. lentils
$^1/_2$ cup chopped onions
$^1/_2$ cup chopped carrots
2 cloves garlic, minced
$^3/_4$ cup olive oil
2 to 3 cups sliced onions
1 to 2 Tbsps. curry powder

Cook lentils in water just to cover, adding more water as lentils become too dry. Cook chopped onions, carrots and garlic with lentils. At the same time, sauté 2 to 3 cups sliced onions in $^3/_4$ cup olive oil until golden. Toward end of cooking, add curry powder to taste. Combine lentils, which should be rather dry, with onions. Serve at room temperature. Serves 8.

Jean Haynes
Down Home . . .
(1989)

GLORIFIED LIMA BEANS

2 cups cooked lima beans
1 Tbsp. butter
2 Tbsps. onions, chopped
2 Tbsps. green pepper, chopped
2 cups cheese sauce
   (white sauce with $^1/_2$ cup cheese added)
bread crumbs
4 strips bacon, cooked

Sauté onions and peppers in butter and add cheese sauce. Pour over limas in casserole; top with buttered bread crumbs. Bake 30 minutes in moderate oven, 350°. Place cooked bacon strips on top. Serves 4.

Janet Livermore
Silver Creek's Own . . .
(Date unknown)

CALIFORNIA SUCCOTASH

Cook 2 cups lima beans in small amount of boiling water 10 minutes. Add corn cut from 4 ears; cook 10 minutes longer. Melt 3 Tbsps. butter or margarine; add $^1/_4$ cup slivered blanched almonds, and brown lightly. Add almonds and $^1/_4$ cup chopped ripe olives to succotash. Season. Serves 4.

Mabel LaFrance
Good Cooking
(1950s)

BAKED BARLEY WITH MUSHROOMS

6 Tbsps. butter
1$^1/_2$ cups barley (pearl)
1 (4 oz.) can mushroom stems and pieces
1 (10 $^1/_2$ oz.) can condensed onion soup
$^1/_2$ cup white table wine or dry vermouth
seasoned salt and pepper to taste
2 cups finely diced celery
2 Tbsps. parsley flakes

Melt 4 Tbsps. butter in a 10" skillet. Add barley and sauté until it is a nice golden brown, stirring frequently. Drain mushrooms, reserving liquid. Mix mushroom liquid, onion soup and wine. Add boiling water to make 4 cups. Season to taste. Add this liquid to barley. Stir well. Bring to a boil.

Pour into greased 2-quart casserole. Cover tightly. Bake in moderate oven for 1 hour. Meantime, sauté celery in remaining 2 Tbsps. butter for 5 minutes. Add to barley at end of 1 hour baking period along with mushrooms and parsley, mixing with fork — lightly! Cover and continue baking another 10 to 15 minutes or until barley is tender and all liquid is absorbed. Serves 6.

Dixie Post
What's Cooking V
(1980)

MUSHROOM CASSEROLE

1 lb. fresh mushrooms
3 Tbsps. lemon juice
$^1/_2$ stick margarine
$^1/_2$ cup finely chopped onion
2 Tbsps. flour
salt & pepper to taste
$^1/_4$ cup wine
10 Tbsps. grated Parmesan cheese
4 egg yolks
2 cups heavy cream
1 cup fine dry bread crumbs

Slice mushrooms and sprinkle with lemon juice. Sauté in melted margarine in skillet for 3 minutes. Add onion, flour, and seasonings and blend. Whisk in wine and 5 Tbsps. cheese until mixture is smooth. Pour into greased baking dish. Beat together the egg yolks and cream. Pour over mushroom mixture. Combine bread crumbs and remaining cheese and sprinkle on top. Dot with butter or margarine and bake at 400° for 15 to 20 minutes. Serves 4 to 6.

Shari Vance
Chautauqua-Allegheny Cookbook
(1990)

MUSHROOMS ON CHEESE TOAST

1 lb. mushrooms
6 slices of bread
6 slices of Old English cheese
$1^1/_2$ cups cream sauce (make your own or use a mix)
Seasonings
$^1/_2$ lb. bacon, cooked crisp
Chopped stuffed olives for garnish

Sauté mushrooms and add to cream sauce. Season to taste. Toast bread on one side. Place on cookie sheet, untoasted side up. Cover each with slice of cheese. Place under broiler until cheese melts. Cover with cream sauce mixture. Garnish with olives and serve with bacon. Serves 6.

Mrs. Robert Tiffany
Wonderful Cooking . . .
(Date unknown)

OKRA CASSEROLE

$1^1/_2$ lb. tender okra, fresh or frozen
3 fresh tomatoes, peeled and chopped
1 onion, chopped fine
1 pepper, chopped fine
5 strips of bacon, uncooked
salt and pepper to taste

Slice the okra in thin rounds. In a large casserole dish, put a layer of okra at the bottom, then a layer of tomatoes. Season with salt and pepper. Sprinkle some of the onion and pepper on top. Repeat layers, ending with the onion and pepper. Cover entirely with bacon, overlapping strips.

Bake at 350° for 1 hour or until brown and tender. Serves 6-8.

Lucille Neveu
Cook Book
Silver Creek
(1977-78)

CHEESE MARINATED ONIONS

3 oz. blue cheese, crumbled
$^1/_2$ cup salad oil
2 Tbsps. lemon juice
1 tsp. salt
$^1/_2$ tsp. sugar
dash pepper and paprika
4 med. onions, thinly sliced
   and separated into rings (4 cups)

Mix all ingredients except onions. Pour mixture over onion rings and refrigerate for 3 to 4 hours. Good with barbecued meats or in green salads. Makes about 1 quart.

Henry Hadley
Stockton ... Cookbook
(Date unknown)

ONIONS AU GRATIN

4 medium mild onions, cut into thick slices
1 beef or chicken bouillon cube
$^3/_4$ cup boiling water
$^1/_4$ tsp. thyme
salt and pepper
1 Tbsp. butter
$^1/_2$ cup fresh bread crumbs
2 Tbsps. melted butter
$^1/_4$ cup grated sharp cheese

Arrange onion slices, overlapping in baking dish. Dissolve bouillon cube in boiling water. Add thyme and pour over onions. Sprinkle with salt and pepper and dot with butter. Cover and bake in a 400° oven for 20 minutes.

Toss bread crumbs in melted butter. Add cheese and sprinkle over onions. Bake uncovered 10 minutes or until crumbs are crisp and golden. Serves 6.

June Wilcox
Eileen McCallister
Favorite Recipes
Mayville
(1982)

ONION PIE

1 (9")baked pie shell
8 slices bacon
2 cups thinly sliced onions
3 eggs, slightly beaten
1 cup sour cream
$^3/_4$ tsp. salt
$^1/_8$ tsp. white pepper
$1^1/_2$ tsps. snipped chives
$^1/_2$ tsp. caraway seeds

Fry bacon until crisp, then crumble. Sauté onions in a little bacon fat until tender. Mix together eggs, sour cream, salt, white pepper and chives. Pour into pie shell along with bacon bits and onion slices and bake 30 minutes at 300°. Sprinkle $^1/_2$ tsp. caraway seeds over top of pie before baking. Let stand a few minutes before cutting. Serves 6-8.

Angela Symula
Cooking by Degrees
(1985)

SCALLOPED ONIONS

Slice onions as for frying; cook them in water a few minutes; drain, and put a layer of onions in a pan, add a layer of bread crumbs, season as you put them in with salt and pepper, butter, cream or milk; put them in the oven, and let brown; are nice; try them if you have any doubt.

Kate Cook
Chautauqua Cook Book
(1882)

PARSNIP BALLS

Boil parsnips in salted water until very tender. Mash and season with salt, pepper and butter. Add a little flour and one or two eggs, according to amount of parsnips used. Shape into balls and fry in butter.

Mrs. Robert B. Ellison
Norden Club
(1930)

PARSNIP CASSEROLE
6 - 8 small parsnips, cooked till soft
$1/_2$ stick butter, softened
1 egg
$1/_2$ cup light cream
$1/_2$ tsp. salt
$1/_4$ tsp. pepper
$1/_4$ tsp. nutmeg (optional)
$1/_4$ cup toasted slivered almonds

Remove skins from parsnips. Put in blender at medium speed and add butter, egg, cream and seasonings. Blend till smooth. Put in casserole, dot with butter and sprinkle with almonds. Heat in 350° oven for 30 minutes. Serves 6.
Editor's Request
Wonderful Cooking . . .
(Date unknown)

CREAMED PEAS AND NEW POTATOES
$1^1/_2$ lbs. tiny new potatoes (about 15)
2 cups shelled peas or 1 (10 oz.) package frozen peas
$1/_4$ cup sliced green onions
2 Tbsps. butter or margarine
1 Tbsp. all-purpose flour
$1/_4$ tsp. salt
dash of white pepper
1 cup milk

Scrub potatoes. Remove a narrow strip of peel around center of each. Cook potatoes until tender; drain. Meanwhile, cook fresh peas until tender; drain. Cook onion in butter or margarine until tender. Stir in flour, salt and pepper. Add milk and cook and stir until thickened and bubbly. Cook and stir 1 to 2 minutes more. Combine vegetables and onion mixture. Makes 4 to 5 servings.
Judy Pearson
"Cookin' From . . ."
(1987-88)

GREEN PEAS à la FRANÇAISE

3 lbs. peas
6 small onions
$^1/_4$ lb. butter
1 small head of lettuce
1 egg yolk
salt and pepper

Shell the peas. Put them in a pan half filled with boiling water. Add onions, lettuce cut in quarters, salt and pepper. When peas are tender, drain out most of the water. Add butter, and when it is melted remove from fire and mix in a well-beaten egg yolk. Serve at once. Serves 6.

Odette's War Recipes
(1940s)

TO PREPARE PEPPERS FOR STUFFING

Cut off the stems and cut at the blossom end a cap, taking out the seeds and insides. Put the peppers in boiling water with a little salt and let cook 20 minutes. Now they are ready to be stuffed. After they are filled, always sprinkle bread crumbs over the top with bits of butter and put in a buttered pan with a little stock or water and let them bake until well browned, about 20 minutes. The following is a list of a few things that may be used for stuffing peppers:

Rice and chicken
Bread prepared as for turkey stuffing
Tomatoes and bread crumbs
Corn pudding
Creamed cauliflower with a little cheese

Celery and Cheese
Any cold chopped meat with bread crumbs
Rice and Tomatoes
Creamed asparagus

They are a little nicer served with a tomato, cream, or brown sauce.

Jessie Ormes Greenlund
Needlework . . .
(1907)

BAKED POTATOES IN CREAM

5 large baking potatoes
1 large garlic clove
2 pints of heavy cream
   ($1^1/_2$ might do, depending on shallowness of baking dish)
1 cup Swiss cheese
salt
freshly ground pepper

Peel potatoes and place in cold water. Preheat oven to 300°. Mince garlic. Butter casserole. Dry and thinly slice one potato at a time. Place a layer of potatoes in casserole. Sprinkle with garlic, salt and plenty of pepper. Pour cream over to just about cover. Repeat procedure. Bake for $1^1/_2$ hours. Sprinkle with cheese and bake for 30 minutes more. Serves 6.

Cindy Coon
Cooking by Degrees
(1985)

ESTHER'S POTATOES

3 lb. little new potatoes
$^1/_2$ cup butter
3 Tbsps. flour
1 tsp. salt
$^1/_4$ tsp. pepper
2 cups water
1 Tbsp. lemon juice
parsley

Cook potatoes just until tender. Cook butter, flour, salt, pepper, water and lemon juice until smooth and clear. Mix with potatoes. Sprinkle with parsley and serve. Serves 6.

Esther Snyder
Finger Lickin' . . .
(1981)

GERMAN POTATO PANCAKES

2 medium onions, grated
2 large potatoes, grated
1½ Tbsps. flour
1 scant tsp. baking powder
2 eggs
1 Tbsp. chopped parsley
salt and pepper to taste

Grate potatoes and onions. Add eggs and mix. Add salt, pepper, flour and baking powder. Mix well. Form into thin cakes and fry slowly in butter until brown. Makes about 8 pancakes.

Helen Trippy
Favorite Recipes
Sherman
(Date unknown)

POTATO BALLS

Take six medium-sized cold cooked potatoes, grate them fine on a grater, add three well-beaten eggs, one-half cup sweet milk or cream, season with salt and pepper and minced parsley; summer savory may or may not be added as chosen; stir enough flour in this, so that with the hand you can shape it into balls the size of a small apple. Have on the stove a kettle half full of boiling water; salt a little. Twenty minutes before serving, drop these balls in the boiling water, and boil over a very hot fire; while these are boiling, put a piece of butter the size of an egg in a frying pan, slice thin a small onion, add to butter and fry a nice brown; then take from the fire and add a cup of sweet cream, and a little salt and pepper; with a skimmer, take out the balls, drain dry and put in a covered tureen; then pour the dressing in the frying pan over them, and serve immediately. They are nice to break each one open before adding dressing. This is a German dish, but I find the Americans very fond of it.

Kate Cook
Chautauqua Cook Book
(1882)

POTATO PATTIES WITH CHEESE AND TOMATO

2 cups hot or cold seasoned, mashed potatoes
1 egg, well-beaten
$^1/_2$ tsp. salt
$^1/_2$ tsp. finely chopped onion
$^1/_2$ cup grated American cheese
4 tomato slices
$^1/_4$ cup dry bread crumbs
2 Tbsps. melted butter or margarine

Combine potatoes, egg, salt, onion, mixing well. Shape into 4 patties and put on greased baking sheet. Make a depression in center of each, fill with cheese. Cover with a slice of tomato, sprinkle with mixture of bread crumbs and butter. Bake at 350° for 30 minutes. Makes 4 patties.

Dorothy J. Near
Cookbook
Westfield
(1986)

WHITE POTATOES HOW DID YOU DO THIS

I think most people believe there isn't much you can do to improve the baking of a white potato. I have news for you all - when I put white potatoes on the table people take a bite and they are delighted and surprised. As often as not, they'll ask me the magic question. Well, here's how it's done. No big mystery to it at all. I make a little basket out of foil for each potato. After I've washed the potatoes and the oven is hot, I just pour a little bit of Italian dressing into that basket under the potato so that the potato is resting in it. As the cooking proceeds, the dressing goes all the way through the potato. You find the flavor delightfully mixed with the potato flavor. The skin of the potato is soft and edible. If you prefer, you can use cooking oil with tiny garlic pieces in it. I keep a jar of that mixture handy at all times, even for salads. The longer it sits, the better it is.

Pearl Bailey
Chautauqua Celebrity . . .
(1980)

SWEET POTATO CASSEROLE

1 cup orange juice
1 Tbsp. lemon juice
2 tsps. lemon rind
$^1/_3$ cup brown sugar
$^1/_3$ cup white sugar
3 Tbsps. butter
1 Tbsp. cornstarch
4 large sweet potatoes, cooked

Heat first seven ingredients and pour over cooked sweet potatoes. Let stand in refrigerator overnight. Bake 45 minutes at 350°. Serves 4.

Mrs. Marshall Larson
What's Cooking I
(1954)

SAUTÉED SCALLIONS

4-6 scallions per serving
olive oil
salt
4 cloves garlic, chopped
lemon juice

Cut off tops of scallions leaving $1^1/_2$ to 3" at top. Wash and pat dry. Sauté garlic in olive oil until golden. Add scallions and sauté over medium heat until scallions are slightly colored on at least one side. Arrange on plate, cool and add lemon juice and salt to taste. Serve cool, but not cold. For added attraction, sauté parsley and oregano with the garlic.

Susan Lord
Favorite Recipes from
Our Best Cooks
(1978)

DUTCH SPINACH

10-oz. package frozen chopped spinach
1 Tbsp. butter
1 Tbsp. flour
$^2/_3$ cup milk
salt
1 Tbsp. finely chopped onion
$1^1/_2$ tsps. cider vinegar

Cook spinach according to package directions; drain well. Melt butter over low heat; stir in flour, add milk; cook, stirring constantly until sauce thickens and bubbles. Add spinach, salt to taste, onion and vinegar; reheat, stirring often. Makes 4 servings.

Margaret Baker
Culinary Delights
(1988-89)

SPECIAL SPINACH

1 lb. fresh spinach
2 Tbsps. butter
$^1/_4$ cup light cream
$^1/_2$ Tbsp. horseradish
$^1/_4$ to $^1/_2$ tsp. lemon juice to taste

Cook spinach; drain and chop. Add 2 Tbsps. butter, cream and horseradish. Heat through. Add lemon juice. Serves 3. Great with fish.

Holly and Ted Butryn
A Cappella Choir . . .
(1986)

CREAMED SPINACH

3 eggs
1 pound small curd cottage cheese
$^1/_2$ pound grated cheddar cheese
$^1/_2$ stick margarine, melted
1 10-oz. package spinach, thawed, and drained well
1 Tbsp. flour
$^1/_4$ tsp. each salt, pepper, onion powder
3 slices crisp fried bacon, broken into small pieces

Beat eggs in large bowl, add remaining ingredients; pour into 1-quart buttered casserole dish. Bake uncovered 1 hour at 350°.

Marilyn Simpson
Post-Journal Cookbook
(1985)

YOU'LL BE SURPRISED SPINACH

Cook 2 packages fresh spinach slightly and drain. Add $^1/_2$ cup sour cream and $^1/_2$ package onion soup mix.
Stir and place in casserole. Cover with buttered crumbs and Parmesan cheese. Bake at 325° for $^1/_2$ hour. Serves 8.

Mary Lou Beatty
Our Culinary Favorites
(1984)

SCALLOPED TURNIP

3 cups turnip, cubed
3 Tbsps. butter
3 Tbsps. flour
$^1/_2$ tsp. salt
$1^1/_2$ cups milk
$^1/_2$ cup grated cheese

Cook turnip in boiling, salted water until it can be pierced with a fork. Make a white sauce of butter, flour, milk and salt. Alternate layers of turnip and sauce in casserole; spread cheese and paprika over each layer. Cover with bread crumbs and bake in moderate oven 20 min. 6 servings.

Mrs. Ray L. Lewis
Victory Cook Book
(1940s)

ALBANIAN VEGETABLE CASSEROLE

4 large potatoes, sliced thin
4 tomatoes, chopped
2 carrots, grated
1 cup chopped onion
1 green pepper, chopped
$^1/_4$ tsp. garlic salt
3 tsps. chopped parsley
2 tsps. salt
fresh ground pepper
2 cups chicken or beef broth
$^1/_4$ cup olive oil

Place potatoes in greased casserole. Put rest of vegetables on top along with seasonings. Add broth. Bake at 350° for 50 minutes. Pour oil on top. Bake 20 minutes longer. Serves 6.

Dee Dee Warriner
Centennial Cook Book
(1987)

CROWD-PLEASING VEGETABLE BAKE

1 (10 oz.) package frozen cauliflower
1 (10 oz.) package frozen cut broccoli
2 cups (8 oz.) shredded Swiss cheese
1 can ($10^3/_4$ oz.) condensed cream of celery soup
1 can (4 oz.) sliced mushrooms, drained
1 (17 oz.) can cream-style corn
1 (17 oz.) can whole kernel corn, drained
$1^1/_2$ cups soft rye bread crumbs (2 slices)
2 Tbsps. butter, melted

Cook cauliflower and broccoli according to package directions; drain. Cut up any large pieces.

Combine both cans of corn, cheese and soup. Fold in cooked vegetables and mushrooms. Turn mixture into a 9"x13"x2" baking dish.

Toss bread crumbs with melted butter; sprinkle on top of casserole. Bake, uncovered, at 375° for 30 to 35 minutes. Let stand 10 minutes before serving. Serves 10 to 12 or more.

Susan Spadaro
Centennial Cook Book
(1987)

GARDEN VEGETABLE STIR FRY

2 medium carrots, cut in thirds
2 cups green beans, bias-sliced in 1" pieces
2 cups sliced cauliflower
2 Tbsps. cold water
$1^1/_2$ tsps. cornstarch
2 Tbsps. soy sauce
2 tsps. sugar
dash of pepper
1 medium onion, cut in wedges
2 Tbsps. cooking oil
1 cup sliced zucchini

You can substitute broccoli, summer squash or your favorite vegetable.

Cut carrots into thin sticks. In covered saucepan, cook carrots and green beans in salted water for 3 minutes. Add cauliflower. Cover and cook 2 minutes more; drain well. In small bowl, blend water and cornstarch; stir in soy sauce, sugar and pepper. Set aside. Preheat a wok or large skillet over high heat; add cooking oil. Stir fry onion in hot oil for 1 minute. Add carrots, green beans, cauliflower, and zucchini. Stir fry for 2 minutes or until vegetables are crisp-tender. Stir soy sauce mixture; stir into vegetables. Cook and stir 3 or 4 minutes or until thickened and bubbly. Serve at once. Serves 6.

Connie Francis
Stockton . . . Cookbook
(Date unknown)

OKLAHOMA VEGETABLE PLATTER

Arrange a head of cauliflower in center of large platter. Pour cream sauce over it and sprinkle paprika in center. Around this place buttered carrots. Make an outer circle of string beans.

Mrs. F. L. Scudder
The Parish Cook Book
(1937)

SPRING CASSEROLE

Cook 8 small new potatoes, 8 baby carrots, 1 small cauliflower broken into small pieces, and 1 cup fresh peas. To 2 cups of hot cream sauce add 4 oz. cubed sharp Cheddar cheese. Stir until smooth. Place vegetables in casserole, pour sauce over them, and place under broiler just long enough to delicately brown the cream sauce. Garnish with parsley. Serves 6.

Odette's War Recipes
(1940s)

SHERRIED BROILED TOMATOES

fresh tomatoes
dry sherry
salt, pepper, oregano
bacon slices
mayonnaise
grated Parmesan cheese or Fontinella cheese

Cut tomatoes in half, let drain. Prick cut surface with fork. Drizzle sherry (about 1 Tbsp. per half) over cut surface. Sprinkle with salt, pepper and oregano. Top with bacon slices. (Can be made ahead to this point; refrigerate.) Broil 5-7 minutes. Top with mayonnaise, sprinkle with grated cheese and brown lightly under the broiler.

Daune M. Palmer
First United . . .
(1978)

ZCRUMPTIOUS ZUCCHINI
4 cups zucchini, in $\frac{1}{2}$" slices

SAUCE:
1 cup sour cream
3 Tbsps. butter
$\frac{1}{2}$ cup grated cheese
3 beaten egg yolks
$\frac{1}{4}$ cup chopped chives
2 Tbsps. chopped parsley

Steam covered zucchini for about 5 minutes, until still firm. Drain well. For sauce combine sour cream, butter, cheese, salt and pepper and stir over low heat till cheese is melted. Remove sauce from heat and stir in egg yolks, chives and parsley. Add to zucchini. Place in buttered casserole. Cover with buttered bread crumbs or sprinkle with additional cheese or your own favorite topping. Serves 6-8.

Fran Ritenburg
Cooking by Degrees
(1985)

FENNEL GRATIN WITH ROBIOLA
2 bulbs fennel trimmed of stalks
2 cup bechamel sauce (white sauce)
4 ounces fontina cheese, grated
8 ounces robiola cheese*
2 ounces fresh bread crumbs, lightly toasted under broiler
Salt and pepper to taste

*If you can't find Robiola cheese, substitute Fontinella (available in local markets).

Preheat oven to 450°. Bring 4 quarts water to boil and add 2 Tbsps. salt. Butter 4 small round (4" diameter) earthenware gratin or shallow sauce dishes.

Halve fennel bulbs and cut into $\frac{1}{4}$ inch thick slices. Place in boiling water and blanche until very tender, 8 to 10 minutes. Drain in a colander over sink and set aside until cool enough to handle. Mix tepid fennel with bechamel sauce and fontina and mix well. Divide evenly among 4 gratin dishes and pat down with back of spoon.

Bake in top half of oven for 25 minutes until bubbling and hot. Remove from oven. Place 2 ounce dollop or square of robiola in center of each dish, sprinkle bread crumbs over robiola and place in oven 5 to 6 more minutes, until robiola is hot and soft and crumbs have melted in. Remove. Allow to stand 3 minutes before serving. Serves 4.

No name given
C.I.A.O. Italian Traditions Cookbook (1980s)

DESSERTS

It comes as no surprise to any of us that, for most of the cookbooks consulted for this compilation, the largest section by far was that for desserts.

It happened again as we were choosing the recipes to include here. More than 300 recipes were initially chosen as possible candidates for the dessert section, and about half of those were for cookies. Regrettably, the section had to be cut drastically. What we have left in are here for good reason, as the following will show.

In our cake repertoires, most of us have readily at hand good recipes for white, yellow, chocolate and sponge cakes. Of course there are hundreds of other specialty cakes. What have been included here are recipes for things most of us remember, and most of which are included in the majority of the cookbooks. To get an idea of what has gone on in cakebaking in Chautauqua County in a hundred years, here are recipes for Crumb Cakes, that Date-Nut-Chocolate Chip cake that is so good, the Heath Bar Cake (subtitled "Mom's Angry Cake," because we get to smash the Heath Bars to bits), Texas Sheet Cake and Wacky Cake, both chocolate, both easy and delicious, and finally — remember it? — Brownie Pudding or Hot Fudge Sundae Cake.

One pie recipe kept recurring, that for Paper Bag Apple Pie, and since apple pie is probably the quintessential American dessert, we included this version. But also here in Chautauqua County were Concord Grape Pie and Betty Latimer Schwertfager's prizewinning 1949 Cherry Pie recipe. Since pie cannot be discussed or showcased without attention to its crust, we have also included all the important variations of pie pastry as used in Chautauqua County, notably that "never-fail" recipe that had a place in most of the cookbooks, the one using an egg and a tablespoon of vinegar to produce the inevitable perfection.

Choosing cookie recipes is like trying to choose among one's children. It's impossible. Yet we tried, and here you'll find some of the popular ethnic cookies known to Chautauqua residents, such as Pineapple Squares (Polish), Italian white and chocolate versions, and others; some remembered from childhood like Snickerdoodles and Whoopie Pies; and other good recipes — all delicious.

In the "other dessert" section, we eliminated many favorites like apple dumplings, icebox cakes (like Jimmy Carter Peanut Cake and "Better than Robert Redford," both of which made the rounds in the 1980s), cobblers and simple fruit desserts. Here, though, are the beloved rice pudding, a steamed pudding, Lemon Bisque, which was a favorite summer dessert in mid-century (and still is) and other favorites. (The "Brownie Pudding" recipe is here, not in the cake section.)

It is worth noting that certain flavors have always been popular in desserts. Pineapple, for instance. Chocolate, of course (see the extensive section of Brownie recipes). Other fruit flavors — peach, pear, berry and rhubarb, notably. And peanuts, surprisingly far more than any other nut, with almonds running a close second.

With this cookbook in hand it's not going to be difficult to satisfy the family sweet tooth.

CAKES

APFELKUCHEN

(Apple Cake-Germany)
1 egg
$^1/_2$ cup butter, melted
1 cup milk
$^1/_2$ tsp. salt
2 Tbsps. sugar
2 cups flour
2 tsps. baking powder
sliced apples
Topping
$^1/_2$ cup sour cream
2 or 3 eggs, beaten well
3 Tbsps. sugar

Mix all ingredients, except apples and those for topping. Spread into two 8x8-inch buttered pans. Cover with sliced apples. Press into top of dough. Bake at 350° - 375° F. for 20 minutes or until fruit is done.

Combine topping ingredients; pour over cake; bake 10 minutes longer. 12-18 servings
Reva Chaffee
Our Country...
(1980s)

BLACKBERRY CAKE

1 cup sugar
$^1/_2$ cup butter
3 eggs
$^3/_4$ cup sour milk
1 tsp. soda
$^1/_2$ tsp. cloves
$^1/_2$ tsp. cinnamon
$^1/_2$ tsp. nutmeg
2 cups flour
1 cup fresh blackberries (mashed)

Mix all ingredients in the order given. Pour into 2 greased 9-inch round cake pans and bake for 35 minutes at 350°. Frost with desired frosting.
Elizabeth Barton Alexander
Pioneer . . .
(1987)

Traveling spice and notions salesman, J.R. Watkins Co., ca. 1910.

A HANDY SPICE AND HERB GUIDE

ALLSPICE: a pea-sized fruit that grows in Mexico, Jamaica, Central and South America. Its delicate flavor resembles a blend of cloves, cinnamon and nutmeg. Uses: (Whole) Pickles, meats, boiled fish, gravies. (Ground) Puddings, relishes, fruit preserves, baking. Essential flavor in "Jerk" - seasoned foods.

BASIL: the dried leaves and stems of an herb grown in the United States and North Mediterranean area. Has an aromatic, leafy flavor. Uses: For flavoring tomato dishes and tomato paste, turtle soup; also use in cooked peas, squash, snap beans; sprinkle chopped over lamb chops and poultry.

BAY LEAVES: the dried leaves of an evergreen grown in the eastern Mediterranean counties. Has a sweet, herbaceous floral spice scent. Uses: For pickling, stews, for spicing sauces and soup. Also use with a variety of meats and fish.

CARAWAY: the seed of a plant grown in the Netherlands. Flavor that combines the tastes of Anise and Dill. Uses: For the cordial Kummel, baking breads; often added to sauerkraut, noodles, cheese spreads. Also adds zest to French fried potatoes, liver, canned asparagus.

CURRY POWDER: a ground blend of ginger, turmeric, fenugreek seed, as many as 16 to 20 spices. Uses: For all Indian curry recipes such as lamb, chicken, and rice, eggs, vegetables, and curry puffs.

DILL: the small, dark seed of the dill plant grown in India, having a clean, aromatic taste. Uses: Dill is a predominant seasoning in pickling recipes; also adds pleasing flavor to sauerkraut, potato salad, cooked macaroni, and green apple pie.

MACE: the dried covering around the nutmeg seed. Its flavor is similar to nutmeg, but with a fragrant, delicate difference. Uses: (Whole) For pickling, fish, fish sauce, stewed fruit. (Ground) Delicious in baked goods, pastries and doughnuts, adds unusual flavor to chocolate desserts.

MARJORAM: an herb of the mint family, grown in France and Italy. Has a minty-sweet flavor. Uses: In beverages, jellies and to flavor soups, stews, fish, sauces. Also excellent to sprinkle on lamb while roasting.

OREGANO: a plant of the mint family and a species of marjoram of which the dried leaves are used to make an herb seasoning. Uses: An excellent flavoring for any tomato dish, especially pizza, chili con carne, and Italian specialties.

PAPRIKA: a mild, sweet red pepper growing in Spain, Central Europe and the United States. Slightly aromatic and prized for brilliant red color. Uses: A colorful garnish for pale foods, and for seasoning Chicken Paprika, Hungarian goulash, salad dressings.

POPPY: the seed of a flower grown in Holland. Has a rich fragrance and crunchy, nut-like flavor. Uses: Excellent as a topping for breads, rolls and cookies. Also delicious in buttered noodles.

ROSEMARY: an herb (like a curved pine needle) grown in France, Spain, and Portugal, and having a sweet, fresh taste. Uses: In lamb dishes, in soups, stews and to sprinkle on beef before roasting.

SAGE: the leaf of a shrub grown in Greece, Yugoslavia and Albania. Flavor is camphoraceous and minty. Uses: For meat and poultry stuffing, sausages, meat loaf, hamburgers, stews and salads.

THYME: the leaves and stems of a shrub grown in France and Spain. Has a strong, distinctive flavor. Uses: For poultry seasoning, in croquettes, fricassees and fish dishes. Also tasty on fresh sliced tomatoes.

TURMERIC: a root of the ginger family, grown in India, Haiti, Jamaica and Peru, having a mild, ginger-pepper flavor. Uses: As a flavoring and coloring in prepared mustard and in combination with mustard as a flavoring for meats, dressings, salads.

"MELT IN YOUR MOUTH" BLUEBERRY CAKE

$^1/_2$ cup butter or margarine
1 cup and 1 Tbsp. sugar
$^1/_4$ tsp. salt
1 tsp. vanilla
2 eggs, separated
$^1/_3$ cup milk
$1^1/_2$ cups and 1 Tbsp. all-purpose flour
1 tsp. double-acting baking powder
$1^1/_2$ cups fresh blueberries

Preheat oven to 350°. Grease an 8" square pan; set aside. Cream butter or margarine and $^3/_4$ cup sugar. Add salt and vanilla. Add egg yolks, beat until creamy. Combine $1^1/_2$ cups flour with baking powder. Add alternately with milk to egg yolk mixture. Beat egg whites until soft, adding $^1/_4$ cup sugar, 1 Tbsp. at a time, and beat until stiff.

Coat berries with 1 Tbsp. flour and add to batter. Fold in egg whites. Pour into prepared pan. Sprinkle top with remaining Tbsp. sugar. Bake for 50 minutes or until toothpick inserted comes out clean. 8 servings.

Ruth Mohney
Adventures in Food
(1977)

BANANA SPLIT CAKE

3 cups flour
2 tsps. baking powder
1 tsp. salt
$^1/_4$ tsp. baking soda
1 cup margarine
$1^1/_2$ cups sugar
1 tsp. vanilla
4 eggs
1 medium banana
$^1/_2$ cup sour cream
$^1/_2$ cup milk
$^1/_2$ cup instant cocoa

STRAWBERRY SAUCE:
4 cups strawberries
1 cup water
2 Tbsps. cornstarch
$^2/_3$ cup sugar

Grease and flour a 10" fluted tube pan. Combine flour, powder, salt and soda in a bowl. Set aside. Beat margarine 30 seconds with electric mixer. Add sugar and vanilla; beat until fluffy. Add eggs 1 at a time, beating for 1 minute after each egg. Combine banana, sour cream, and milk. Add dry ingredients and banana mixture alternately. Fold cocoa into 1 cup of batter. Pour plain batter into pan. Spoon cocoa batter on top. Do not spread. Bake in 350° oven for 60-70 minutes. Cool 10 minutes. Remove from pan and cool thoroughly. Serve with strawberry sauce.

SAUCE: Crush 1 cup berries. Add 1 cup water. Cook for 2 minutes. Sieve. Combine sugar and cornstarch. Stir into sieved mixture. Cook until bubbly, and cook 2 minutes. Halve remaining 3 cups strawberries. Stir into sauce. Chill.

Lois Scott
Sugar 'N Spice . . . (1987)

CARROT CAKE

1 cup vegetable oil
$^1/_4$ cup honey
2 eggs
1 tsp. vanilla
$1^1/_2$ cups whole wheat flour
$1^1/_2$ tsps. baking soda
$1^1/_2$ tsps. ground cinnamon
2 tsps. nutmeg
1 tsp. ground cloves
1 tsp. ground allspice
$^1/_2$ tsp. salt
$1^1/_2$ to 2 cups grated carrots
$1^1/_2$ cups walnuts, chopped fine
handful of chopped apricots
handful of raisins
1 small can (drained) crushed pineapple

Grease Bundt pan or angel food cake pan and dust with flour. Combine oil, honey, eggs, vanilla in bowl. Add flour, baking soda, and spices, stir in carrots, walnuts, apricots, raisins and pineapple. Mix to blend and turn into pan. Bake 1 hour at 350°.

Carol Adams
First United...
(1978)

CARAMEL CAKE

$^3/_4$ cup butter
2 cups sugar
2 cups cake flour
2 tsps. baking powder
1 cup cold water
6 egg whites
Vanilla

CARAMEL ICING:
3 cups light brown sugar
$^2/_3$ cup cream
$^1/_2$ cup butter

Cream butter and 2 cups sugar, less 2 Tbsps. Sift flour and baking powder. Add to creamed mixture along with the cup of cold water and flavoring. Beat 6 eggs whites until they will stand in peaks. Add the 2 Tbsps. sugar saved from the 2 cups. Fold eggs into the rest of the mixture. Pour mixture into two 9-inch pans. Bake at 350° until cake leaves the side of the pan.

Mix and boil until forms a ball. Stir to cool and frost between layers and top and sides. Serves 12-14

Mrs. C. W. Green
Best/Brocton
(1960s)

CHOCOLATE ZUCCHINI CAKE

$^1/_2$ cup margarine
$^1/_2$ cup oil
$1^3/_4$ cups sugar
2 eggs
$^1/_2$ cup sour milk
1 tsp. vanilla
$2^1/_2$ cups flour
$^1/_2$ tsp. baking powder
1 tsp. soda
$^1/_2$ tsp. cinnamon
$^1/_2$ tsp. cloves
4 Tbsps. cocoa
2 cups grated zucchini
$^1/_2$ cup chocolate chips
$^1/_2$ cup nutmeats

Cream margarine, oil, and sugar together. Add eggs, sour milk and vanilla. Sift together flour, baking powder, soda, cinnamon, cloves, and cocoa. Add to mixture. Stir in zucchini. Put in well-greased 9 x 13-inch pan. Sprinkle with chocolate chips and nut meats. Bake at 325° for 45 minutes. Serves 12-16.

Jean Beale
Warm Your Heart...
(1987)

MY MOTHER'S CRUMB CAKE

$1^1/_2$ cups brown sugar
$^1/_2$ cup shortening
$2^1/_2$ cups flour
1 tsp. baking powder
$^1/_4$ tsp. salt
1 tsp. vanilla
1 cup sour milk
1 tsp. baking soda

8x8-inch pan — 350° — 45 minutes.

Combine brown sugar, shortening, flour, baking powder and salt in mixing bowl. Blend as for pie dough. Take out 1 cup of mixture to be saved as topping. Add vanilla and sour milk (having put the baking soda into sour milk beforehand) to ingredients in mixing bowl. Beat until foamy. Then stir lightly, adding $^1/_2$ cup of reserved crumbs. DO NOT BEAT! Pour into 8 x 8-inch baking pan and cover with remaining $^1/_2$ cups of crumbs.

Donald B. Bube
A Cappella Choir...
Jamestown
(1986)

PENNSYLVANIA DUTCH CRUMB CAKE

4 cups sifted flour
2 cups sugar
4 tsps. baking powder
$1/2$ tsp. salt
1 cup butter
4 eggs, separated
1 cup milk
$1/4$ cup melted butter
2 tsps. cinnamon

With a pastry blender, blend first 4 ingredients with the 1 cup butter. Measure 1 cup of this mixture and set aside for topping. Beat egg yolks and mix with milk and remaining dry mixture. Fold in beaten egg whites. Turn batter into two greased 9x9x2-inch pans, sprinkle each with $1/2$ of reserved crumbs. Bake at 375° for 20-25 minutes.   Sprinkle top of each cake with $1/2$ the butter-cinnamon mixture.

Ann Mullikin
Sugar 'N Spice . . .
(1987)

DATE-NUT-CHOCOLATE CHIP CAKE

Mix:
1 cup cut-up dates
1 tsp. baking soda
$1^1/2$ cups boiling water
Let cool.
Cream:
$1/2$ cup margarine
1 cup granulated sugar
2 eggs
Sift together:
$1^1/4$ cup plus 3 Tbsps. flour
$1/4$ tsp. salt
$3/4$ tsp. baking soda

Combine:
Flour mixture
Creamed mixture
Dates and water
Mix gently but thoroughly with wooden spoon. Spread in 8x12 inch pan.
Mix:
1 cup walnut meats, chopped
6 oz. chocolate chips
$1/2$ cup granulated sugar
Sprinkle over dough. Bake 40 to 45 minutes at 350°.

Lois Hern
Cookbook
Westfield
(1986)

GRAPE LAYER CAKE

2 cups plus 2 Tbsps. flour
1 1/2 cups sugar
3 1/2 tsps. baking soda
1 tsp. salt
1/2 cup shortening
1 cup milk
1 tsp. vanilla
4 egg whites

Sift dry ingredients into bowl. Add shortening, milk and vanilla. Beat 2 minutes. Add egg whites. Beat 2 more minutes. Pour into prepared 8- or 9-inch layer pans. Bake at 350° until lightly browned and cake springs back when touched.

FILLING:

1/2 cup grape juice
1 1/3 cup water
3 1/2 Tbsps. cornstarch
1/4 tsp. salt
1/2 cup sugar
2 Tbsps. lemon juice
1 Tbsp. butter

Scald grape juice and water in top of double boiler. Mix cornstarch, salt and sugar and add to grape juice, stirring with a whisk. Cook over direct heat until thick, then return to double boiler and cook 15 minutes longer, stirring occasionally. Remove from heat and add lemon juice and butter. Cool.

FROSTING:

1 egg white
1/2 tsp. light corn syrup
3 Tbsps. grape juice
3/4 cup sugar

Mix all ingredients in top of a double boiler. Place over rapidly boiling water and beat until mixture will hold a peak. Remove from heat and beat until thick enough to spread. Spread cooled filling between layers and spread the frosting on top and sides of cake. (You may use a white cake mix in place of cake above.) Serves 12.

Helen Burch
Chautauqua-Allegheny Cookbook
(1990)

Remember to handle baking powder dough as little as possible. Sour milk and soda products are improved by adding a little baking powder.

TIP

Cookbook, Jamestown (1920s)

HEATH BAR CAKE

2 cups brown sugar
2 cups flour
$1/2$ cup margarine
2 eggs
1 tsp. vanilla
1 cup milk
1 tsp. baking soda
$1/4$ cup chopped pecans
10 miniature Heath bars (6 oz. total)

Blend together brown sugar, flour and margarine. Set aside 1 cup of this mixture for topping. To the remaining mixture add eggs, vanilla and milk to which baking soda has been added. Pour into 9x12-inch greased pan. Sprinkle the remaining topping over the batter. Chop Heath bars and mix with nuts and sprinkle on top. Bake at 350° for 30-40 minutes.

Lucille Labert
Sugar 'N Spice . . .
(1987)

TRADITIONAL HONEY CAKE
FOR JEWISH NEW YEAR

2 cups honey
1 cup sugar
3 eggs
2 Tbsps. oil
grated rind and juice of 1 lemon and 1 orange
$4^1/2$ cups flour
2 tsps. baking powder
1 tsp. baking soda
1 tsp. nutmeg
1 tsp. ginger
1 tsp. cinnamon
1 tsp. salt
$1^1/4$ cups strong black coffee

Mix honey and sugar and then add slightly beaten eggs and oil. Add rind and juice of lemon and orange. Sift together in a separate bowl the flour, baking powder, baking soda, spices and salt. Add dry ingredients, alternately with black coffee, to the honey mixture. Pour into a large greased angel food pan. Bake at 350° for $1^1/4$ hours. This is like a quick bread and splits in the center. Use a toothpick to test for doneness. Also can use 2 bread pans or 2 quick bread pans plus 1 smaller loaf pan, then bake for 50-60 minutes. Serves 12-16.

Diane Burkowsky
Dames in the Kitchen
(1975)

OATMEAL CAKE

CAKE
1¼ cups boiling water
1 cup oatmeal
½ cup shortening, softened
1 cup white sugar
1 cup brown sugar
1 tsp. vanilla
2 eggs
1½ cups sifted flour
1 tsp. soda
½ tsp. salt
¾ tsp. cinnamon
¼ tsp. nutmeg

FROSTING:
¼ to ½ cup butter, melted
½ cup brown sugar
3 to 4 Tbsps. cream
⅓ cup chopped nuts
¾ to 1 cup shredded coconut
1 tsp. vanilla

Pour boiling water over oats; cover and let stand 20 minutes. Beat shortening until creamy; add sugars and beat until fluffy. Blend in vanilla and eggs. Add oat mixture; mix well. Sift together flour, soda, salt, cinnamon and nutmeg. Add to creamed mixture. Mix well. Pour batter into well-greased and floured 9-inch square pan. Bake in preheated 350° oven 50 to 55 minutes. Do not remove cake from pan. Immediately spread following frosting on cake and broil until bubbly.

Combine all ingredients for frosting. Spread evenly over baked cake, and broil until bubbly.

Arkwright Jr. Grange No. 514
Cooking Favorites
Arkwright
(1960s)

GENERAL MIXING RULES

TIP

If butter is used as basis of cake, be sure to cream well at first.
Egg yolks are lightest if beaten with a Dover or a twirling egg beater.
Egg whites should always be whipped with a wire egg whip because the result is lighter and fluffier.
If egg whites are to be used in any cooked dish such as cakes, souffles, meringues, etc., beat until egg whites are stiff, but stop before that wet stiffness changes to a dry glazed appearance.
Never stir stiffly beaten egg whites into any mixture. This will break walls of egg white and much of the carefully caught air will be lost. Always use a spoon or a spatula, cut down and fold over the beaten egg white, working from outside toward center.

Cook Book
Cassadaga (1950)

A very old recipe for a truly wonderful delicious cake!

FRENCH ORANGE CAKE

1 cup sugar
$1/_8$ tsp. salt
$1/_2$ cup unsalted margarine
1 egg, well-beaten
$1/_2$ cup skim milk
2 cups sifted flour
rind of 1 orange, grated
$1/_3$ cup chopped English walnuts
1 ($7^3/_4$ oz.) package pitted dates
1 tsp. soda
$1/_2$ cup boiling water
Juice of 1 orange
$3/_4$ cup sugar

Cut each date into halves or thirds. Dissolve soda in boiling water and pour over dates in small bowl. Blend margarine and sugar until light and fluffy. Add salt and well-beaten egg and beat until fluffy. Add part of the flour and all the milk alternately to the sugar mixture. Blend in orange rind and date mixture, then the remaining flour and nuts. Pour batter into 9" ring mold pan which has been well sprayed with oil and dusted with flour. Bake in a 350° preheated oven for 45-50 minutes or until cake tests done. Remove from oven and unmold cake on a platter which has been covered with aluminum foil. Mix $3/_4$ cup sugar and 3 Tbsps. orange juice; pierce top of the cake all over with small diameter meat skewer; pour orange mixture over warm cake. Let stand until glaze has hardened before placing on serving plate. Serves 20.

Thyra Grey Howard
Favorite Recipes . . .
Findley Lake   (1981)

STRAWBERRY POUND CAKE RING

$3/_4$ cup butter ($1^1/_2$ sticks)
1 cup sugar
4 eggs
$3/_4$ tsp. vanilla
$1/_2$ tsp. finely grated lemon rind
$2^1/_4$ cups sifted cake flour
$1/_2$ tsp. baking powder
$1/_4$ cup milk
Orange Whipped Cream*
1 pt. fresh strawberries

Butter and lightly flour 6 cup ring mold. Cream butter and sugar until light and fluffy. Add eggs, all at once and beat for 3 minutes. Blend in vanilla and lemon rind. Sift flour and baking powder. Add to creamed mixture alternately with milk, beginning and ending with dry ingredients. Bake in 325° preheated oven for 35 to 40 minutes. Cool 10 minutes, remove from mold to wire rack to cool.   Wash, hull strawberries; slice enough to make 1 cup; reserve remainder for garnish. Slice ring into 2 layers.   Spread $1/_2$ Orange Whipped Cream on each layer; arrange 1 cup sliced strawberries on bottom layer; place top layer over it. Swirl remaining cream over top of ring. Garnish with whole strawberries. Serve with additional Orange Whipped Cream and berries, if desired.

*In chilled bowl, whip cream until almost stiff; add sugar and beat until stiff. Blend in rind.

Martha Laughlin
Cookbook
Westfield
(1986)

PLUM CAKE

$^1/_2$ cup softened butter
$1^1/_4$ cups flour
1 tsp. baking powder
$^1/_4$ tsp. salt
2 Tbsps. sugar
2 egg yolks beaten with
2 Tbsps. milk
3 cups fresh plums, pitted and sliced ($1^1/_2$ lbs.)
2 Tbsps. sugar
$^1/_2$ tsp. cinnamon
butter

Preheat oven to 350°. Cream butter until it is light and fluffy. Gradually add the flour, baking powder, salt and sugar and blend in thoroughly. Add the egg yolks and mix them in well. Using your fingers, press the dough evenly into an ungreased 8-9" pan. Cover dough with even rows of sliced plums. Sprinkle the plums with the sugar and cinnamon mixture, using additional sugar if the fruit is especially tart. Dot generously with butter and bake 35-40 minutes. Serve the plum cake warm or cold. Serves 9-12.

This cake is simple to make and it provides a perfect foil for any kind of fruit. You can substitute canned plums or apricots when fresh fruit is not in season.

Lotte Morse
Dames in the Kitchen
(1975)

PASTELES DE CACAO

(Pound Cake)
$^1/_2$ cup butter
1 cup sugar
3 eggs
$^3/_4$ cup cocoa
$1^1/_2$ cups flour
3 tsps. baking powder
pinch of salt
$^2/_3$ cup milk
1 tsp. vanilla

Beat butter until creamy. Add sugar gradually, beating until light and fluffy. Add eggs one at a time, beating well after each. Sift cocoa, flour, baking powder, salt. Add this alternately with milk. Beat in vanilla. Pour into 2 buttered and floured small loaf pans ($2^3/_4$" x 5"). Bake at 375° for 20 minutes or until cake tester comes out clean.

Pat Toner
"Someone's in . . ."
(1980s)

PRUNE CAKE

CAKE
1 1/2 cups flour
1 tsp. soda
1/2 tsp. salt
1/2 tsp. nutmeg
1 cup white sugar
1/2 cup shortening
2 eggs
1 tsp. vanilla
1/2 cup buttermilk
1 cup prunes, cooked
some of the prune juice

FROSTING:
1/4 cup butter
1/2 cup brown sugar
1 tsp. vanilla
cream or milk
powdered sugar

Have all ingredients at room temperature. Sift together the flour, soda, salt, nutmeg and sugar. Add shortening, eggs, vanilla, buttermilk, prunes and prune juice. Beat well. Bake in greased sheet cake pan at 350° for 30 minutes.

After cake is cooled, melt together the butter and brown sugar. Add vanilla, cream or milk and powdered sugar to make the right consistency. Frost cake. Serves a crowd.

Becky Snider
Chautauqua Motet . . .
(1985)

TIP

STEPS FOR MIXING BUTTER CAKES
Cream the butter.
Add sugar gradually, creaming well.
Add egg yolks, beat mixture well.
Sift dry ingredients.
Add alternately dry ingredients and liquid.
Add flavoring, beat cake well.
Cut and fold in beaten egg whites.

STEPS FOR MIXING SPONGE CAKES
Beat the egg yolks until frothy and orange colored.
Add sugar and cream well.
Add liquid alternating with the well sifted dry ingredients.
Add flavoring.
Cut and fold in stiffly beaten egg whites.

Cook Book
Cassadaga (1950)

RASPBERRY CONTINENTAL

$1/_2$ cup butter
1 egg, beaten
1 tsp. vanilla
$1^1/_4$ cups all-purpose flour
1 cup sugar
$1/_4$ cup milk
$1/_2$ tsp. salt
$1/_4$ cup toasted blanched almonds, chopped

RASPBERRY FILLING: Combine in saucepan $1/_4$ cup sugar, 2 Tbsps. cornstarch. Add 1 package (10 ounce) frozen red raspberries. Cook, stirring constantly, until thick. Cool completely.
BUTTER FILLING: Cream $1/_2$ cup butter. Gradually add $1^1/_2$ cups sifted confectioners' sugar, creaming well. Add 1 whole egg and beat until fluffy.
WHIPPED CREAM: Beat 3/4 cup whipping cream until thick. Stir in 3 Tbsps. sugar. Continue beating until stiff. Sprinkle $1/_2$ cup chopped walnuts on assembled cake.

Cream butter and gradually add sugar and cream well. Add beaten egg, vanilla and salt. Add milk. Stir in flour and almonds. Turn into 8" square pan, greased. Bake at 350° for 30-35 minutes. Remove from pan and cool on rack. Cut in half horizontally with sharp knife to make 2 thin layers. Spread bottom layer with butter filling and then raspberry filling. Top with second layer, then whipped cream. Chill for 4 hours.

Freezes well in tight container. Serves 9.

(Dust a little cornstarch on your cakes before icing to hold the icing on the cake.)

Mildred Szabo
Favorite Recipes . . .
Findley Lake
(1981)

WACKY CAKE

$1^1/_2$ cups flour
1 cup sugar
3 Tbsps. cocoa
1 tsp. soda
$1/_3$ cup oil
1 Tbsp. vinegar
1 tsp. vanilla
1 cup cold water

Mix all ingredients. Put into 9x9-inch square pan. Bake at 350° for 30 minutes. Serve with vanilla ice cream. Top with chocolate syrup.

Betsy Hudson
Warm Your Heart . . .
(1987)

RHUBARB CAKE

$1^1/_2$ cups sugar
$^1/_2$ cup shortening
2 eggs
$^1/_3$ cup milk
1 tsp. soda
1 tsp. cinnamon
$^1/_4$ tsp. cloves (ground)
$^1/_4$ tsp. allspice (ground)
dash of salt
2 cups flour
2 cups rhubarb (raw), cut up

Mix everything together adding the rhubarb last. You may use either fresh or frozen rhubarb. Dough will be very stiff. Put in a 9x13 pan. (I use a glass pan because the rhubarb discolors metal ones.) Bake at 325° for about 35 minutes.

TOPPING:
About $^1/_2$ cup sugar
About 1 tsp. cinnamon
About $^1/_2$ cup nuts

Mix together and put on the dough before you bake it.

Helen Peterson
Our Favorite . . .
(1970s)

TEXAS SHEET CAKE

2 cups flour
2 cups sugar
2 sticks margarine
4 Tbsps. cocoa
1 cup water
$^1/_2$ cup sour cream
2 eggs
1 tsp. vanilla
dash of salt
1 tsp. baking soda

Mix flour and sugar. Set aside. Mix margarine, cocoa and water. Bring to a boil and take off heat. Mix this with sugar and flour, add sour cream, eggs, vanilla, salt, and baking soda. Mix well. Bake at 375° for 15-20 minutes in a greased 18x12-inch pan. After cake bakes 5 minutes begin making icing.

1 stick margarine
4 Tbsps. cocoa
6 Tbsps. milk
1 box powdered sugar
1 tsp. vanilla

Mix margarine, milk and cocoa. Bring to a boil and remove from heat. Add powdered sugar and vanilla. Beat well. Ice cake as soon as it comes from oven.

Kathy Swanson
Euclid Avenue . . .
(1980)

PUDDINGS, CHEESECAKES, AND MORE

BLACKBERRY PUDDING

Grease 2 quart casserole with butter. Put 3 cups black-berries in the casserole.
Batter:
3 Tbsps. butter
1/2 cup milk
1 cup flour
2 tsps. baking powder
Mix and put evenly over berries. Then mix:
1 cup sugar
1 Tbsp. cornstarch
salt

Pour sugar mixture over the batter, then pour 1 cup of boiling water over all. Bake at 350° for 1 hour. Blueberries may also be used.

Miss Eleanor Burtch
What's Cooking I
(1954)

BROWNIE PUDDING

1 cup flour
2 tsps. baking powder
1/2 tsp. salt
3/4 cup white sugar
2 Tbsps. cocoa
1/2 cup milk
1 tsp. vanilla
2 Tbsps. melted shortening
3/4 cup chopped nuts
3/4 cup brown sugar
1/4 cup cocoa
1 3/4 cups hot water

Sift together dry ingredients. Add milk, vanilla and shortening. Mix until smooth and add nuts. Pour into tin 8"x8". Mix brown sugar and cocoa and spread over batter. Pour hot water over all. Bake at 350° for 40-45 minutes. Serve warm, topped with whipped cream or ice cream. Serves 8.

Marion Erick
Favorite Hometown . . .
(Date unknown)

BUTTERCREME TORTE
(Frankfurter Kranz)
1 cup flour
$^1/_2$ cup cornstarch
1 tsp. baking powder
1 cup sugar
5 large eggs

FILLING:
$2^1/_2$ cups milk
1 package vanilla pudding
2 Tbsps. vanilla
$^1/_2$ cup chopped nuts
$^1/_2$ lb. butter
$^1/_2$ cup sugar

Break eggs into large mixing bowl. Add sugar and beat at high speed, until light and fluffy. Fold flour, cornstarch and baking powder into egg mixture and pour into well buttered springform pan (or Angel Food pan), which has been sprinkled with fine bread crumbs.

Bake in a preheated oven at 350° for 45 minutes.

Combine in saucepan, milk, sugar, vanilla and pudding mix. Cook until pudding is thickened; cool to room temperature. Stir occasionally so it stays smooth. Cream butter and stir by spoonfuls into pudding. Watch! Stir; do not beat!

Cut cake into 3 layers and spread layers with apricot preserves, thinned with water or rum. Spread with filling, fairly thick; frost top and sides with remaining filling. Sprinkle top and sides with chopped nuts.

Liselotte A. Kelley
Cooking with . . .
Dunkirk
(1972)

PRUNE WHIP
$^1/_2$ lb. prunes
Stew until tender without sugar.
3 egg whites
scant $^1/_2$ cup sugar

Put cut prunes, whites of eggs and sugar in a bowl and whip until light and stiff. Serve with whipped cream.

Caroline Secor
Pilgrim's Treasure . . .
(1952)

THE BEST CHEESECAKE YOU EVER TASTED

1 lb. cottage cheese
1 lb. cream cheese
$1/4$ cup softened butter
$1^1/_3$ cups granulated sugar
1 cup sour cream
4 eggs
1 Tbsp. vanilla
3 Tbsps. cornstarch
3 Tbsps. flour

RASPBERRY TOPPING
1 qt. raspberries
$1^1/_3$ cups sugar
$2^1/_2$ Tbsps. cornstarch
1 Tbsp. lemon juice

In a large bowl blend together cream cheese, cottage cheese and butter. Add the sugar. Beat in the eggs, vanilla, cornstarch and flour. Lastly blend in sour cream. Pour into a 9-inch buttered springform pan. Put in *cold* oven. Set at 325°; bake 70 minutes. Don't open the oven door. Leave oven closed 2 hours. Remove from oven and chill. Top with canned cherry pie filling or raspberry topping. (Recipe follows.) This cheesecake freezes well.

Crush berries to equal 2 cups prepared. Mix sugar and cornstarch together in a medium saucepan. Stir in berries and lemon juice. Cook over medium heat until mixture boils and thickens. Stir constantly while cooking. Cool slightly. Spread on cheesecake and cool thoroughly.

Deborah Johnson
Favorite Recipes . . .
Mayville
(1982)

LEMON BISQUE

1 can evaporated milk
1 package lemon Jell-o
$1^1/_2$ cups boiling water
$1/3$ cup honey
$1/8$ tsp. salt
3 Tbsps. lemon juice
Grated rind (lemon)
2 cups Vanilla Wafer crumbs

Chill milk. Dissolve gelatin in boiling water. Add honey, salt, lemon juice, rind. Set aside to cool until it begins to gel. Beat milk stiff and fold into gelatin. Spread pan (10x12 inch) with most of the wafer crumbs. Add lemon mixture and sprinkle with remaining crumbs. Set in refrigerator to chill. Makes 12 servings.

Gene Chaffee
Westfield Jayncees . . .
(1983)

RICOTTA CREAM CHEESE CAKE

CRUST:
1/2 cup graham cracker crumbs
3/4 stick butter
dash cinnamon

Mix together and press in 8" square pan 2" deep. Retain about 2 heaping Tbsps. of mixture for topping.

FILLING:
1 lb. ricotta cheese
2 (8-oz.) packages cream cheese, softened
1/2 cup sugar
1/4 cup cornstarch
1/2 tsp. salt
1 Tbsp. lemon juice
4 eggs

In a mixing bowl, cream ricotta and cream cheese with spoon. Blend in remaining ingredients. Beat in mixer for about 10 minutes. Pour batter in graham cracker crust, and bake at 375° for 20 minutes. Take out and let stand for 15 minutes.

TOPPING:
1 pint sour cream
1/4 cup sugar
1 tsp. vanilla

Mix together and spread on top of cake. Sprinkle with remaining 2 Tbsps. of graham cracker mixture. Bake for 10 minutes. Cool in oven for 15 minutes and remove.

If you prefer something different — try spreading one can of cherry or blueberry pie filling as a topping, instead of sour cream mixture.

Carmen J. Basile
Wonderful Cooking . . .
(Date unknown)

FORGOTTEN DESSERT

Grease an 8x8x2" pan. Preheat oven to 450°. Beat stiff 5 egg whites, 1/2 tsp. salt, 1/2 tsp. cream of tartar. Measure 1 1/2 cups sifted sugar and add a tablespoonful at a time to egg mixture. Beat 15 min. after all sugar has been added. Add 1 tsp. vanilla. Pour into pan, place in oven and immediately turn off heat. Leave overnight without opening oven door. In the morning whip 1/2 pt. of cream and frost meringue. Put in refrigerator. When ready to serve, pile fresh fruit on top.

Mrs. Violetta Coons
Kiantone Cookbook
(1969)

CREAMY RICE PUDDING

(Swedish)

$^1/_2$ cup raw rice
$2^1/_2$ cups boiling water
$^3/_4$ tsp. salt
3 eggs
$^1/_3$ cup sugar
$^1/_2$ cup raisins
$1^1/_2$ tsps. grated lemon rind
2 tsps. vanilla
$3^1/_2$ cups milk
1 tsp. nutmeg
2 Tbsps. butter

Heat oven to 300°. Add washed rice to water and cook until tender. Drain. Beat eggs, stir in sugar, raisins, rind and vanilla. Add milk to rice, add egg mixture, and mix. Put into 2-quart casserole, sprinkle with nutmeg. Dot with butter. Set into pan of water 1 inch from top. Bake 1 hour and 25 minutes, stirring once after first $^1/_2$ hour. Done when knife comes out clean.

Priscilla Nixon
Cookbook
Westfield
(1986)

STEAMED PUDDING

1 beaten egg
$^1/_2$ cup water
$^2/_3$ cup dark molasses
1 tsp. soda
1 cup flour
$^1/_4$ tsp. salt
1 tsp. vanilla
$^1/_2$ tsp. cinnamon

Sift flour, soda, salt, cinnamon. Mix egg, water, molasses, and vanilla. Combine liquid and dry ingredients and blend well. Pour into buttered 1-quart mold. Cover with waxed paper; tie securely. Place in shallow pan on oven rack; pour hot water around it 1 inch deep. Keep water at this level. Bake at 350° about 2 hours.

SAUCE FOR STEAMED PUDDING
1 cup confectioners' sugar
2 Tbsps. butter
1 beaten egg
$^1/_2$ cup whipped cream

Mix together thoroughly confectioners' sugar, butter and egg. Fold in whipped cream. Serve with pudding.

Mary Potter
Pioneer...
(1987)

DROP AND ROLLED COOKIES

BUTTERNUT DROPS
$1/2$ cup butter
$1/4$ cup sugar
1 egg, separated
$1/4$ tsp. vanilla
$1/4$ tsp. salt
1 cup cake flour
1 Tbsp. lemon juice
2 Tbsps. grated orange rind
1 Tbsp. grated lemon rind
$1/2$ cup Brazil nuts, ground fine
candied cherries

Cream butter and sugar well. Add egg yolk and vanilla. Beat well. Sift dry ingredients together and add with lemon juice and rinds. Mix thoroughly and place in covered bowl. Chill. Roll into tiny balls ($1/2$ tsp. dough per ball). Dip balls into slightly beaten egg white. Roll in ground nuts. Place on greased cookie sheet 1 inch apart. Press $1/2$ candied cherry on top of each and bake at 350° for 25 minutes. Makes 40.

Mrs. Andrew Scalise
What's Cookin'...
(1964-65)

CHOCOLATE COOKIES
$2/3$ cup brown sugar
$1/2$ cup butter
1 well-beaten egg
$1/2$ cup milk
2 cups cake flour
$1/2$ tsp. soda
$1/4$ tsp. almond extract
$1/2$ tsp. vanilla
3 squares chocolate, melted
pinch of salt

FROSTING
2 cups powdered sugar
4 Tbsps. cocoa
cream, as needed, start with 1 tsp.

Cream butter and sugar, add beaten egg. Add sifted dry ingredients alternately with milk and flavorings. Stir in melted chocolate. Drop from teaspoon. Bake at 350° for 7 to 10 minutes. Then frost and place pecan half on top of each cookie.

Mix powdered sugar, cocoa and cream until of spreading consistency.

Mrs. Richard N. Lindbeck
What's Cooking I
(1954)

BUTTERSCOTCH WHIRLS

Sift together:
4 cups flour
1 tsp. soda
1 tsp. salt
Cream together:
1 cup butter or shortening
2 cups brown sugar
Then add:
2 eggs
1 tsp. lemon juice
1 tsp. vanilla

Add creamed mixture to dry ingredients. Divide dough in two parts. Roll each portion to $1/2$ inch thickness. Spread with date filling. Roll as for jelly roll and chill. Cut in thin slices and bake at 400° for 10 minutes.

FILLING:
$1^1/_4$ cups dates
1 cup water
$1/_2$ cup sugar
1 Tbsp. lemon juice
$1/_2$ cup nut meats

Cook until thick and cool before using.

Mrs. Ralph T. Mee, Sr.
Kennedy's Favorite Recipes
(1950)

FIG FILLED COOKIES

1 cup sugar
1 cup sweet cream
$1/_2$ cup shortening
$1/_2$ cup milk
1 egg
$3^1/_2$ cups flour
2 tsps. cream of tartar
1 tsp. baking soda
$1/_2$ tsp. salt
1 tsp. vanilla

Mix all together. Roll thin. Cut with round cutters and put cookies on greased cookie tin and place a teaspoon of filling on each cookie. Place another cookie on top and bake at 350° until done. Test after 8 minutes.

FILLING:
2 cups figs
$1/_2$ cup sugar
$1/_2$ cup water
1 tsp. flour

Soak figs in warm water until soft enough to grind through chopper. Add sugar, water and flour. Cook until thick, stirring constantly so it does not burn.

Sharing Our Best
(1987)

Clark and Lewis Families at Dessert, Ellery, ca. 1900.

Jack T. Ericson

CALIFORNIA RANGER COOKIES

1 cup shortening
1 cup sugar
1 cup brown sugar
2 eggs
1 tsp. vanilla
1 Tbsp. milk
2 cups flour
1 tsp. baking soda
$^1/_2$ tsp. baking powder
$^1/_2$ tsp. salt
2 cups rolled oats
2 cups corn flakes
1 cup shredded coconut
1 cup chopped nuts
1 cup raisins
1 cup chopped dates

Gradually combine ingredients, form balls and place on greased cookie sheet. Press with floured fork. Bake at 350° for 8 to 10 minutes.

Mrs. Leonard Mackowiak
Sharing Our Best
(1987)

CHOCOLATE MERINGUES

2 egg whites
1 tsp. vanilla
$^1/_8$ tsp. salt
$^1/_8$ tsp. cream of tartar
$^3/_4$ cup sugar
1 (6 oz.) pkg. (1 cup) semisweet chocolate pieces
$^1/_4$ cup chopped walnuts

Beat first 4 ingredients until soft peaks form. Add sugar gradually, beating till stiff peaks form. Fold in chocolate pieces and nuts. Cover cookie sheet with a brown paper bag. Drop mixture by rounded teaspoonfuls. Bake at 300° for 25 minutes. Cool slightly before removing from paper. Makes 24.

Lois Gilson
Tidbit Tea
(1968)

CHOCOLATE PEANUT BUTTER BALLS

3 cups Rice Krispies
3 cups powdered sugar
3 cups crunchy peanut butter
1 stick margarine, melted
1 (12 oz.) bar sweet chocolate
6 oz. semisweet chocolate chips
$1/_2$ piece canning wax

Mix together Rice Krispies and sugar. Melt margarine and peanut butter together and mix with Rice Krispies and sugar. Roll into small balls about 1". Melt chocolates and wax together. Dip balls in chocolate mixture. Dry on waxed paper.

Dorothy Roman
East Dunkirk . . .
(Date unknown)

FUDGE MELTAWAYS

$1/_2$ cup butter
1 (1 oz.) square unsweetened chocolate
$1/_4$ cup sugar
1 tsp. vanilla
1 egg, beaten
2 cups graham cracker crumbs
1 cup coconut
$1/_2$ cup chopped nuts (optional)

Melt $1/_2$ cup butter and 1 square chocolate in saucepan. Blend sugar, vanilla, egg, graham cracker crumbs, coconut and nuts into butter-chocolate mixture. Mix well and press into ungreased 9-inch square pan. Refrigerate.

TOPPING

$1/_2$ cup chopped nuts (optional)
$1/_4$ cup butter
1 Tbsp. milk or cream
2 cups sifted confectioners' sugar
1 tsp. vanilla
2 (1-oz.) squares unsweetened chocolate

Mix butter, milk, confectioners' sugar and vanilla. Spread over crumb mixture. Chill. Melt 2 squares chocolate and spread over chilled mixture. Sprinkle with nuts. Chill again. Cut into squares before completely firm. Makes 12 meltaways.

Kathy Poweska
Favorite Hometown . . .
(Date unknown)

CRANBERRY-PINEAPPLE COOKIES

$^1/_2$ cup margarine
$1^1/_2$ cups brown sugar
3 Tbsps. buttermilk
1 tsp. vanilla
2 eggs
$^1/_2$ tsp. salt
$^3/_4$ cup crushed pineapple, drained
2 cups cranberries, chopped fine
1 cup walnuts, finely chopped or put in blender
3 tsps. grated orange peel
2 tsps. orange juice
3 cups flour
1 tsp. soda

Mix all ingredients well. Drop by teaspoonfuls on greased cookie sheet. Bake at 350° for 8-12 minutes.

Virginia Wareham Dean
Cookbook
Westfield
(1986)

DANISH BROWN SUGAR COOKIES

2 cups sifted flour
1 cup butter
1 egg yolk
$^3/_4$ cup brown sugar, firmly packed

Cream butter until softened. Add the brown sugar gradually, creaming after each addition. Blend in egg yolk thoroughly. Add the flour gradually, mixing thoroughly. Shape batter into balls about 3/4-inch in diameter. Place about 2 inches apart on greased cookie sheets. Using the back of a fork, flatten with criss-cross marks. Press a pecan or walnut half on top of each cookie. Bake at 375° about 8 minutes. Cool on pans about 2 minutes, then remove to wire rack to cool completely. Makes about 40 cookies.

Mrs. Raymond Norberg
What's Cookin' . . .
(1964-65)

ELEGANT RAINBOW SQUARES

8 oz. almond paste (not marzipan)
$1^1/_2$ cups (3 sticks) unsalted butter, softened
1 cup sugar
4 eggs, separated
1 tsp. almond extract
2 cups sifted flour
$^1/_4$ tsp. salt
green food coloring
red food coloring
1 (12 oz.) jar apricot preserves
6 oz. semisweet chocolate chips

Preheat oven to 350°. Grease 3 (13x9-inch) baking pans. Line pans with waxed paper. Grease paper. Using fork, break up almond paste in large mixer bowl. Add butter, sugar, egg yolks and almond extract. Beat with electric mixer until light and fluffy, about 5 minutes. Beat in flour and salt.

In a medium bowl, beat egg whites with mixer until stiff peaks form. Fold into almond mixture, using turning motion. Remove $1^1/_2$ cups batter. Spread evenly in one of the prepared pans. Remove another $1^1/_2$ cups batter to a small bowl. Tint to a medium shade of green using green coloring. Spread in second prepared pan. Tint remaining batter with red food coloring until it is a medium pink color and spread in a third pan. Layers will be $^1/_4$-inch thick.

Bake in preheated oven for 15 minutes or until edges are lightly golden. Immediately remove cakes from pans by lifting edges of waxed paper. Invert layers onto wire racks and remove waxed paper. Place another wire rack on top and invert once again and let cool, right side up, on racks. Layers are very delicate so be very careful in handling them. Cool thoroughly. Place green layer on flat cookie sheet or upturned jelly roll pan. Heat apricot preserves in small saucepan; strain. Spread half the warm preserves over green layer to edges. Place yellow layer on top. Spread with remaining preserves. Place pink layer, top side up, on yellow layer. Cover with plastic wrap. Weight down the cake with large cutting board or tray. Place large catalog on top for more weight. Refrigerate overnight.

Melt chocolate chips in microwave or in top of double boiler over hot water. Trim cake edges even. Cut cake across width into 1-inch wide strips. Frost top (pink) layer with chocolate. Turn strip on side. Frost bottom (green) layer. Let strips stand until chocolate is dry. Cut into 1-inch pieces. Repeat with remaining strips. Keep refrigerated until serving time.

Debbie Gneshin
"Cookin' from . . ."
(1987-88)

GINGER CREAMS

$1/_2$ cup shortening
1 cup sugar
1 egg
1 cup molasses
4 cups all-purpose flour
$1/_2$ tsp. salt
1 tsp. nutmeg
1 tsp. cloves
1 tsp. cinnamon
2 tsps. ginger
2 tsps. soda mixed into 1 cup hot water

Cream shortening and sugar. Add egg and molasses and mix well. Sift together flour, salt and spices and stir into shortening mixture alternately with the soda-water mixture. Chill dough. Then drop by teaspoon onto greased cookie tin and bake 10 minutes at 400°. Makes 5-6 dozen cookies.

ICING FOR GINGER CREAMS
1 Tbsp. melted butter
2 cups confectioners' sugar
3-4 Tbsps. cream
Blend until spreading consistency and frost cookies.
Mrs. Franklin W. Bigelow
What's Cooking I
(1954)

HAMENTASHEN

$3/_4$ cup sugar
2 cups sifted flour
2 tsps. baking powder
$1/_4$ tsp. salt
$1/_2$ cup shortening
1 egg, beaten
2 Tbsps. orange juice

Sift flour, sugar, baking powder and salt into a bowl. Work in shortening by hand. Add egg and orange juice, mixing until dough is formed. Chill overnight, if possible, or at least 2 hours. Roll dough to about an eighth-inch thickness on lightly floured board and cut into three-inch circles. Place a heaping teaspoon filling in the center. Pinch three edges of dough together, leaving a little of the filling showing. Place on greased cookie sheet. Cover with a towel and let stand half an hour. Bake in a 400° oven for about 20 minutes or until lightly browned on top.

FILLING:
$1^1/_2$ cups mashed prunes
$1/_2$ cup sugar or honey
$1/_2$ cup coarsely chopped nuts
1 tsp. lemon juice
$1/_4$ tsp. allspice
Cook prunes and sugar together until mixture is thick. Add other ingredients and cool.
Margot G. Heinemann
Home Town Recipes
(1989)

OLD-TIME GINGER SNAPS

$^3/_4$ cup shortening
$^3/_4$ cup brown sugar
$^3/_4$ cup molasses
1 egg
3 cups sifted flour
$^1/_4$ tsp. salt
$1^1/_2$ tsps. baking soda
$^1/_4$ tsp. cloves
1 tsp. cinnamon
1 tsp. ginger

Cream shortening and add sugar gradually. Add molasses and egg and mix well. Add sifted dry ingredients and blend thoroughly. Drop by teaspoon on ungreased cookie sheet or fill cookie press and form cookies on ungreased cookie sheet. Sprinkle with sugar, if desired.

Bake at 375° for 10-12 minutes. Remove cookies from sheet at once. Makes about 7 dozen small or 4 doz. large cookies.

Martha Woolley
Cooking Favorites
Arkwright
(1960s)

HALLOWEEN DINGBATS

$1^1/_2$ cups dates, chopped
1 cup sugar
$^1/_4$ cup butter
1 egg, beaten
$^1/_4$ cup water
2 cups Rice Krispies
1 tsp. vanilla
1/2 cup pecans, chopped
1 (4 oz.) can coconut, tinted yellow

Mix dates, sugar, butter, and egg. Stir to blend well. Stir in water. Cook slowly over medium heat for 10 minutes. Stir in cereal, vanilla and pecans. Cool. Drop by teaspoon into bowl of coconut. Roll into balls. Can be frozen. Can also use red and green tinted coconut for Christmas.

Margaret Bigler
Warm Your Heart . . .
(1987)

ITALIAN COOKIES

6 heaping tsps. baking powder
$2^1/_2$ lbs. flour
3/4 lb. shortening, melted
6 eggs
1 lb. sugar
$^1/_2$ tsp. baking soda
2 tsps. vanilla
1 pint milk

Beat eggs; add sugar and melted shortening. Beat again and add vanilla and milk. Mix flour, soda and baking powder in a mound on board or counter. Make a well in center and pour egg mixture into well and mix to make a soft dough that can be rolled. Roll thin and cut with a cookie cutter. Bake on ungreased cookie sheets at 375° until golden brown. Frost. Makes a large batch of cookies.

FROSTING
1 box powdered sugar
1 Tbsp. buttermilk
1 tsp. vanilla

Mix together until spreading consistency.
Sharing Our Best
(1987)

CHOCOLATE ITALIAN COOKIES

5 cups flour
$1^1/_4$ cups sugar
$^3/_4$ cup cocoa
$1^1/_2$ Tbsps. baking powder
1 Tbsp. baking soda
1 Tbsp. cinnamon
1 cup shortening
3 eggs
$^1/_4$ cup strawberry jam
1 cup raisins, optional
handful chopped nuts, optional
$^1/_2$ cup milk, as needed

Sift together dry ingredients. Blend in shortening. Add eggs, jam, raisins and nuts. Add milk to moisten as needed. Shape into small-medium balls. Bake on greased cookie sheet at 375° for 10-12 minutes. Frost when cool. Makes about 100 cookies.

FROSTING
1 stick margarine
1 lb. confectioners' sugar
pinch of cream of tartar
1 tsp. vanilla or almond extract
$^1/_2$ cup warm milk

Beat all ingredients together until smooth and of spreading consistency.
Carla Howie
Sugar 'N Spice . . .
(1987)

KIFLI

(from Hungary)

1 cup soft sweet butter
$^1/_2$ lb. (8 oz.) soft cream cheese
$^1/_4$ tsp. salt
2 cups sifted flour
1 cup chopped walnuts
$^1/_2$ cup sugar
1 Tbsp. cinnamon

DAY BEFORE: Mix butter, cheese, and salt until creamy. Mix in flour, shape into 14 balls. Refrigerate overnight. Bake next day as follows:

Heat oven to 350°. On lightly floured cloth-covered board, roll each cream-cheese ball to 6" circle. Cut each circle into quarters.

Mix nuts, sugar, cinnamon; drop a rounded teaspoon of this nut mixture on each quarter of dough. Pinch edges of dough together, enclosing filling, then form into crescents.

Place crescents on ungreased cookie sheet. Bake 12 min. or until light brown. Best served soon after baking. Makes about 5 dozen.

Violet Swanson
Tidbit Tea
(1968)

LEMON REFRIGERATOR COOKIES

1 cup shortening
2 cups white sugar
2 Tbsps. lemon rind
2 Tbsps. lemon juice
2 eggs
4 cups flour
2 tsps. baking powder
$^1/_8$ tsp. salt
$^1/_8$ tsp. nutmeg

Cream shortening, sugar, lemon rind and lemon juice together until light and fluffy. Add eggs, one at a time, beating well after each addition. Sift flour with baking powder, salt, and nutmeg. Add to first mixture. Blend well. Chill dough in refrigerator, then shape into 3 rolls, each roll about 2 inches in diameter. Wrap in waxed paper. Chill, or the wrapped dough may be frozen. Slice thin and bake as needed. Remove from pan immediately after baking. Cookies will be crisp. Bake at 400° for 8 to 10 minutes. Yields 5 dozen.

Mrs. Judy VanVorst
Kiantone Cookbook
(1969)

ORANGE CHOCOLATE CHIPPERS

1 cup shortening
1 cup sugar
1 (3 oz.) package cream cheese, softened
2 eggs
1 Tbsp. grated orange peel
2 tsps. vanilla
2 cups sifted enriched flour
1 tsp. salt
1 (6 oz.) package semisweet chocolate chips
$^1/_2$ cup chopped nuts, optional

Cream shortening, sugar, cream cheese. Add eggs, orange peel, vanilla; beat well. Sift flour and salt; add to mixture, mix well. Stir in chips and nuts. Drop from teaspoon 2 inches apart on lightly greased cookie sheet. Bake at 350° for 12 minutes. Can be frozen. Makes about 4 dozen cookies.

Barbara J. Reid
Cookbook
Westfield
(1986)

ORANGE DROP COOKIES

$1^1/_2$ cups brown sugar
2 eggs, well-beaten
1 cup Crisco
$1^1/_2$ cups nuts, chopped (also dates, if desired)
grated rind of an orange
1 tsp. soda
$3^1/_2$ cups sifted flour
3 tsps. baking powder
pinch of salt
1 cup sour milk

ICING
grated rind of 1 orange
1 Tbsp. lemon juice
3 Tbsps. orange juice
1 egg yolk

Combine sugar and Crisco, add beaten eggs, then add dry ingredients alternately with milk. Grated rind and nuts may be added last. Drop by spoonfuls on greased cookie sheet and bake at 350° for about 10 minutes. Makes about 5 dozen.

Combine ingredients and add enough powdered sugar for right consistency to spread. Then add 1 Tbsp. butter.

Mrs. John A. Hall
What's Cooking I
(1954)

PEANUT BLOSSOMS

$1^3/_4$ cups flour
1 tsp. baking soda
$^1/_2$ tsp. salt
$^1/_2$ cup sugar
$^1/_2$ cup firmly packed light brown sugar
$^1/_2$ cup shortening (margarine)
$^1/_2$ cup creamy peanut butter
1 egg
2 Tbsps. milk
1 tsp. vanilla
48 milk chocolate kisses (unwrapped)

In large mixer bowl, stir in flour, soda and salt. Add remaining ingredients, except kisses. Beat at low speed until mixed well. Chill dough 30 minutes. Preheat oven to 375°. Roll small amounts of dough into 1 inch balls. Place on ungreased cookie sheet. Bake 12 minutes or until light brown. Remove from oven and immediately press a kiss into the center. (Cookie will crack around edges.) Makes 48 cookies.

Burdella Warner
Warm Your Heart . . .
(1987)

PEANUT COOKIES

1 egg, slightly beaten
1 cup brown sugar
$^3/_4$ cup melted margarine
$1^1/_4$ cups flour
$^1/_2$ cup cornflakes
$^1/_2$ tsp. baking soda
$^1/_2$ tsp. baking powder
$^1/_4$ tsp. salt
$1^1/_2$ cups oatmeal
$^3/_4$ cup peanuts (Spanish with skins)

Cream together the first 3 ingredients; add dry ingredients and blend. Add oatmeal, cornflakes and peanuts; blend well. Drop by teaspoon. Bake at 400° for 10 minutes. Makes 3-4 dozen.

Frances Haas
Cooking Favorites . . .
Arkwright
(1960s)

PUMPKIN COOKIES

1¹/₂ cups sugar
¹/₂ cup shortening
1 egg
2¹/₂ cups flour
1 tsp. baking powder
1 tsp. soda
¹/₂ tsp. salt
1 tsp. nutmeg
1 tsp. cinnamon
2 cups pumpkin puree (canned or made fresh)
1 cup raisins
¹/₂ cup nuts
1 tsp. vanilla

Cream shortening and sugar. Add egg, vanilla and spices. Mix well. Sift flour with baking powder, salt, soda. Add to creamed mixture alternately with pumpkin. Fold in raisins and nuts. Drop on ungreased cookie sheet. Bake at 350 degrees for 12 to 15 minutes. Makes 4 dozen cookies.

Florence Morris
Cookbook
Westfield
(1986)

SNICKERDOODLES

¹/₂ cup butter or margarine, softened
¹/₂ cup shortening
1¹/₂ cups sugar
2 eggs
2¹/₄ cups flour
2 tsps. cream of tartar
1 tsp. soda
¹/₄ tsp. salt
2 Tbsps. sugar
2 tsps. cinnamon

Heat oven to 400 degrees. Beat butter or margarine, sugar, and shortening; add eggs. Blend in flour, cream of tartar, soda and salt. Shape dough by rounded teaspoon into balls. Roll in mixture of sugar and cinnamon. Place 2" apart on ungreased baking sheet. Bake 8-10 minutes. Immediately remove from baking sheet. Makes 6 dozen.

Sharon Fisher
100 Years of Cooking . . .
(1986)

STOCKTON HOTEL SOUR CREAM COOKIES (1890)

1 cup sugar
$^1/_2$ cup butter
1 egg
1 tsp. baking soda
1 cup sour cream
$^1/_2$ tsp. baking powder
1 scant tsp. nutmeg
4 cups flour

Cream sugar and butter. Add egg and beat well until fluffy. Mix soda with sour cream and add to sugar mixture. Mix well. Sift baking powder, nutmeg and flour together. Add to mixture and mix well. Chill dough. Roll out dough and cut with large round cookie cutter. Put a raisin in middle and sprinkle with sugar. Bake at 300° for 10 minutes.

Cook Book
Mayville
(1981)

SUNFLOWER SEED COOKIES

$^1/_2$ cup softened butter or margarine
$^1/_2$ cup packed brown sugar
$^1/_2$ cup white sugar
1 egg
$^1/_2$ tsp. vanilla
$1^1/_2$ cups quick oats
$^3/_4$ cup whole wheat flour
$^1/_2$ tsp. soda
$^1/_4$ tsp. salt
$^3/_4$ cup sunflower seeds

Cream butter and sugar. Add egg and vanilla, beat well. Mix together oats, flour, soda and salt. Stir into first mixture. Gently blend in sunflower seeds. Form into two rolls, $1^1/_2$ inches in diameter. Wrap in waxed paper and chill thoroughly. Slice $^1/_4$ inch thick and bake on ungreased cookie sheet at 350 degrees for 10 minutes.

Ruth F. Steese
Cooking By Degrees
(1985)

WHEATIES COOKIES
(original 1936 recipe)
1 cup shortening
1 cup brown sugar
1 cup white sugar
2 eggs
$2^1/_2$ cups flour
$^1/_2$ tsp. baking powder
$^1/_2$ tsp. salt
1 tsp. baking soda
1 tsp. vanilla
1 to $1^1/_2$ cups shredded coconut
4 cups Wheaties cereal

Cream shortening, eggs and sugars together. Add baking soda, baking powder, salt and vanilla; mix. Add flour. Mix until well-blended. Mix in coconut and Wheaties with spoon or fork. Drop walnut-sized pieces onto cookie sheet. Bake at 350 degrees until light brown. Cool on rack. Yield: 6 dozen.

Dorothy Humes
Our Country . . .
(1980s)

WHOOPIE PIES
6 Tbsps. shortening
1 cup sugar
1 egg
1 cup milk
1 tsp. vanilla
2 cups sifted flour
$1^1/_2$ tsps. soda
5 Tbsps. cocoa
1 tsp. salt

FILLING:
$^1/_2$ cup shortening
2 Tbsps. marshmallow fluff
$^3/_4$ cup powdered sugar
$^1/_4$ to $^1/_2$ cup milk

Cream shortening, sugar and egg. Add remaining ingredients and mix well. Drop by tablespoon on an ungreased cookie sheet. Bake 8 minutes at 400 degrees.

FILLING: Beat shortening, marshmallow fluff, powdered sugar and milk until consistency of cream. (Add milk a little at a time.) Spread filling on top of 1 cookie and top with another, sandwich-style, with cream in the middle. Makes 24 double cookies.

Angie Banes
Sts. P. & P. Family . . .
(1988)

BAR COOKIES

APRICOT BARS

$^1/_2$ cup soft margarine
$^1/_4$ cup sugar
1 cup flour

1 cup brown sugar, packed
2 eggs, well-beaten
$^2/_3$ cup dried apricots
$^1/_3$ cup flour
$^1/_2$ tsp. vanilla
$^1/_2$ tsp. baking powder
$^1/_4$ tsp. salt
$^1/_2$ cup chopped nuts

Mix until crumbly, pack into 7x11 inch pan. Bake at 350 degrees about 25 minutes until brown.

Rinse apricots; cover with water, boil 10 min. Drain, chop when cool. Sift together flour and baking powder and salt. Gradually beat brown sugar into eggs; add flour mixture; mix well. Mix in vanilla, nuts and apricots. Spread over baked layer. Bake 30 min. until done. Cool. Cut into squares. Sprinkle with powdered sugar.

Cora Rogger
Adventures in Food
(1977)

BLACK WALNUT BROWNIES

Melt in a pan $^1/_2$ cup butter. Add 2 cups brown sugar. Stir until dissolved. Cool slightly. Beat in:
2 eggs
1 tsp. black walnut extract or 2 tsps. vanilla
Sift, then measure 1 cup bread flour. Resift with:
2 tsps. baking powder
1 tsp. salt

Stir into butter mixture. Add 1 (4-oz.) can black walnuts. Pour into 2 greased 8x8-inch tins, lined with waxed paper. Bake 30 minutes at 350 degrees. Makes 18 brownies.

Mrs. Walter Gunkler
What's Cooking I
(1954)

BLACK AND WHITE BROWNIES AND ICING

1 cup margarine
$1^1/_2$ tsps. vanilla
2 cups sugar
2 squares chocolate, melted
4 eggs
2 cups flour
$1^1/_2$ tsps. baking powder
$^1/_2$ tsp. salt
$^1/_2$ cup chopped walnuts or pecans

Cream first 3 ingredients. Add eggs, flour, baking powder, salt and nuts. Divide batter and add melted chocolate to $^1/_2$ of batter. Drop light and dark batter into 13x9x2 inch greased pan, alternating in checker-board pattern. Run knife through batter several times to marbleize. Bake at 350 degrees, 30 to 35 minutes or until done.

CHOCOLATE ICING
3 Tbsps. cocoa
4 Tbsps. margarine
4 Tbsps. milk
6 Tbsps. brown sugar
1 tsp. vanilla
confectioners' sugar

Boil first 4 ingredients for 2 minutes. Add vanilla and confectioners' sugar for spreading consistency.

Grace Nordine.
Favorite Recipes . . .
Mayville
(1982)

CHOCOLATE MINT SQUARES

2 squares unsweetened baking chocolate
$^1/_2$ cup butter
$^3/_4$ cup flour
1 cup sugar
2 eggs, slightly beaten
1 tsp. vanilla

Melt butter and chocolate over low heat. Cool slightly. Mix flour and sugar; stir into chocolate mixture. Add eggs and vanilla, mixing well. Pour into greased 8- or 9-inch square pan. Bake at 350 degrees for 20 minutes. Cool.

MINT CREAM FILLING
$1^1/_2$ cups powdered sugar, sifted
3 Tbsps. butter, softened
2 Tbsps. evaporated milk or heavy cream
$^3/_4$ tsp. peppermint flavoring
green food coloring (desired amount)

Beat ingredients until smooth and spread over cookie layer. Chill until firm and then top with glaze.

CHOCOLATE GLAZE
3 oz. German's sweet chocolate
2 Tbsps. butter
1 (1-inch) piece paraffin wax
1 tsp. vanilla

Melt ingredients together in top of double boiler. Spread mixture over mint cream layer. Chill and cut into 1-inch squares. Makes 16 squares.

Martha J. Kolstee
Bemus Point . . .
(1986-87)

BLONDE BROWNIES

$^1/_3$ cup butter
1 cup flour
$^1/_2$ tsp. baking powder
1 Tbsp. milk
$^1/_2$ cup chopped pecans
1 cup firmly packed brown sugar
1 egg
$^1/_2$ tsp. salt
1 tsp. vanilla

Melt butter in 8" square pan, stir in brown sugar with fork. Remove from heat, add remaining ingredients. Stir until well blended (will be stiff). If desired, sprinkle with $^1/_4$ cup semisweet chocolate bits. Bake at 350 for 30 -35 minutes. Makes 9-12 brownies.

FOR CHOCOLATE CRUNCH TOPPING:
Top hot baked brownies with 4 Tbsps. peanut butter and $^1/_2$ cup semisweet chocolate pieces. Let stand 10 minutes. Spread with $^1/_2$ cup corn flakes, slightly crushed, or Rice Krispies cereal.

Beth Greenbaum
Our Cooking Favorites
(1965-66)

BROWNIES BY THE DOZEN

3 cups margarine
$5^1/_2$ cups sugar
1 tsp. vanilla
12 eggs
3 cups flour
$1^3/_4$ cups cocoa
$2^3/_4$ cups nuts

Beat sugar and margarine until fluffy. Add eggs one at a time, stirring after each one. Add vanilla; sift flour and the cocoa. Add to first mixture. Fold in nuts. Grease and flour two 17 $^1/_2$ x 14-inch cookie sheets with sides. Divide batter in pans. Bake for 35 minutes at 350°. Cool and frost if desired. Each pan makes 4 dozen.

Caroline Peterson
Sugar 'N Spice . . .
(1987)

SPECIAL 3 LAYER BROWNIES

FIRST LAYER

1 cup (2 sticks) butter or margarine, softened
1 (3-oz.) package cream cheese, softened
$1^2/_3$ cups sugar
3 eggs
1 tsp. vanilla extract
1 cup all-purpose flour
$^2/_3$ cup cocoa
$^1/_2$ tsp. salt
$^1/_4$ tsp. baking powder

SECOND LAYER (ALMOND FILLING)

$^1/_2$ cup (1 stick) butter or margarine, softened
2 cups powdered sugar
1 Tbsp. milk
$^1/_2$ cup sliced almonds, toasted
$^1/_2$ tsp. almond extract

THIRD LAYER (FUDGE FROSTING)

6 Tbsps. light cream
$^1/_3$ cup butter or margarine, softened
3 cups powdered sugar
$^2/_3$ cup cocoa
dash of salt
1 tsp. vanilla extract

Heat oven to 325°. Grease bottom of a 13x9" baking pan. In a large mixing bowl, beat butter, cream cheese and sugar until well-blended. Add eggs and vanilla, beat until light and fluffy. Sift together flour, cocoa, baking powder and salt. Gradually add to butter mixture, beating until well-blended. Spread batter into prepared pan. Bake 30 to 35 minutes or until wooden pick inserted in center comes out clean. Cool completely in pan on a wire rack.

To toast almonds spread a thin layer in a shallow baking pan. Bake in a preheated 350° oven for 8 to 10 minutes, stirring occasionally until light golden brown. Cool. In a small mixing bowl, beat butter, powdered sugar and milk until creamy. In food processor or blender, grind almonds. Stir almonds and almond extract into butter mixture. Spread almond filling over brownies, refrigerate.

In a small saucepan, heat cream until bubbles form around the edge of the pan. In a small mixer bowl, beat butter until creamy. Combine powdered sugar, cocoa and salt, add to butter alternately with hot cream, beating to spreading consistency. Stir in vanilla. Spread fudge frosting over top of brownies, let stand until set. Cut into bars. Cover, store in refrigerator. Makes about 36 bars.

Andy Chambers
Here's What's Cooking . . .
(1988)

JEWELED CHEESECAKE BARS

CRUST
$^1/_3$ cup cold butter
$^1/_3$ cup light brown sugar, firmly packed
1 cup flour

FILLING
1 package (8-oz.) cream cheese, softened
$^1/_4$ cup sugar
1 egg
1 Tbsp. lemon juice
$^1/_4$ cup glazed red and green cherries, chopped

Cut butter in chunks, add brown sugar and flour. Mix well at low speed. Reserve $^1/_2$ cup crumb mixture for topping. Press remaining crumb mixture into 8-inch square baking pan. Bake 10 to 12 minutes in preheated 350° oven.

To prepare filling, beat cream cheese, sugar, egg and lemon juice in a mixing bowl. Beat at medium speed until fluffy. Stir in chopped cherries.
Spread filling over crust and sprinkle with remaining crumbs. Continue baking for 18-20 minutes, or until filling is set and top is lightly browned. Cool. Chill and store in refrigerator. Makes 9-12 bars.

Lucille Piper
Chautauqua Motet . . .
(1985)

RASPBERRY MERINGUE BARS

1 cup butter (2 sticks)
$^1/_2$ cup firmly packed brown sugar
1 egg
2 cups flour
1 (12 oz.) jar raspberry preserves
$^1/_2$ cup seedless raisins
$^1/_2$ tsp. almond extract
3 egg whites
$^3/_4$ cup sugar
$^1/_2$ cup flaked coconut
$^1/_2$ cup sliced almonds

Cream butter and brown sugar until light and fluffy. Blend in egg. Stir in flour and mix well. Spread dough in buttered 13x9-inch baking pan. Bake for 25 minutes at 325°.
Combine preserves, raisins and almond extract. Spread over slightly cooled, baked cookie base.
Beat egg whites until foamy. Gradually beat in sugar and continue beating until stiff peaks form. Gently fold in coconut and almonds. Spread over raspberry mixture. Return to oven and bake at 325° until meringue is lightly browned, about 20 minutes. Cool in pan and cut into 48 bars.

Judy Bennett
Cooking by Degrees
(1985)

COCONUT DREAM BARS

$1^1/_2$ cups flour
$^1/_2$ cup brown sugar
$^3/_4$ cup butter or shortening

2 eggs
1 cup brown sugar
3 Tbsps. flour
$^1/_2$ tsp. baking powder
$^1/_4$ tsp. salt
$1^1/_2$ cups coconut
$^1/_2$ cup nut meats

Mix as for pie crust and spread in 9x13" baking pan and bake 15 minutes at 400 degrees.

Mix together and spread on top of first mixture which has been cooled slightly and return to oven for 15 minutes. Cool and cut into squares.

Beryl Mee
Kennedy's Favorite Recipes
(1950)

DATE STICKS

4 eggs, separated
$^1/_4$ cup milk
$1^1/_2$ tsps. baking powder
$1^1/_2$ cups coarsely chopped nuts
$^1/_2$ cup sugar
1 cup flour
1 lb. coarsely chopped dates
1 tsp. vanilla

Beat yolks thoroughly, add sugar and beat well. Add vanilla, and milk, then sifted dry ingredients. Add nuts and dates. Last, fold in stiffly beaten egg whites. Pour into a 9x13-inch pan that is lined with waxed paper. Bake about 30 minutes in a pre-heated 350-degree oven. Cool; while cake is still warm carefully turn upside down and remove paper. Cool. Cut cake into strips and roll in powdered sugar.

Ruth Weinstein
Our Cooking Favorites
(1965-66)

LEMON SOURS

1 cup sifted cake flour
2 Tbsps. sugar
$\frac{1}{8}$ tsp. salt
$\frac{1}{3}$ cup margarine, softened
2 eggs, slightly beaten
1 cup (firmly packed) dark brown sugar
$\frac{1}{2}$ cup chopped pecans
$\frac{1}{2}$ cup grated coconut
$\frac{1}{2}$ tsp. vanilla
GLAZE:
2 cups confectioners' sugar
2 Tbsps. lemon juice
1 tsp. grated lemon rind

Sift flour, sugar and salt into bowl. Cut in margarine until mixture resembles coarse meal. Press firmly in greased 9-inch square pan. Bake at 350° for 15 minutes or until lightly browned. Mix eggs, brown sugar, pecans, coconut, and vanilla. Pour over baked mixture. Bake for 30 minutes or until firm. Cool for 15 minutes.

Combine all glaze ingredients; mix until smooth. Spread over baked mixture.

Carmen Ellsworth
Food for . . .
(1987)

PINEAPPLE SQUARES

CRUST
2$\frac{1}{2}$ cups flour
1 tsp. salt
1 cup shortening
$\frac{1}{2}$ cup milk
FILLING
1$\frac{1}{2}$ cups crushed pineapple, drained
$\frac{1}{2}$ cup pineapple juice
5 Tbsps. instant tapioca
1 cup sugar
ICING
1 cup confectioners' sugar
2 Tbsps. milk
1 tsp. vanilla

Mix crust ingredients with fork. Divide in half and roll between 2 sheets of wax paper. Put half on bottom of 9x13 pan.

Mix filling and pour over crust. Cover with remaining dough. Seal edges. Bake for 30 minutes at 375°.

Mix icing ingredients until smooth and spreadable. Frost squares while still warm. Makes about 24 squares.

Lorraine Miley
Here's What's Cooking . . .
(1988)

SOUR CREAM ORANGE BARS

Cream together:
1 cup sugar
$^1/_2$ cup margarine
Beat in the following:
1 egg
1 Tbsp. orange rind
1 tsp. vanilla
Stir in dry ingredients, alternately with sour cream.
$1^1/_2$ cups flour
$^1/_2$ tsp. baking soda
$^1/_4$ tsp. salt
$^1/_3$ cup sour cream

Add $^1/_3$ cup orange marmalade. Spread in a 9x13-inch greased pan. Sprinkle with 1/2 cup finely chopped nuts. Bake 25-30 minutes at 350°.

Meanwhile, stir together:
3 Tbsps. sugar
3 Tbsps. orange juice

As soon as batter has finished baking, stir sugar and juice again to dissolve sugar and dribble over hot, baked batter. Let cool and cut into bars.

Gladys (Dee) Ogden
Cooking with . . .
Dunkirk
(1972)

SOUR CREAM RHUBARB SQUARES

$^1/_2$ cup white sugar
1 Tbsp. melted butter
$1^1/_2$ cups brown sugar
1 egg
$^1/_2$ tsp. salt
$1^1/_2$ cups raw rhubarb (cubed)
$^1/_2$ cup chopped nuts
1 tsp. cinnamon
$^1/_2$ cup shortening
2 cups flour
1 tsp. baking soda
1 cup sour cream

Mix white sugar, chopped nuts, melted butter and cinnamon together and set aside. Cream shortening, brown sugar, then add egg and stir well. Blend dry ingredients, alternating with sour cream into other mixture. Add cubed rhubarb and then pour into 9x13" pan. Sprinkle top with sugar-nut mixture. Bake at 350° for 45-50 minutes.

Helen Locke
Favorite Recipes
Findley Lake
(1981)

SPICE BARS

3 cups flour
1 tsp. baking powder
1 tsp. baking soda
1 tsp. salt
1 tsp. cinnamon
$^1/_2$ tsp. cloves
$^1/_4$ tsp. allspice
6 Tbsps. shortening
1 cup brown sugar, not packed
2 eggs
1 to 1$^1/_4$ cup hot coffee
$^1/_2$ cup raisins
$^1/_2$ cup nuts

Sift flour, baking powder, soda, salt, spices. Cream shortening and sugar. Add eggs, coffee. Add flour mixture, then raisins, nuts. Spread onto greased cookie sheet with sides and bake at 350° for 15 minutes.

FROSTING
1$^1/_2$ cups packed brown sugar
$^3/_8$ cup milk
6 Tbsps. margarine
1 tsp. vanilla
In pan, mix sugar, milk, margarine. Bring to rolling boil, add vanilla. Cool and beat until thick. Spread on bars.

Ree Evans
Cookbook
Westfield
(1986)

THREE-LAYER COOKIES

LAYER 1
1 cup flour
1/2 cup butter
Mix and pat down on bottom of pan (7x11-1/2).
Bake in 350° oven until light brown (10 min.).

LAYER 2
2 eggs
1 1/2 cups brown sugar
1/4 tsp. baking powder
1 Tbsp. flour
1/2 tsp. salt
1/2 cup nut meats
1/2 cup coconut
Beat eggs. Mix in rest of ingredients. Spread on baked crust and bake again for 20 minutes or less at 325°. Let cool and then cover with layer 3.

LAYER 3
Beat together
1 cup (heaping) powdered sugar
2 Tbsps. melted butter
2 Tbsps. orange juice

Dorothy Beckstrom
Tidbit Tea
(1968)

PIES

PAPER BAG APPLE PIE

1 unbaked 9-inch pastry shell
3 or 4 large baking apples (about $2^1/_2$ lbs.)
$^1/_2$ cup sugar (for filling)
2 Tbsps. flour (for filling)
2 Tbsps. lemon juice
$^1/_2$ tsp. nutmeg
$^1/_2$ cup sugar (for topping)
$^1/_2$ cup flour (for topping)
$^1/_2$ cup (1 stick) butter or margarine

Make an unbaked 9-inch pie shell. Pare, core and quarter apples, then halve each quarter crosswise to make chunks (you should have about 7 cups). Place in large bowl. Make filling. Combine $^1/_2$ cup sugar, 2 Tbsps. flour and nutmeg in cup. Mix. Sprinkle over apples; toss to coat well, spoon into pastry shell, drizzle with lemon juice. Combine $^1/_2$ cup sugar and $^1/_2$ cup flour for topping in small bowl. Cut in butter or margarine. Sprinkle over apples to cover top. Slide pie into a heavy brown paper bag, large enough to cover pie loosely. Fold open end over twice and fasten with paper clips or bobbie pins. Place on large cookie sheet for easy handling. Bake in 425° oven for 1 hour (apples will be tender and top bubbly and golden). Split bag open. Remove pie. Cool on wire rack. Serve plain or with cheese or ice cream. Serves 10.

Gladys Aldrich
Cooking Favorites . . .
Fredonia
(1960s)

APPLE PASTRY SQUARES

$2^1/_2$ cups flour
1 tsp. salt
1 cup plus 2 Tbsps. margarine
1 egg yolk
milk
1 cup crushed corn flakes
8 cups (2 quarts) peeled, sliced apples
$^2/_3$ cup sugar
$^1/_2$ tsp. ground ginger
$^1/_2$ tsp. ground cinnamon
1 egg white, stiffly beaten
GLAZE:
1 cup confectioners' sugar
$^1/_2$ tsp. vanilla
1 to 2 Tbsps. water

Preheat oven to 400°. In large bowl, stir flour and salt together. Cut in margarine until crumbly. Beat egg yolk lightly with fork in measuring cup. Add milk to yolk to make 2/3 cup. Stir into flour mixture. Mix with fork until mixture holds together. Divide dough into 2 parts. Roll $^1/_2$ to line 15x10x1-inch pan. Place in pan to form bottom crust. Sprinkle crust with corn flakes. Combine apples, sugar, ginger and cinnamon in a large bowl. Spread apple mixture over bottom crust. Roll out remaining dough and place over apples. Pinch edges to seal. Brush with egg white. Bake 50 to 60 minutes or until golden brown. Make glaze; frost while slightly warm. Serves a crowd.

Cathy Wojcinski
Berry-Good . . . (1977)

APRICOT COCONUT CREAM PIE

baked pie crust
1 envelope unflavored gelatin
1 cup apricot juice
2 (16-oz.) cans apricot halves, drained
$1/_2$ cup sugar
$1^1/_4$ cups cornstarch
$1^3/_4$ cups milk
1 Tbsp. butter
$1/_2$ cup coconut
$1/_4$ tsp. salt
4 egg yolks, beaten
$1/_2$ tsp. vanilla

TOPPING:
Cool Whip, mixed with 3 Tbsps. melted
  apricot preserves
$1/_2$ cup coconut

In small bowl sprinkle gelatin over $1/_4$ cup apricot juice. Let stand to soften. In larger bowl cut up 1 can of apricots in small pieces. In blender combine remaining apricots and remaining juice and blend until smooth. In medium saucepan combine sugar, cornstarch and salt. Stir in milk and blended apricot mix. Heat to a boil until it begins to thicken, stirring constantly. Remove from heat and blend in small amount of egg yolk, then pour entire contents of the saucepan into the egg yolk mixture, then bring to boil for 2 minutes, stirring constantly. Remove from heat and stir in butter, vanilla and gelatin mixture. Fold in $1/_2$ cup coconut. Refrigerate 30 minutes or until slightly thickened. Fold in apricot pieces and spoon entire mixture into baked pie crust. Cover and refrigerate 45 minutes or until partially set.

Combine Cool Whip and preserves by folding thoroughly and pile on top of pie. Sprinkle with remaining $1/_2$ cup coconut. Refrigerate 3 or 4 hours before serving.

Ellen Johnson
Down Home . . .
(1989)

NEVER-FAIL PIE CRUST

Blend together:
2 cups flour
1 cup shortening*
$1/_2$ tsp. salt
Whip together with fork:
1 Tbsp. vinegar
3 Tbsps. cold water
1 egg

Form a well in flour mixture and add liquid. Mix together and roll out. Makes 2 crusts.
*If using lard, $3/_4$ cup is enough.

Kitty Mistretta
Favorite Hometown . . .
(Date unknown)

BOURBON PIE

5 egg yolks
$^3/_4$ cup sugar
1 envelope unflavored gelatin
$^1/_4$ cup water
$^1/_3$ cup bourbon
2 cups heavy cream, whipped
1 baked 9" pie shell, cooled
1 square unsweetened chocolate, shaved

Beat the egg yolks and gradually add the sugar. Beat constantly until the mixture turns a light yellow. Soften the gelatin in the water and heat over boiling water until gelatin dissolves. Add to the egg yolk mixture and mix well. Add the bourbon, then fold in the whipped cream and pour into the pie shell. Sprinkle with the chocolate shavings and chill for six hours. 6-8 servings.

Lotte Morse
Dames in the Kitchen
(1975)

'49 CHAMPION CHERRY PIE

PIE CRUST
2 cups sifted flour
$^3/_4$ tsp. salt
$^1/_2$ cup vegetable fat
$^1/_4$ cup lard
6-8 Tbsps. water or milk

Sift flour and salt into a bowl. Cut in fat. Add liquid enough to moisten. Collect dough, divide, roll out.

FILLING
$^3/_4$ cup cherry juice
3 cups cherries (drained)
3 Tbsps. cornstarch
$^1/_8$ tsp. salt
1 cup sugar

Make a paste of cornstarch and cherry juice. Add sugar and salt. Boil until thick and clear. Cool and combine with cherries. Arrange in pastry lined pie pan. Dot lightly with butter. Apply top crust. Brush cream on top. Bake at 425° approximately 40 minutes.

Betty Lou Latimer Schwertfager
To the Town's Taste
(1964)

CONCORD GRAPE PIE
WITH CRUMB TOPPING
$3^1/_2$ cups grapes
1 cup sugar
$^1/_4$ cup flour
$^1/_4$ tsp. salt
1 Tbsp. lemon juice
$1^1/_2$ Tbsps. melted butter
8-in. pastry shell (unbaked)

Wash grapes. Slip skins. Cook pulp, strain through sieve to remove seeds. Combine flour, sugar, salt, butter. Add skins, lemon juice, and grape pulp. Pour into pie shell.

Sprinkle crumb topping over pie. Topping: Sift $^3/_4$ cup flour, $^1/_2$ cup sugar. Cut in $^1/_3$ cup butter until crumbly. Bake in hot oven (450°) for 10 minutes. Reduce to 350° and bake 25 minutes more.

Mrs. Bessie Dennison
Kiantone Cookbook
(1969)

COCONUT-SHORTBREAD CHOCOLATE PIE
$^1/_3$ cup butter
2 Tbsps. sugar
1 egg yolk
1 Tbsp. cream
1 cup sifted flour
1 cup shredded coconut, cut fine

FILLING:
$^3/_4$ cup sugar
3 Tbsps. cornstarch
$1^1/_2$ tsp. salt
$2^1/_2$ cups milk
2 squares unsweetened chocolate
3 beaten egg yolks
1 Tbsp. plus 1 tsp. vanilla

Cream butter and sugar. Blend in egg yolk and cream. Add gradually the flour. Blend in coconut. Pat evenly in 9-inch pie pan. Bake at 350° for 20 to 22 minutes. Cool.

In double boiler combine sugar, cornstarch and salt. Blend in milk gradually. Add chocolate. Cook over boiling water, stirring occasionally, until thick. Stir in egg yolks, cook 2 minutes, stirring constantly. Add vanilla and cover and cool. Pour into shell and chill. Top with whipped cream and toasted coconut.

Mrs. Arthur Purol
Sharing Our Best
(1987)

Making Fruit Butter, ca. 1905.

Jack T. Ericson

CITRUS CHIFFON PIE

2 tsps. unflavored gelatin
$^1/_4$ cup cold water
$^1/_3$ cup sugar
$^1/_3$ cup lemon and orange juice (equal parts)
pinch of salt
3 egg yolks
$^1/_2$ tsp. grated lemon rind
$^1/_2$ tsp. grated orange rind
$^1/_4$ cup sugar
3 stiffly beaten egg whites
$^3/_4$ cup heavy cream

Soften gelatin in water. Combine $^1/_3$ cup sugar and fruit juices. Add salt to egg yolks and beat until thick. Add fruit juice mixture; beat well. Cook in double boiler until mixture coats spoon. Remove from heat; add softened gelatin and stir until dissolved. Add grated rinds. Chill until partially set. Slowly beat $^1/_4$ cup sugar into beaten egg whites. Fold into custard and pour into pastry shell. Chill until set. Whip cream, spread over top; sprinkle with orange rind. Makes one 9-inch pie.

Betty Traver
To the Town's Taste
(1964)

LEMON CURD

The juice of a dozen lemons, the grated rind of eight lemons, four pounds of lump sugar, the yolks of two dozen eggs and the whites of sixteen eggs, one pound of butter; put all into a saucepan and stir over a slow fire till it is the consistency of honey. Put into small jars and when cold cover it like jam. Then it is ready to be put into tarts.

Belle Warner
The Parish Cook Book
(1937)

PRIZE PEACH PIE
CRUST:
1$^1/_4$ cups all-purpose flour
$^3/_4$ cups enriched corn meal
$^3/_4$ tsp. salt
$^1/_2$ cup shortening
$^1/_2$ cup cold water

PEACH FILLING:
6 cups fresh peach slices
$^3/_4$ cup sugar
$^1/_3$ cup half & half or light cream
$^1/_4$ cup flour

Combine flour, corn meal and salt. Cut in shortening until mixture resembles coarse crumbs. Add water, a tablespoon at a time, stirring lightly with a fork until mixture forms a ball. Roll half of dough onto lightly floured surface to form a 13-inch circle. Fit loosely into a 9-inch pie plate. Trim. Roll remaining dough to 13-inch circle; cut steam vents.

Combine peaches, sugar, half & half and flour; mix lightly, just until peaches are coated. Spoon mixture into pie crust. Place rolled dough over peach mixture. Trim; flute edges. Bake in pre-heated oven at 400° for 40 minutes or until crust is lightly browned. Serves 8.

Lylla Berndt
Chautauqua-Allegheny Cookbook
(1990)

PIECRUST MIX
(Absolutely foolproof!)
3 cups flour
$^1/_2$ tsp. salt
2$^1/_2$ tsps. sugar
$^1/_8$ tsp. baking soda
1 cup fine quality lard
1 egg
2 Tbsps. lemon juice
2 Tbsps. water

Mix together the flour, salt, sugar and baking soda. Cut in the lard. Mix together the egg, lemon juice and water and cut into flour mixture. This pie dough may be handled without fear and may be frozen beautifully. Makes 2 10" pie crusts or 3 9" crusts. Brush pie crust with beaten egg white and sprinkle with a little sugar before baking for an attractive pie.

Liz Schabel
Dames in the Kitchen
(1975)

PEACH PIE

1 unbaked pie shell
2 Tbsps. butter
3-5 fresh peaches, peeled
1 cup sugar
2 eggs, beaten
2 Tbsps. flour
cinnamon

BLUEBERRY (or Rhubarb) Variation
Use 4 cups blueberries or rhubarb
1 1/2 cups sugar
3 beaten eggs
3/4 tsp. nutmeg instead of cinnamon,
   added to custard mixture.

Dot unbaked pie crust with butter. Slice peaches into crust. Mix well the sugar, beaten eggs and flour. Pour over peaches and sprinkle with cinnamon. Bake at 425° for 15 minutes. Lower heat to 350° and bake another 20-30 minutes or until pie tests done (custard is set and peaches are tender).

Bake at 400° for 50 to 60 minutes.
Lois McGill Pickett
(1970)
Jack Ericson
(1980s)

PEANUT BUTTER PIE

1 cup butter
4 eggs
$1^1/_2$ cups powdered sugar
1 cup peanut butter
$^1/_2$ tsp. vanilla

Beat butter, add sugar and beat. Add eggs, one at a time, and beat. Add peanut butter and beat. Add vanilla and beat. Pour into baked pie shell and chill.
   Garnish with whipped cream, peanuts, or chocolate sauce.
Stanley N. Lundine
Chautauqua Celebrity . . .
(1980)
NOTE: If using raw eggs is a problem, substitute Eggbeaters or equivalent (which are pasteurized and, therefore, safe) in place of raw eggs.

PASTRY

Make pastry in a cool atmosphere and on a cool surface. The quantity of water depends on the quality of the flour, but beware of making it too moist as it will be heavy. Use best pastry flour. If baking powder is used, get in oven as quickly as possible, but with a liberal supply of fat, it improves by being set aside an hour or so before using. The heat of the oven should in most cases be moderate, and the door opened only when absolutely necessary while baking. In baking crusts before putting in filling, prick well to prevent blistering.

SHORT CRUST

1 large cup sifted flour, rub 3 ounces of butter, lard or dripping finely into it, add 1 teaspoonful baking powder, and pinch of salt, then gradually add just enough very cold water to form a moderately stiff paste. Roll out once only and bake in quick oven.

PUFF PASTE

Pass $1/_2$ pound flour through a sieve on to baking board, add a pinch of salt. Cut 5 ounces of butter into pieces 1 inch square, then put all into a basin, making into a stiff paste with a little cold water and a few drops of lemon juice, added gradually. Put a little flour on your board, roll out the pastry, fold in 3, turn the rough edges toward you and roll out again. Roll from you, never from side to side. Continue this for 5 times. This may be used at once, but is better by setting in a cold place 3 times, 20 minutes each time between the rollings. All kinds of puff paste are improved by standing a few hours in a cold place. Bake in quick oven.

Miss Mary Brewer
Sherman Cook Book
(1908)

NEVER WEEP MERINGUE

1 Tbsp. cornstarch
2 Tbsps. cold water
$^1/_3$ cup water
3 egg whites
sprinkle of salt
6 Tbsps. sugar
$^1/_2$ tsp. vanilla

Mix cornstarch with ice cold water. Add remaining water and cook over low heat, stirring constantly, until mixture is thick and clear. Add salt and cool. *Do not chill.* Beat whites with beaters until stiff. Add vanilla. Reduce beater speed and gradually add sugar. Add cornstarch mixture and beat at high speed until well blended. Place over pie, spreading to the edge, and bake in a 400° oven to brown.

Elizabeth Wise
Warm Your Heart . . .
(1987)

OIL PASTRY

(Quick, easy, lower in cholesterol.)
$1^3/_4$ cup unsifted flour
1 tsp. salt
$^1/_2$ cup vegetable oil
3 Tbsps. cold water

Mix flour and salt. With fork stir in oil. Sprinkle with the cold water and mix to a ball. Roll between 2 sheets of waxed paper, wiping counter with a damp cloth to keep paper from slipping. Makes 2-crust 8" or 9" pie (For 1 pie shell, use 1 cup plus 2 Tbsps. flour, 1/2 tsp. salt, 1/3 cup oil and 2 Tbsps. water.)

Flora McMullen
Dames in the Kitchen
(1975)

SOUTHERN PASTRY

2 cups sifted flour
$^1/_2$ tsp. salt
6 Tbsps. ice water
1 cup butter or other shortening

Mix flour and salt; work shortening lightly into flour. Add ice water a tablespoon at a time, using only enough to make a workable paste. (Too little will leave it crumbly.) This pastry, being exceedingly rich, must be handled very deftly.

Roll and line pie plate. Makes 2 (9-inch) pastry shells or pastry for 1 two-crust (9-inch) pie.

Mrs. Robert Barger
What's Cooking I
(1954)

SUNKIST PASTRY PIE CRUST

3 cups sifted flour
1 tsp. salt
1 cup shortening

Cut shortening into flour-salt mixture until crumbly. Add 1 slightly beaten egg combined with 3 tsps. Sunkist lemon juice. Add gradually ice water just enough to blend dough together (about 5 Tbsps.).

Bake in hot oven (475°) 15-20 minutes. Makes three 8-inch pie shells.

Evelyn Krieger
Favorite Hometown . . .
(Date unknown)

SWEET PASTRY

$1^1/_2$ cups flour
1 tsp. baking powder
2 Tbsps. sugar
$^1/_2$ cup shortening
1 egg yolk
4 Tbsps. ice water

Sift dry ingredients together. Add shortening and cut in with pastry blender. Add egg to ice water; beat with a fork, then add to dry ingredients. Knead lightly. Chill in refrigerator before rolling. Makes 1 crust.

Audrey Worden
Warm Your Heart . . .
(1987)

MISCELLANEOUS

As space limitations began to restrict recipe choices, I asked, "Does anyone make pickles any more?" And got a surprising, to me, chorus of response: "I do!" I do!" I do!"

So, back to the choosing of recipes for condiments, relishes, enhancements for the recipes occurring earlier in the book.

The invention or discovery of freezer jam was perhaps the best thing to happen in the century for turning fruits and even vegetables into sweet somethings to go with morning bread or dinnertime meat. The selections in this chapter are the more interesting examples in this category encountered in the cookbooks.

We chose a sampling of pickle recipes which could be made easily by time-pressured cooks while still providing imaginative complements for the dinner plate.

When it came to relishes, the rules for green tomato "Chowder," green tomato Mincemeat, and something called "Club Sauce," appeared in at least half of the cookbooks consulted — testimony, certainly, to their popularity and also to the garden bounty that we in Chautauqua County enjoy.

In this day of salsas (just a more exotic name for "sauce"), some of the old-time, tried and true versions like Raisin Sauce or Mushroom Sauce deserve to be revisited. Also, wonderful hot fudge sauce and Texas Hot Sauce, which is popular, still, with Jamestown Hot Dog vendors and customers.

Finally, sandwiches: We couldn't leave out sandwiches, especially when the cookbooks offered so many interesting and delicious examples.

By the time you reach and peruse this chapter, there will be no doubt that cooking in Chautauqua County, from the tea sandwiches and pickles of Kate Cook's time, to the Salad Sandwiches and Hoisin Marinade of the 1980s, has always been very, very good.

JAMS, CONSERVES, ETC.

OVEN APPLE BUTTER

26 cups applesauce, unsweetened
13$\frac{1}{2}$ cups sugar
6 tsps. cinnamon
3/4 tsp. ground cloves
2 Tbsps. boiled cider (can omit)
$\frac{1}{2}$ cup strong vinegar
Red food coloring

Put all ingredients into large roaster pan and mix well with spoon. Bake at 300° to 325° for 3$\frac{1}{2}$ hours, or until desired thickness. Stir every 15 minutes. Seal in canning jars. Makes about 14 pints.

Teri Ochs
Sts. Peter and...
(1988)

SPICED PEACH BUTTER

4 lbs. peeled peaches, quartered
1 cup water
juice of 1 lemon
$\frac{2}{3}$ cup sugar per cup pulp
2 tsps. cinnamon
$\frac{1}{2}$ tsp. each cloves, allspice

Cook peaches with water until soft, put through food mill, and measure. Add lemon juice, sugar, spices. Cook rapidly until thick and clear, stirring occasionally. Seal in clean, hot jars.

You may also use equal parts peaches and plums. Makes three pints.

Nancy Zastrow
Adventures in Food
(1977)

BARLEY DEW JAM

1 quart raspberries
1 quart cherries
1 quart gooseberries
1 quart currants
sugar

Wash, mash and measure fruit. Add equal amount of sugar. Cook until thick. Put in jelly glasses.

Myrtle Beck
To the Town's Taste
(1964)

FROZEN JAM

3$\frac{1}{2}$ cups mashed strawberries or raspberries
6$\frac{1}{2}$ cups sugar
1 pkg. Sure Jell
1 cup water

Mix strawberries and sugar. Mix and boil Sure Jell and water one minute, stirring constantly. Remove and add berries and sugar. Stir for 5 minutes and let cool. Pour cold mixture into jars or containers and store in freezer. Keep frozen until ready to use. Good for sundaes.

Mrs. Margaret Dorsey
Cook Book I
Frewsburg
(1964)

ZUCCHINI JAM

6 cups grated zucchini
5 cups sugar
$\frac{1}{2}$ cup lemon juice
1 cup crushed pineapple, drained
2 (3 oz.) packages of apricot Jell-o

Cook the first 4 ingredients for 10 minutes after it starts to boil, stirring occasionally. Remove from heat, and add Jell-o. Let stand to cool. Pour into containers, plastic or glass. Freeze.

Cindy Allen
Here's What's Cooking . . .
(1988)

PEACH AND TOMATO PRESERVES

12 peaches, cut up
9 tomatoes, cut up
6 cups sugar
nuts, if desired

Boil until real thick, about 1 hour. Pack and seal hot.

Marge Goldhardt
Adventures in Food
(1977)

PEAR AMBER

4 cups diced Bartlett pears (about 5 pears)
1 large orange
1 (9 oz.) can crushed pineapple, plus juice
$^1/_4$ cup sliced maraschino cherries
6 cups sugar
1 pkg. powdered pectin (3$^1/_2$ oz.)

Prepare glasses or $^1/_2$ pint jars. Measure sugar into dry dish to be used later. Prepare fruits: Wash and peel pears, cut in small pieces. Wash orange, dice or put through food grinder, using whole orange. Add sliced cherries, crushed pineapple and juice. Measure prepared fruits into large kettle. Total amount of fruit should be 6 cups. Add pectin and stir well. Place over highest heat and bring to boil, stirring constantly. Now add measured sugar and mix well. Continue stirring and bring to a full rolling boil. Boil exactly 4 minutes. Remove from heat; let boil subside. Stir and skim by turns for 5 minutes to cool slightly and to prevent floating fruit. Pour into prepared glasses. Seal.

Art/Dunkirk
(1960s)

GRAPE CONSERVE

$^1/_2$ peck grapes
2 oranges (juice and rind)
2 lemons (juice and rind)
1 cup chopped nuts
sugar
$^1/_2$ tsp. salt

Wash grapes before removing skins. Remove skins from pulp. Cook pulp for 10 minutes, then run through food mill to remove seeds. Strain to remove seeds. Put strained pulp in kettle. Extract juice from oranges and lemons. Put rind through the food chopper. Add juice and rind to grape mixture. Cook for 1 hour. Measure and add equal quantity of sugar. Add nuts and salt; pour into glasses and seal while hot.

Marion Mackie
To the Town's Taste
(1964)

Canning Day in Chautauqua County. Carrie Pickett uses the out-of-doors to keep the heat and mess out of her kitchen, ca. 1910.

STRAWBERRY-RHUBARB CONSERVE

2 quarts strawberries
2 quarts rhubarb
12 cups sugar

Cut rhubarb into $1/_2$ inch pieces, being careful not to peel. Mix together strawberries, rhubarb, and sugar. Cook mixture slowly until it is thick and clear. Pour into clean, hot jars and seal at once.

Mrs. C.W. Carlson
Adventures in Food
(1977)

MYSTERY MARMALADE

(Meat accompaniment)
2 cups finely chopped cucumbers
4 cups sugar
$1/_3$ cup lime juice
2 Tbsps. grated lime peel
5-8 drops green food coloring
$1/_2$ bottle liquid fruit pectin

Peel and chop cucumbers; measure into large enamel saucepan. Add sugar, lime juice and lime peel. Place over full flame; add food coloring. Bring to a full rolling boil and boil hard for two minutes, stirring constantly with wooden spoon. Remove from heat; add fruit pectin at once. Skim off foam; continue stirring and skimming for five minutes to cool slightly. (This prevents floating particles.) Ladle quickly into hot sterilized jars. Seal at once. You will know your jars are sealed when the seal becomes concave. Makes about 5 quarter pints.

Connie Swanson
Favorite Hometown...
(Date unknown)

AMBER OR ORANGE MARMALADE

Peel 6 oranges, 3 lemons, 1 grapefruit very thin, rejecting nothing but cores and seeds (cut the fruit in four, then core and seeds are easily taken out). Measure fruit and skin and add three times the quantity of water.
Let stand in an earthen dish over night and next morning boil until skins are tender. Stand another night and the next morning add pint for pint of sugar and boil steadily until it jellies.

Mrs. J.W. Unsworth
English Cookbook
(1911)

CANDIED ORANGE PEEL

4 oranges
$3/_4$ cup water
1 cup sugar
Granulated sugar

Remove peel from oranges in lengthwise sections. Cover with cold water in saucepan. Bring to boiling point, then simmer until soft. Drain. Remove white part with spoon and cut peel in thin strips with scissors. Place sugar, water and peel in saucepan and simmer until clear (230°). Cool on plate and roll in granulated sugar.

Mr. & Mrs. James A. Lord
Favorite Recipes...
Dunkirk
(1978)

PICKLES AND RELISHES

CHOWDER

1 peck green tomatoes, 1 dozen onions, 8 green peppers, 2 red peppers. Chop all together, add 1 cupful salt, let stand overnight, drain. Put in a porcelain kettle with 1 lb. brown sugar, $^1/_2$ teacupful grated horseradish, 1 tsp. ground black pepper, 1 tsp. mustard, 1 tsp.whole white mustard seed, 1 Tbsp. celery seed. Cover with vinegar and boil gently 1 hour. Editor's Note: Does not need to be sealed. Will keep in a crock. Cover and keep in refrigerator.

Mrs. Ernest J. Seaburg
Norden Club
(1930)

SWEDISH DILL PICKLES

Take medium sized cucumbers. Soak in salt water overnight, drain. Arrange layer of cucumbers, then layer of dill and a few pieces of horseradish, to fill a crock. Cover with following: Make a brine, strong enough to float an egg. Add $^1/_4$ cup of alum, $^1/_2$ pkg. mixed spices, 1 cup sugar, $^1/_2$ gal. vinegar. Cover with a weight.

Mrs. Thure Anderson
Norden Club
(1930)

GARLIC DILL PICKLES

Wash and put to soak overnight in cold water the cucumbers, using 1 Tbsp. salt to 1 quart water.
Wash pickles, wipe with cloth. Pack in jar with dill and 4 whole cloves of garlic to the quart.

2 cups salt
4 quarts water
2 quarts vinegar

Heat boiling hot and pour over pickles. Seal. If you use bag salt, with no cornstarch added, pickles will keep better.

Georgia Whitford
Strictly Personal
(Date unknown)

DILL PICKLES MADE INTO SWEET PICKLES

1 quart dill pickles
1$^1/_2$ cups sugar
$^1/_3$ cup vinegar
garlic powder

Drain 1 quart jar of dill pickles, then slice the pickles and put back into the quart jar. In bowl, mix sugar and vinegar and pour over pickles in jar. If liquid doesn't cover the pickles, add a little water. Sprinkle desired amount of garlic powder and shake well. Put in refrigerator and, later on, shake the jar again. You will have to do this a couple of times. Refrigerate.

Evelda Meyer
"Cookin' From...
(1987-88)

EASY REFRIGERATOR PICKLES

6 cups thinly sliced cucumbers, skins on
2 cups thinly sliced onions
1$^1/_2$ cups sugar
1$^1/_2$ cups vinegar
$^1/_2$ tsp. salt
$^1/_2$ tsp. mustard seed
$^1/_2$ tsp. celery seed
$^1/_2$ tsp. turmeric

In a crockery pot or bowl alternate layers of cucumber and onion. In a medium saucepan combine sugar, vinegar and rest of ingredients and boil and stir till sugar dissolves. Pour mixture over cucumbers and onions. Cool slightly. Cover tightly. Refrigerate 24 hours before serving. Store up to 1 month in refrigerator. Makes 7 cups.

Monica Sauer Karsten
Centennial Cook Book
(1987)

WATERMELON RIND PICKLES

6 cups water
9 cups rind
4 cups sugar
$1/_4$ tsp. oil of cinnamon
$1/_4$ tsp. oil of cloves
1 cup white vinegar

Cut green off of the white rind, cut in cubes.

1st day, heat water to boiling, add rind and cook 15 minutes.

Drain well and place rind in a large glass bowl. Boil rest of ingredients and pour over rind. Repeat next 3 days (drain the syrup from the rind into a kettle and bring it to a boil and pour over rind.)

4th day: Drain and boil syrup, add rind. Bring to a boil. Put in jars. Process to seal.

Mary Muench
Fredonia's Hottest...
(1988)

MOCK MINCEMEAT

3 lbs. green tomatoes
3 lbs. apples, chopped
4 lbs. brown sugar
2 lbs. raisins
2 Tbsps. salt
1 cup suet

1 cup vinegar
2 Tbsps. cinnamon
2 tsps. cloves
2 Tbsps. nutmeg
Orange peel, if desired

Chop tomatoes and drain well, measure the juice and discard, add the same amount of water as juice discarded. Bring to a boil, drain off the liquid, measure it again, discard and add same amount of fresh water. Repeat twice this process of adding fresh water, bringing to a boil and draining. (Bring to a boil three times.) Add remaining ingredients of apples, sugar, raisins, salt and suet. Cook until mixture is clear. Add the next ingredients. Cook the mixture for 5 minutes. Process in boiling water bath for 10 minutes.

Carrie Prince
Cooperative Extension Bulletin
Ellicottville
(1975)

PEAR MINCEMEAT

6 lbs. winter pears
3 lbs. light brown sugar
2 lbs. seedless raisins
1 Tbsp. cloves, ground
2 Tbsps. ground cinnamon
1 cup vinegar
2 oranges
1 tsp. salt

Put well washed pears with blossom ends removed and oranges through food chopper. Cook fruit about 10 minutes, then add sugar, spices, vinegar, salt. Cook until mixture thickens, then add raisins and cook until mixture is thick enough for pie. Pour into hot jars and seal. Makes 8 pints.

Miss Celestine Pilkey
Best/Brocton
(1960s)

AUNT VERNA'S WHITE MOUNTAIN PICCALILLI

5 lbs. green tomatoes (3 quarts)
2 large onions, chopped
1 large sweet red pepper, chopped
$^1/_3$ cup salt
3 cups cider vinegar
2 cups white sugar
1 cup light brown sugar
1 tsp. cinnamon
1 tsp. allspice
1 tsp. ground ginger
$^1/_2$ tsp. dry mustard
Pinch of pepper

Wash, remove stems and chop the tomatoes. Put in stone crock or enameled kettle. Add onions, pepper. Add and mix the salt. Let stand overnight. Drain. Mix in large kettle the vinegar, sugars. Tie cinnamon, allspice, ginger, mustard and pepper in small cheesecloth or organdy bag and add to vinegar. Bring to boil and cook 5 minutes to blend spices. Add drained vegetables. Simmer 25 minutes. Discard bag. Can in hot sterilized jars. Seal. Makes 5 pints.

Audrey Dowling
Cookbook
Westfield
(1986)

BEET RELISH
Chop 1 quart cooked beets, 1 quart raw cabbage
Add 1 cup grated horseradish
1 cup sugar
1 tsp. salt
$1/2$ tsp. pepper

Mix very thoroughly and add only enough vinegar to moisten.

Mrs. Wayne Janes
Favorite Recipes I
Ripley
(1965)

SHOE PEG RELISH
1 (12 oz.) can Shoe Peg corn (white), drained
1 (12 oz.) can small peas, washed and drained
1 (No.2, 20 oz.) can French-style greens beans, drained
1 (2 oz.) jar sliced pimientos, drained
1 cup chopped celery
$1/2$ cup chopped green onion
$1/2$ cup chopped green pepper
$1/4$ tsp. salt
$1/4$ tsp. pepper
$1/4$ tsp. garlic powder
1 Tbsp. parsley flakes
$3/4$ cup wine vinegar
$3/4$ cup sugar
$1/2$ cup oil

Combine all ingredients and marinate overnight or as long as 1 week. Pour off excess liquid before serving.

Dina Errico
Soup and Salad . . .
(1989)

SAUERKRAUT RELISH

1 1-lb. can (2 cups) sauerkraut
$1/_3$ cup Italian salad dressing
2 Tbsps. Sugar
1 Tbsp. instant minced onion
1 tsp. caraway seed

Drain and snip sauerkraut. Add salad dressing, sugar, onion and caraway. Refrigerate 4 hours or overnight. Serve over grilled sausages or hot dogs.

Verena Sanner
Euclid Ave. . . .
(1980)

RED SAUCE

30 large ripe tomatoes
4 sweet red peppers
$4^1/_2$ cups vinegar
$2^1/_2$ Tbsps. salt
8 medium sized onions
Boil 1 hour. Add
5 cups sugar

Boil all until thick.

Mrs. Frank Russell
Favorite Recipes I
Ripley
(1965)

SANDWICH SPREAD

1 pint green tomatoes, ground fine. Let come to boil in 1 cup vinegar. Drain and rinse. Grind fine 1 pint carrots, 1 medium onion, 2 red sweet peppers, 6 green peppers, 1 small bottle olives. Add 1/2 tsp. salt, 1/2 tsp. celery salt, $1^1/_2$ cups vinegar. Cook all together with tomatoes for 10 min. Add $1/_2$ jar prepared mustard, 1/3 cup flour to other ingredients; boil 5 minutes. Add 1 pint mayonnaise. Heat through and can. Seal and store.

Editor's Note: This is akin to what is still sold as "sandwich spread" in the stores. Use it as a garnishing spread on meat, fish or vegetable sandwiches, or use it on its own as a sandwich filling.

Mrs. Edna Barber
Favorite Recipes I
Ripley
(1965)

SANDWICHES

HOT SANDWICHES

1. Broiled pineapple slices, sliced hot chicken or turkey on whole wheat bread.
2. Hot roast veal and grilled tomato on rye.
3. Grilled tomato with Cheddar cheese on rye toast.
4. Scrambled eggs with minced ham, dried beef, liver sausage or salmon.
5. Broiled meat loaf with gravy on toast.
6. Broiled hash on toast with cole slaw.
7. Minced chicken livers and giblets with chopped bacon on toast.

To The Town's Taste
(1964)

CUCUMBER SANDWICH

1 medium cucumber
1 tsp. minced onion
mayonnaise
4 hard boiled eggs, chopped
salt
paprika

Pare the cucumber, cut lengthwise, remove seeds, chop cucumber. There should be 1 cup of pulp. Add onion and eggs. Moisten with mayonnaise to spreading consistency. Season to taste. Spread on buttered slices of white bread. Garnish with paprika.

Lavina Wilder
Adventures in Food
(1977)

BARBECUED CHIPPED HAM

2 Tbsps. margarine
1 medium onion, chopped
$^1/_2$ cup celery, chopped
1 piece garlic
$^3/_4$ cup water
1 cup catsup
2 Tbsps. vinegar
2 Tbsps. lemon juice
2 Tbsps. Worcestershire sauce
2 Tbsps. brown sugar
1 tsp. dry mustard
1 tsp. salt
$^1/_4$ tsp. pepper

Melt margarine, add onions and fry until soft. Add remaining ingredients, then add 1 lb. chipped chopped ham.

Terri Larson
Kiantone Cookbook
(1989)

CUCUMBER SANDWICHES

Cucumber, peeled and sliced very thinly
Party rye bread
1 pkg. Good Season's Italian dressing mix
3 Tbsps. mayonnaise
8 oz. cream cheese

Mix dressing mix, mayonnaise and cream cheese. Spread on rye slices, top with cucumber.

David Bills
First Presbyterian
(1986)

ANIMAL CRACKER SANDWICHES

1. Sort out the animal crackers in pairs - two lions, two tigers, two bears, and so on.
2. Put one package of cream cheese in a bowl and grate a little orange rind into it.
3. Add a tablespoonful of cream and mix the cheese with a spoon until it is soft enough to spread.
4. Now for the fun! Spread the flat side of each animal cracker with the cheese.
5. Press each two animal crackers together sandwich fashion and arrange them on a tray or plate.

Even if you don't have a back-yard stand, they would be jolly to make for your next party or just to eat with your supper. Grownups like them too.

From "Children Can Cook"
The Parish Cook Book . . .
(1937)

VITAMIN SANDWICH

One-half cup grated raw carrot, one-half cup chopped raisins, one cup peanut butter. Mix and spread between whole-wheat bread.

Nancy Olmstead
The Parish Cookbook . . .
(1937)

BOYS' HIKING SANDWICHES

Mash cold baked beans to a paste, season with tomato catsup or prepared horseradish. Add enough finely chopped onion to flavor to taste and moisten with mayonnaise. Use as filling between medium thin slices of rye bread that has been spread lightly with prepared mustard. Wrap each sandwich in waxed paper and wrap with it a dill pickle or deviled egg. This sandwich is original with Mrs. Anderson. Its title is highly descriptive. We feel there is no doubt that you boys would not like it at all if we failed to place it with the recipes you will most quickly turn to. We also have a feeling that your sisters will more than once borrow the idea for their own food needs on hike or picnic.

Grace V. Anderson
The Parish Cook Book . . .
(1937)

HAM SALAD

Mince fine some cold boiled ham, add twice its bulk of celery, lettuce or cabbage, prepared the same as for chicken salad. Put in saucepan one small cup vinegar, one coffee cup thick sour cream free from milk, a piece of butter the size of a hickory nut, or a piece of fat boiled from the ham, of the same size, one teaspoon sugar, a little salt, one even teaspoon black pepper, or, if too much, use less; mix a small tablespoon of mustard smooth with a little cold water; add the yolks of two eggs, well beaten; stir this carefully into the cream and vinegar; stir until as thick as starch; do not let boil, as it will curdle. Take from the stove, set in cold water or on ice. When cold, pour over the salad, and mix well.

Kate Cook
Chautauqua Cook Book
(1882)

"HAM" SALAD

Grind in a food grinder or food processor 1 pound bologna. Run 1 medium onion through the grinder after the bologna. Add 1 cup diced celery, 1/2 cup sweet pickle relish or chopped dill pickle (it's good both ways), and enough mayonnaise to bind the mixture together and make it spreadable. Chill to blend flavors, then use as a sandwich filling on your favorite bread.

VARIATION: Add 2 cups ground or shredded Cheddar cheese to mixture. Generously fill hamburger buns. Wrap buns in foil and heat in a 350° oven for 20 minutes. Makes a wonderful and easy hot sandwich for a party or a picnic.

Joanne Schweik
"The Artful Kitchen"
(1980s)

CRAB DEVONSHIRE

1 lb. crabmeat
$^1/_2$ tsp. salt
$^1/_2$ tsp. dry mustard
dash Worcestershire sauce
$^1/_4$ tsp. Accent
3 Tbsps. butter
5 to 6 slices toast
Devonshire sauce (2 cups White Sauce, seasoned with 1/2 tsp. salt, 1/2 tsp. dry mustard, 1/4 tsp. poultry seasoning, and 1/2 cup shredded sharp Cheddar Cheese)

Pick over crabmeat to remove all cartilage and flake. Combine crabmeat and seasonings. Melt butter in pan, add crabmeat. Cook over low heat until heated through. Spread on toast. Place on heat proof platter or plate. Cover with Devonshire Sauce. Sprinkle with Parmesan cheese and paprika mixture. Bake at 350° for 10 minutes. Yields: 5 to 6 sandwiches

Mrs. Frank Campbell
What's Cooking I
(1954)

CUCUMBER SHRIMP SANDWICH SPREAD

$^1/_2$ cup finely chopped unpeeled cucumbers
1 tsp. chopped olives
1 tsp. mayonnaise
1 can shrimp cleaned and minced
1 Tbsp. French dressing

Make open sandwiches of thinly sliced bread cut in fancy shapes.

Margaret Gailewicz
To the Town's Taste
(1964)

BUMSTEADS

Chop finely:
2 Tbsps. green pepper
2 Tbsps. stuffed olives
2 Tbsps. onions
2 Tbsps. sweet pickle relish
Dice:
3 hard-boiled eggs
$^1/_4$ lb. American cheese
Add: $^1/_2$ cup mayonnaise, 1 can tuna fish.

Mix all ingredients. Fill hot dog rolls, wrap in foil and bake for about 20 min. at 350°.

Mrs. Joan Spontaneo
Kiantone Cookbook
(1969)

A VISIT WITH A NEW OLD FRIEND

Peanuts are not a product of the Chautauqua-Allegheny region of New York State, but peanut butter and grape jelly are. Concord grape jelly is world-famous, made in New York, of course. And a few years back, peanut butter from the Red Wing Company in Fredonia made world news, so to speak, when William Buckley testified to his love for it in an autobiographical essay published in *The New Yorker*. It was with considerable interest, therefore, that we re-discovered the following 20 "Different Ways to Make a Peanut Butter Sandwich," originally printed in the 1964-65 Jamestown Jayncees Cookbook. No credit is given in the original, so whoever was the imaginative cook remains a mystery. But the sandwiches are still good— and good for us in this too-cholesterol-conscious age.

1. Peanut butter and bacon
2. Peanut butter and mustard
3. Peanut butter and mayonnaise (Lite, that is)
4. Peanut butter and marshmallow creme
5. Peanut butter and dill pickle (Editor's choice)
6. Peanut butter and jelly
7. Peanut butter and cheese
8. Peanut butter and raisins
9. Peanut butter and green pepper
10. Peanut butter and celery
11. Peanut butter and banana
12. Peanut butter and luncheon meats
13. Peanut butter, cold cuts and cheese
14. Peanut butter and Cheese Whiz
15. Peanut butter and sandwich spread
16. Peanut butter and sardines
17. Peanut butter, lettuce and tomato
18. Peanut butter mixed with light corn syrup
19. Peanut butter mixed with jam
20. Toasted peanut butter and jelly

And we'll add:
21. Peanut butter and chicken or turkey, a la an Indonesian Satay

Chautauqua-Allegheny...
(1990)

A FEW RULES FOR SANDWICHES

Bread for sandwiches should be at least 24 hours old.
Cream butter before spreading.
Do not have filling too moist.
If sandwiches are not to be used immediately, wrap in damp cloth and place in cool place.
Cook Book IV, Jamestown   (1920s)

282

PARTY SANDWICHES

1 (8 oz.) pkg. cream cheese
$^1/_4$ cup chopped green pepper
$^3/_4$ cup chopped walnuts, toasted, if desired
$^1/_4$ cup chopped onion
3 Tbsps. chopped pimiento
3 hard cooked eggs, chopped
1 Tbsp. catsup
$^3/_4$ Tbsp. salt
Dash of pepper

Remove crusts from thin slices of bread. Spread generously with mixture and cut into triangles or any desired shape.

Susie Glutch
St. Peter's....
(1979)

OLIVE FILLING

1 cup ground cucumber pickles, $^1/_2$ cup stuffed olives (ground), 2 hard cooked eggs (ground), mix with mayonnaise and spread on bread.

Mrs. C.G. Anderson
Home Bureau
(1929)

DELICIOUS SANDWICHES

2 heads of crisp celery, chopped very fine. Set away to become very cold. Add $^1/_2$ cup of grated cheese; $^1/_2$ cup of cream, after being whipped stiff. Very good.
These are particularly appetizing for traveling lunches, as they keep moist so long.

Mrs. Seldon E. Stone
The Fredonia Cook Book
(1899)

PIMIENTO SANDWICHES

Take sweet red bell peppers fully ripe, place them in the stove on a tin plate until they are slightly brown, or at least the skin will slip off. Peel them and take out the seed and ribs, mash them to a pulp, grate a big slice of cheese and add to the pepper with a little salt and butter. Cut thin slices of light bread. Spread the pimiento and cheese, after you have buttered your bread, over the piece of bread and cover with another piece of bread, with a fresh lettuce leaf between. I am sure you will like it.

Parish Cook Book
(1937)

NUT SANDWICHES

Mix equal parts of grated Swiss cheese and chopped English walnut meat, season with salt and cayenne, spread between thin slices of bread slightly buttered and cut in fancy shapes.

Sweets and Meats
(1917)

MARY PICKFORD SANDWICH

Wash one-half cup apricots and cook over low flame until soft. Force through a sieve, sweeten to taste with honey and cook to a thick jam. Cool. Put one-fourth cup preserved ginger and one-fourth cup English walnuts through food chopper, using the medium blade. Combine the two mixtures. Spread lightly between thin slices of bread. Cut off crusts. Good with afternoon tea.

Mrs. J.L. Oakes
Parish Cook Book . . .
(1937)

BETTY'S FAVORITE SANDWICH

Remove stones from dates and large prunes. Have an equal weight of dates, prunes and figs. Pass through meat chopper. For each cup add one-half cup finely chopped English walnut meats. Moisten with orange marmalade. Use as filling between thinly sliced and buttered steamed brown bread. Cut in small triangles and serve with cocoa or five o'clock tea.

TWO-TONED FANCIES

Spread rounds of brown bread with butter creamed with French Mustard. Spread rounds of white bread, cut to fit the former, with butter and nippy cheese creamed together. Press together in pairs and serve with coffee.

Grace V. Anderson
Parish Cookbook . . .
(1937)

A DELICIOUS SANDWICH

2 cups cold cooked beef, 8 or 10 pimientos, 2 Tbsps. mayonnaise, $1/_2$ tsp. salt. Run beef and pimientos thru meat grinder, using medium grinder. Add salt, mayonnaise and mix thoroughly. Spread between slices of white and graham bread.

MEXICAN OR DENVER SANDWICHES (DELICIOUS)

Put in a skillet one onion and 1 green pepper chopped fine, and brown, add 1 lb. chopped ham, fry just a little. Then add 3 beaten eggs and scramble. Serve between hot bread, lettuce and mayonnaise on 1 slice and hot filling on the other slice. Cut into halves. Green peppers may be omitted.

Mrs. Arthur Gill
Newland Ave. . . .
(1926)

SALAD SANDWICHES

For each sandwich: Spread one slice of whole wheat bread with cream cheese, then thinly with cottage cheese.
Top with thinly-sliced tomato and avocado, or asparagus spears (cooked or canned) and leaf lettuce.
Top with a second slice of whole wheat bread, spread with blue cheese dressing.

Florence Clark McClelland
Cooking by Degrees
(1985-86)

SAUCES

BARBECUE SAUCE (CHICKEN)

1 egg
1 cup cooking oil
2 cups cider vinegar
3 Tbsps. salt
1 Tbsp. poultry seasoning
1 tsp. pepper
1 tsp. oregano
1 tsp. sage
1 tsp. garlic salt
1 tsp. parsley flakes

Beat egg, add oil and beat again. Add all other ingredients and beat again. Brush on chicken and turn every 15 minutes. (This is enough sauce for 8 to 10 chicken halves). Cook about 2 hours at medium heat on grill. (This is the famous Cornell chicken barbecue sauce found in many cookbooks. Ms. Newhouse, however, has added oregano, sage and garlic salt to the original ingredients. This is also good on pork.)

Betty Newhouse
Favorite Recipes . . .
Mayville
(1982)

BASIC WHITE (CREAM) SAUCE

To make 2 cups of medium white sauce:
3 Tbsps. butter or margarine
3 Tbsps. White flour
2 cups milk
salt and pepper to taste

Melt the butter over medium heat in a heavy saucepan. Add the flour, stir with a whisk until well-blended with the butter and cook for five minutes or so until the mixture bubbles and becomes fragrant. Slowly add the milk to the pan, stirring all the while with a whisk. Continue to heat, whisking frequently, until mixture bubbles and has thickened. Keep warm over hot water (in a double boiler), stirring occasionally, or add immediately to the ingredients you wish to sauce.

Note: This is the basic Bechamel sauce. If made with broth or broth and wine, instead of milk, it is called Veloute sauce. $^1/_2$ cup grated cheese (Cheddar, Swiss or Parmesan) added turns it into a cheese sauce, such as might be used to sauce vegetables.

BROWN SAUCE WITH MUSHROOMS

$^1/_4$ lb. of bacon
1 Tbsp. flour
1 Tbsp. Worcestershire sauce
$^1/_2$ pint stock
1 Tbsp. mushroom catsup
1 Tbsp. sherry
Salt and pepper to taste.
1 cup fresh or canned mushrooms, chopped

Slice the bacon, put in frying pan and try out all the fat. Take out the bacon, add flour and stir until smooth. Add the stock; stir continually till it boils. Then add the Worcestershire sauce, mushroom catsup, salt, pepper and the mushrooms. When mushrooms are thoroughly heated, take from the fire and add the sherry. If the mushrooms are fresh, cook first in a little butter, stirring all the time.

Mrs. Barrett-Howard
The Fredonia Cook Book
(1899)

CRÈME FRAÎCHE

1 cup heavy cream
2 Tbsps. buttermilk or plain yogurt

Combine cream and buttermilk or yogurt in a pint jar with a cover. Shake vigorously for two minutes. Allow to stand at room temperature with the cover ajar 8 hours or overnight. Shake once or twice, cover loosely and store in the refrigerator. Keeps 4 to 6 weeks refrigerated. Serve on a dish of fresh fruit, on a wedge of pie or as a simple sauce on a freshly cooked vegetable.

Elaine Laughlin
Goodbye Dining Hall . . . (1982)

CLUB SAUCE

10 medium tomatoes, peeled and quartered
1 tsp. salt
$2^1/_2$ cups sugar
2 cups vinegar
5 sweet red peppers
2-3 medium onions
1 hot red pepper (if hot sauce is desired)

In pan, boil tomatoes, salt, sugar and vinegar for 1 hour. If too juicy, continue cooking a little longer. Grind peppers and onions; add to tomato mixture and cook for 20 minutes longer. Seal in freshly cleaned jars. (*Note:* A version of this sauce appeared in many of the cookbooks consulted.)

Alice Gundlach
From Our Kitchen . . .
(1986)

MAGIC CHOCOLATE SAUCE

1 can (14 oz.) sweetened condensed milk
2 (1 oz.) squares unsweetened chocolate
1/8 tsp. salt
$^1/_2$ to 1 cup hot water
$^1/_2$ tsp. vanilla extract

In top of double boiler, put condensed milk, chocolate and salt. Cook over rapidly boiling water, stirring often, until thickened. Remove from heat. Slowly stir in hot water until sauce is of desired thickness (be careful to add slowly; usually for a thick sauce, it only takes $^1/_2$ cup at most). Stir in vanilla extract. Serve hot or chilled.

Debbie Johnson
Our Country . . . (1980s)

HOISIN AND GINGER MARINADE
for flank steak, round steak, pork chops or steak, ribs, chicken wings, drumsticks or thighs

In a covered jar, combine and shake to mix:
2 Tbsps. hoisin sauce
$^1/_4$ cup soy sauce
$^1/_4$ cup honey
$^1/_4$ cup sherry or whiskey
1 Tbsp. minced ginger root
2 Tbsps. sesame seeds
1 Tbsp. sesame oil
1 tsp. garlic powder <u>or</u>
3 minced garlic cloves

Put the meat in a double plastic food bag and add the marinade. Squeeze out most of the air, twist-tie and put in a dish or pan (in case of leaks) and refrigerate several hours or overnight.

If you're cooking beef or pork chops or steak, broil indoors or grill outdoors. Baste with the marinade.

If you're cooking pork ribs, chicken parts, etc., bake at 350°-375° in a flat baking dish or pan until cooked thoroughly and brown, basting often.

Elaine Laughlin
Goodbye Dining Hall . . .
(1982)

CREAMED MUSHROOM SAUCE
Slice 2 lbs. mushrooms and sauté in 4 Tbsps. of butter. Sprinkle with 4 Tbsps. flour. Stir in gradually 2 cups of rich milk/cream. Permit sauce to boil and season with salt, paprika and a pinch of herbs (marjoram or parsley).

Kris Beal
Dames in the Kitchen
(1975)

PEPPER SAUCE
1 dozen red peppers, 1 dozen green peppers, 15 onions. Chop peppers and put boiling water over them. Drain and cover with cold water. Bring to a boil and drain again. Add 1 quart vinegar and onions, $1^1/_2$ cups sugar and $1^1/_2$ Tbsps. salt. Cook down until like preserves.

Mrs. Emily E. Sellstrom
Norden Club . . .
(1930)

NANA'S FRUIT SALAD DRESSING

(Good on any salad)
1 medium onion
$^1/_2$ cup sugar
1 cup oil
$^1/_2$ cup cider vinegar
1 tsp. salt
1 tsp. celery salt
1 tsp. dry mustard
1 tsp. "Salad herbs" by Durkee or Spice Islands

In a food procesor with a steel blade, mince the onion. Add rest of ingredients and blend until creamy.
To make by hand, mince onion; put all ingredients in a jar and shake. It will not be as creamy or smooth.

Jane D. Kidder
Butter and Love I . . .
(1984)

PIZZA SAUCE

2 green peppers
1 hot pepper
2 medium onions
2 cloves garlic
2 cups salad oil
$^1/_2$ bushel plum tomatoes
4 (12 oz.) cans tomato paste
$1^1/_2$ cups sugar
$1^1/_2$ Tbsps. Italian seasoning
$^1/_4$ cup salt

Combine first 5 ingredients; cook for $^1/_2$ hour. Mix all ingredients; cook 3 hours or until desired thickness. Cool and freeze in one-meal containers.

Linda Lawrence
Our Country....
(1980s)

RAISIN SAUCE

1 cup apple juice
$^1/_2$ cup raisins
1 tsp. lemon juice
3 Tbsps. brown sugar
1 Tbsp. cornstarch
$^1/_4$ tsp. salt
$^1/_4$ tsp. ground cloves
$^1/_8$ tsp. cinnamon
Few grains of nutmeg

Put all ingredients into a saucepan. Bring to a boil over moderate heat, stirring constantly, until sauce thickens. Spoon warm sauce over sliced ham or pork.

Barbara Whitehead
Warm Your Heart...
(1987)

TEXAS HOT SAUCE

4 Tbsps. oil
$^1/_2$ lb. ground pork and beef
3 diced all-meat skinless weiners
1 medium onion, chopped
2 cloves garlic, chopped
$^1/_2$ tsp. Kitchen Bouquet or Maggi seasoning
$^1/_2$ tsp. Gravymaster seasoning
1 tsp. black pepper
1 Tbsp. and 1 tsp. salt, or to taste
1 can tomato paste
10 cups water
3 tsps. paprika
2 tsps. chili powder
4 tsps. cinnamon
$1^1/_2$ cups fine dry bread crumbs

Brown onion and garlic in oil in a large pot. Add ground beef and pork, chopped weiners, and brown them, mashing well into a crumbly mixture. Add next 6 ingredients. (Two more cups of water can be added if additional volume is wanted without a major effect on flavor.) Simmer one hour.

Add spices; simmer 10 min. Let cool. Add bread crumbs to thicken. Use of a portable mixer helps take out any lumps.

Makes 1 gallon.

Jim Mohney
Adventures in Food
(1977)

A SAUCE FOR OVER RICE

1 can cream of chicken or mushroom soup
$1/_2$ cup light cream, evaporated milk, or milk
$1/_2$ cup apple or orange juice
1 tsp. curry powder
1 tsp. Worcestershire sauce
$1/_4$ tsp. seasoned salt
1 (6 oz.) can sliced mushrooms, drained
1 can pineapple tidbits
$1/_2$ cup green grapes (optional)

Mix all ingredients together in a medium saucepan.
Heat and serve over rice.
We love to serve this with chicken.

Joyce Blakeslee
Food For . . .
(1987)

TOMATO SAUCE, MARINARA STYLE

$1/_2$ medium onion, chopped
1 clove garlic
2 Tbsps. oil
1 small carrot, grated
2 Tbsps. green pepper, chopped
1 bay leaf
$1/_2$ tsp. thyme
1 tsp. oregano
$1/_4$ tsp. basil
2 Tbsps. chopped fresh parsley
2 cups tomatoes, fresh or canned
1 (6 oz.) can tomato paste
1 tsp. salt
$1/_4$ tsp. brown sugar
$1/_8$ tsp. pepper

Sauté onion and garlic clove in oil until onion is soft.
Discard garlic. Add carrot, green pepper, bay leaf, and
herbs. Stir well, then add tomatoes, tomato paste and
seasonings. Simmer $1/_2$ hour. Remove bay leaf.
Makes about 2 cups.

Excellent for pizza; thin down a little for spaghetti.

Valery Thaden
Centennial Cookbook
(1987)

BIBLIOGRAPHY

NOTE: C1-C128   numbered cookbooks housed in Archives, Reed Library, State University College, Fredonia, NY.

             F1-F29   owned and loaned by Carmela Frame, Fredonia, NY.

             M1-M4   owned and loaned by Ruth Mohney, Fredonia, NY.

             U1-U25, U27   unnumbered (some cataloged) cookbooks housed in Archives, Reed Library, State University College, Fredonia, NY.

             U26   owned and loaned by Marty Hegner, Dunkirk, NY.

Note also: The Roman numerals in parentheses following some of the numbers are for those cases where more than one cookbook has the same title. The numerals indicate which title (I, II, etc.) belongs to which book.

C1   *Our Cooking Favorites*. Compiled by the Sisterhood of Temple Hesed Abraham, Jamestown, NY (1965-66).

C2   *The New World of Welch's*. Introductory page signed "Office of the President, Welch Foods, Inc." (n.d.).

C3(I)   *Cook Book: Favorite Recipes from our Best Cooks*. Compiled by St. Paul's Episcopal Churchwomen, Mayville, N.Y. (Circulation Service, Shawnee Mission, Kansas, 1981).

C4   *The Chautauqua Motet Choir Presents a Medley of Party Favorites*. (Chautauqua, NY, 1985).

C5   *Cooking by Degrees*. American Association of University Women, Dunkirk-Fredonia Branch. (1985-86).

C6   *Pioneer Homemakers Cookbook*. Busti Historical Society. (1987). (Second edition of first book published in 1975).

C7   *Our Country Cookbook*. Compiled by Edwards Chapel United Methodist Church Women, Clymer, NY. (Walters Publishing Company, Waseca, MN, n.d.).

C8   *Bemus Point Cookbook*. Bemus Point P.T.A. (Fundcraft Publishing, Inc., Collierville, TN, 1986-87) .

C9   *Cooking with John W. Rogers Auxiliary #327*. Westfield, NY. (Women's Clubs Publishing Co., Inc., Chicago, IL, 1987) (See U25).

C10   *Food for My Household*. Findley Lake United Methodist Church. (Cookbook Publishers, Inc., Olathe, KS, 1987).

C11(I) *Treasured Recipes*. Relief Society of the Church of Jesus Christ of Latter Day Saints. (Fundcraft Publishing, Inc., 1988).

C12   *Warm Your Heart, Fill Your Tummy*. Sylvan Chapter No. 258, O.E.S. (Cookbook Publishers, Inc., 1987).

C13   *Sharing Our Best*. St. Hedwig's Ladies Society, St. Hedwig's Church, Dunkirk, NY. (Fundcraft Publishing, 1987).

C14   Schweik, Joanne L. *The Artful Kitchen*. Fredonia, NY, 1987.

C15   *Sugar 'N Spice Cookbook*. Bethel Baptist Christian Academy, Jamestown, NY, (1987).

C16   *Chautauqua Local 807 C.S.E.A. Cookbook and 1948-1988 History*. (1988).

C17   *Berry-good Recipes*. The Families and Friends of St. Elizabeth Ann Seton School, Dunkirk, NY. (Fundcraft Publishing, Inc., 1977).

C18   *JCC Alumni Cookbook*. JCC Alumni Board of Directors, (n.d.).

C19   *"Cookin' From Scratch"*. Elementary School Four PTO, Dunkirk, NY. (Fundcraft Publishing, Inc., 1987-88).

C20   *Fredonia's Hottest Recipes*. Fredonia Fire Dept. Ladies Auxiliary. (Circulation Service, Inc., Leawood, KS, 1988).

C21   *Our Daily Bread.* Holy Trinity Women's Guild, Dunkirk, NY. (Fundcraft Publishing, Inc., 1988).

C22   *Sts. Peter & Paul Family Cookbook*, Jamestown, NY. (G & R Publishing Co, Waverly, IA, 1988).

C22a   Same, but under different title, *Here's What's Cooking at Our House.*

C23   *Down Home Cooking.* Brocton-Portland Civic Association. (Fundcraft Publishing, Inc., 1989).

C24   *Home Made Cooking Good 'Nuff for Sharing.* Friends & Neighbors of Open Meadows Methodist Church, Ashville, NY. (Circulation Service, Inc., n.d.).

C25   *Stockton Community Church, Awana Clubs #5128 Cookbook.* Stockton, NY. (Women's Clubs Publishing Co., Inc., n.d.).

C26   *Kiantone Cookbook.* Kiantone Ladies Aid, Kiantone Congregational Church, Jamestown, NY. (Walter's Cookbooks, Waseca, MN, 1989).

C27   *Culinary Delights.* A Collection of Favorite Recipes from the families and friends of Bethel Baptist Christian Academy, Jamestown, NY. (Morris Press, Kearney, NE, 1988-89).

C28   *The Dunkirk Irish Society Presents "Favorite Recipes".* (Fundcraft Publishing, Inc., n.d.) .

C29   *Home Town Recipes.* Collected by the Daughters, Historical Society of Dunkirk, NY. (Women's Clubs Publishing Co., Inc., 1989) .

C30   *All You Can Eat.* A Collection of favored recipes from the families and friends of Chautauqua Day Care Project. (Arkwright Printing, Arkwright, NY, 1983).

C31   *Dayton Delights.* Town of Dayton Historical Society, Dayton, NY. (Cookbook Publishers, Olathe, KS, 1990).

C32   *Newland Avenue Parent-Teachers Association Cook Book.* (Jamestown, NY, 1926).

C33   *Falconer Home Bureau Unit Cook Book.* (Falconer, NY, 1929).

C34   *Choice Recipes Compiled for the Ladies' Aid Society.* Methodist Church. (Bemus Point, NY, n.d.).

C35   *Norden Club Ladies Auxiliary Cook Book.* (Jamestown, NY, 1930).

C36   *The Lutheran Cook Book.* Published for the Benefit of the Proposed Lutheran Home for the Aged. (Jamestown, NY, 1929).

C37   *From Our Kitchen to Your Kitchen.* Chautauqua County Women's Federated Republican Club. (Fundcraft Publishing, Inc., 1986).

C38   Davison, A.W., *Davison's Little Candy Maker.* (Jamestown Publishing Company, Jamestown, NY, n.d.).

C39   *Tried and True Recipes.* The Nursery Mothers of the First Baptist Church. (Jamestown, NY, n.d.).

C40(I)   *What's Cooking.* Compiled by the January Group World Service Guild of the First Presbyterian Church, Jamestown, NY. (North American Press, Kansas City, MO, 1954).

C41(II)   *What's Cooking?* Charles Street P.T.A. (Jamestown, NY, 1966).

C42(I)   *Butter 'n Love Recipes.* Washington Elementary Parents and Teachers, Jamestown, NY. (Fundcraft Publishing, Inc., 1984).

C43   *Strictly Personal: The Family Book.* Lady of the Lake Rebekah Lodge No. 450, Lakewood, NY. (Continental Publishing Company, Mission, KS, n.d.).

C44   *The Euclid Ave. Family Cookbook.* Euclid Elementary School P.T.A. (Jamestown, NY, 1980).

C45   *Soup and Salad Cookbook.* Bemus Point Study Club. (Fundcraft Publishing, Inc., 1989).

C46   *Chautauqua-Allegheny Cookbook.* Chautauqua County Vacationlands Association, Mayville, NY. (Long and Holbrook Printers, 1990).

C47   *Delectable Collectables.* The Fed-Ettes. Busti Federated Church. (Jamestown, NY, 1970).

C48   *Kennedy's Favorite Recipes.* Ladies Auxiliary of Kennedy Fire Company, Kennedy, NY. (Bev-Ron Publishing Co., Kansas City, MO, 1950).

C49   *Old-Fashioned Cook Book*. Cherry Creek Mother's Club. (n.d.).

C50(I) *Favorite Recipes*. Women's Society of Christian Service, Ripley Methodist Church. (Ripley, NY, 1965).

C51(II) *Treasured Recipes*. Chautauqua County Chapter, NY State Association for Retarded Children, Inc. (Gateway Publishing Co., Ltd., Winnepeg, CA, n.d.).

C52   *Dames in the Kitchen*. Faculty Dames, State University College at Fredonia. (Fredonia, NY, 1975).

C53(I) *Cook Book*. Cowan Service Guild, Frewsburg Methodist Church. (Frewsburg, NY, 1964).

C54   *Cooking Favorites of Dunkirk*. Our Lady of Sorrows Society, Dunkirk, NY. (Women's Club Publishing Co., Inc., n.d.).

C55   *The Art of Cooking in Brocton*. Brocton Fire Dept. Auxiliary. (Women's Club Publishing Co., Inc., n.d.).

C56   *The Art of Cooking in Dunkirk*. Fraternal Order of Eagles Auxiliary, Dunkirk, NY. (Women's Club Publishing Co., Inc., n.d.).

C57(II) *Cookbook*. Spirit Lifters Circle of United Methodist Church, Brocton, NY. (Circulation Service, Kansas City, MO, 1974).

C58   *Tidbit Tea*. Evening Circle, First Covenant Church. (Jamestown, NY, 1968. Reprinted in 1972).

C59   (Duplicate of C40).

C60   *The Best in Cooking in Brocton*. The Brocton Guild. (Brocton, NY, n.d.).

C61   *Cooking Favorites of Fredonia*. Golden Sceptre Rebekah Lodge #184. (Fredonia, NY, n.d.).

C62   *First United Presbyterian Church, Dunkirk, NY.* (Women's Clubs Publishing Co., Inc., 1978).

C63   *Home Cooking Secrets of Forestville*. St. Rose of Lima Christian Mothers Altar Rosary Society, Forestville, NY. (Women's Clubs Publishing Co., Inc., n.d.).

C64(IV) *What's Cookin' In Forestville, NY*. J. Carter Knapp Unit No. 953 American Legion Auxiliary. (Forestville, NY, 1965).

C65   *Cooking Favorites of Arkwright*. Arkwright Grange No. 1249, Arkwright, NY. (Women's Clubs Publishing Co., Inc., n.d.).

C66   *Kiantone Cookbook*, Second Edition. The Kiantone Ladies Aid and Missionary Society, Kiantone Congregational Church. (1969).

C67   *Wonderful Cooking from the Auxiliary* (and prized recipes from local men). (Jamestown, NY, n.d.).

C68   *Victory Cook Book*. Women's Society of Christian Service of the Methodist Church. (Jamestown, NY, n.d.).

C69   *Bigelow's Katherine Kay Cook Book*. (Jamestown, NY, 1946).

C70   *Come Out of the Kitchen and Vote!*. Sponsored by the Republican Women of Chautauqua County. (n.d.).

C71   *To The Town's Taste*. The Women's Association of the First Presbyterian Church, Fredonia, NY. (The Fredonia Censor, n.d).

C72   *"The Best in Cooking" in Fredonia*. Women's Auxiliary, Trinity Episcopal Church. (Fredonia, NY, n.d.).

C73   *Pilgrim's Treasure of Personal Recipes*. Compiled by the Women's Guild of Pilgrim Memorial Congregational Church, Jamestown, NY. (Bev-Ron Publishing Co., Kansas City, MO, 1952).

C74   *Crèche Cooks*. The Crèche, Inc., Jamestown, NY. (Calico Kitchen Press, Hartwell, GA, 1986).

C75(III) *What's Cookin'*. Jamestown Jaycees. (1964-65).

C76   *Jamestown's Own International Cook Book*. The Young Adult Civic Council, Jamestown, NY (n.d.).

C77   *Saint Peter's Cook Book*. Compiled by the Parishioners, St. Peter's Episcopal Church, Westfield, NY. (Cookbook Publishers, Inc., Lenexa, KS, 1979).

C78(II) *Cook Book*. Favorite Recipes from Our Best Cooks. Compiled by Frewsburg Area Jaycees. (Circulation Service, 1968).

C79   *From Allen Park Kitchens*. Allen Park Women's Club. (Jamestown, NY, n.d.).

C80(III) *Cook Book*. Second Edition. Business and Professional Women's Club, Jamestown, NY. (Stever Company, n.d.).

C81   *Cookie Recipes*. Jamestown Girls Club. (Jamestown, NY, n.d.).

C82   *Good Cooking*. Ellery Senior Citizens. (Ellery, NY, n.d.).

C83(IV) *Cook Book*. Service Philathea Class, First Baptist Church. (Jamestown, NY, n.d.).

C84   *Sherman Cook Book*. Compiled by the Ladies of the Presbyterian Church, Sherman, NY. (Dormon Printing Company, 1908).

C85   Laughlin, Elaine. *Goodbye Dining Hall, Hello Homestyle*. (Elaine Laughlin's Country Cuisine Cooking School, Westfield, NY, 1982).

C86   *Lakewood and Celeron Ladies' Cook Book*. Prepared by Lakewood and Celeron Ladies of the Methodist Church. (Lakewood, NY, 1910).

C87   *Harvest Supper*. Sponsored by Evening Circle, First Covenant Church. (Jamestown, NY, 1969. Reprinted 1972).

C88   *Suburban Cookie Book*. Sponsored by Women's Society of Christian Service, Methodist Church. (Watts Flats, NY, n.d.).

C89 (II) *Butter 'n Love Recipes*. State Line United Methodist Women. (Fundcraft Publishing, Inc., 1987).

C90   *North Harmony Cookbook*. North Harmony Methodist Church Women. (1977).

C91   *Sweets and Meats*. The Thelian Society, First Presbyterian Church. (Jamestown, NY, n.d.) (See U4).

C92(V)   *Cook Book*. Cassadaga Ladies Chorus. (Cassadaga, NY, 1950).

C93   *The Philergian Cook Book*. Published by The Philergian Society of the First Congregational Church, Jamestown, NY. (The Electric Printing House, 1888).

C94(II) *Favorite Recipes*. Women's Fellowship, St. John's United Church of Christ. (Dunkirk, NY, n.d.).

C95   *Book from Charles St. School*. (Probably Jamestown, NY, probably 1950s.).

C96   *A Festival of Cooking*. The Jamestown YWCA and the Pennsylvania Gas Company. (n.d.).

C97   *Jamestown Post Cooking School*. (April 4, 5, 6, 7, 1939).

C98   *Wholesome Cooking Without Waste*. Welch Foods (Chicago, IL, n.d.).

C99   *Welch's Mother-Daughter Cook Book*. (Welch Grape Juice Co., 1946).

C100   *The Wonderful World of Welch's*. (Welch Foods, Inc., 1968).

C101   *The New World of Welch's*. (Welch Foods, Inc., 1975).

C102   *Jamestown Post-Journal Cookbook Editions* (8) (Jamestown, NY, 1984-1992).

C103   *The Fredonia Cookbook*. Compiled by the Ladies of the Trinity Parish Guild. (Fredonia Censor, 1899).

C104   *Needlework Guild Cookbook*. Compiled by the Needlework Guild of the First Presbyterian Church, Jamestown, NY. (Journal Printing Co., 1907).

C105   *Needlework Guild Cookbook*, 3rd edition.

C106   Duplicate of C104.

C107   Duplicate of C65.

C108   *Favorite Recipes from our Town & Country*. Altar and Rosary Society, Sherman, NY. (Women's Clubs Publishing Co., Inc., n.d.)

C109   Nutt, Cheryl. *New York State Tasty Maple Syrup Recipes*. (Jamestown, NY, 1983).

C110   *Our Favorite Recipes.* Compiled by the Parent-TeacherOrganization, R. R. Rogers School, Jamestown, NY. (Walter's Publishing Co., Waseca, MN, n.d.).

C111(VI)   *Cook Book.* Ladies Auxiliary to the John T. Murray V.F.W. Post 1017. (Dunkirk, NY, 1978).

C112   *Our Own Cookbook.* Compiled by the Parent-Teachers' Club of School Seven, Dunkirk, NY. (Cookbook Publishers, Inc., Lenexa, KS, 1986).

C113   *Westfield Area Jayncees' Cookbook.* Westfield, NY. (Cookbook Publishers, Inc., 1983).

C114   *Centennial Cook Book, 1887-1987.* St. Paul Lutheran Church, Fredonia, NY. (Circulation Services, 1987).

C115   *Dunkirk's Recipe Roundup.* The Guild, First Presbyterian Church, Dunkirk, NY. (Bev-Ron Publishing Co., 1954).

C116   *Forestville's Favorite Recipes.* W.S.C.S. of the Methodist Church, Forestville, NY. (Bev-Ron Publishing Co., 1950).

C117   *Kitchen Kapers.* Junior W.S.C.S. (No place given, n.d.).

C118   Duplicate of C71.

C119   *Cook, Bake and Be Merry.* St. Hedwig's Mother's Club. (Dunkirk, NY, 1962. Duplicate, more or less, of C13.).

C120   Duplicate of C64.

C121   Duplicate of C37.

C122   *Favorite Hometown Recipes.* Compiled by the Ladies of the Elks and Friends. Elks Lodge, No. 922, Dunkirk, NY. (Walter's Publishing Co., n.d.).

C123(V)   *What's Cooking at the Dale.* Lily Dale Auxiliary. (Cookbook Publishers, Inc., 1980).

C124   *Brocton Cook Book.* (No publishing information. n.d.).

C125   *Favorite Recipes from Our Best Cooks.* Young people of St. John the Baptist (Episcopal) Church, Dunkirk, NY. (Circulation Service, 1978).

C126   *Chautauqua County Home Bureau Cookbook.* Third Edition. Home Bureau Chapters. (No publishing information, 1972).

C127(VI)   *What's Cookin' in Irving, New York.* Ladies' Auxiliary of the Irving Volunteer Fire Department. (Bev-Ron Publishing Company, 1966).

C128   *Home Cooking Secrets of Sherman.* Stanley Hose Auxiliary, Sherman, NY. (Women's Clubs Publishing Co., Inc., 1972).

F1(III)   *Favorite Recipes from Findley Lake Families and Friends.* (G & R Publishing Company, Waverly, IA, 1981).

F6(II)   *Favorite Recipes from Our Best Cooks.* Compiled by Daughters of Eve of Mayville United Methodist Church. (Circulation Service, Shawnee Mission, KS, 1982).

F9   *Finger Lickin' Good Cookin'.* Collected by the Cassadaga Parents' Organization. (Cookbook Publishers, Lenexa, KS, 1981).

F13   *Bicentennial Cookbook–1776-1976.* AFS International Scholarships, Silver Creek Chapter. (Wimmer Bros., 1975).

F17   *Out of Silver Creek Kitchens.* Silver Chapter No. 288, Order of Eastern Star. (1962).

F28   *Chautauqua County Fair Cookbook.* Compiled by Women's Committee of the Chautauqua County Fair. (Circulation Service, Shawnee Mission, KS, 1979).

F29   *Our Culinary Favorites.* Shorewood Country Club Women's Association. (1984).

M1   *Recipes from East Dunkirk.* East Town of Dunkirk Ladies Fire Auxiliary, East Dunkirk, NY. (Women's Clubs Publishing Co., Inc., n.d.).

M2   *Cooking With.... Sylvan Chapter No. 258, Order of the Eastern Star in Dunkirk, NY.* (Bev-Ron Publishing Company, 1972).

M3   *100 Years of Cooking Cooking Cooking.* Lutheran Social Services, 1886-1986. (Jamestown, NY, 1986).

M4   *Jamestown High School A Cappella Choir Cookbook.* Jamestown, NY. (G & R Publishing Company, Waverly, IA, 1986).

U1   *An English Cookbook*. Compiled and published by the Adelphian Society of the Unitarian Church, Jamestown, NY. (Journal Press, 1911).

U2   Duplicate of C82.

U3(VII) *Cook Book*. Ellery Senior Citizens. (Ellery, NY, n.d.).

U4   *Sweets and Meats and Other Good Things To Eat*. Philathea Class, Grace United Brethren Church. (Jamestown, NY, 1917).

U5   *Crèche Cooks*. (See C74).

U6   *Cook Book: Favorite Recipes from Our Best Cooks*. Compiled by Friends of the Silver Creek Senior High Band, Silver Creek, NY. (Circulation Service, Shawnee Mission, KS, 1977-78).

U7(VIII) *Cookbook*. First Presbyterian Church, Westfield, NY. (General Publishing and Binding, Iowa Falls, IA, 1986).

U8   Duplicate of C84.

U9   *Anniversary Treasure of Personal Recipes*. First Congregational Church, Portland, NY. (Bev-Ron Publishing Company, 1952).

U10   *Home Cooking Secrets of Ripley*. Published by Presbyterian Women, Ripley, NY. (n.d.).

U11   *What's Cooking in Mayville & Vicinity*. Compiled by St. Monica's Guild of St. Paul's Episcopal Church. (Mayville, NY, n.d.).

U12   *Adventures in Food*. Members and Friends of Grace Evangelical Lutheran Church, Dunkirk, NY. (Walter's Publishing Co., 1977).

U13   *"Someone's in the Kitchen"*. By the Parents Advisory Group of Creative Arts for the Learning Preschool Program. (Westfield, NY, n.d.).

U14   *Chautauqua Celebrity Cookbook for The Elegant Eighties*. (Chautauqua Institution, Chautauqua, NY, 1980).

U15   Cook, Kate. *Chautauqua Cook Book*. (Martin Merz, Jamestown, NY, 1882. Revised in 1886; revised and enlarged in 1889 and 1896.).

U16   *Odette's War Recipes*. (No publishing information, n.d.).

U17(IX) *Cook Book*. Diana Lodge, No. 114, Jamestown, NY. (Circulation Service, Kansas City, MO, 1961).

U18(IV) *Favorite Recipes*. Diana Lodge, No. 114, Jamestown, NY. (Circulation Service, 1968).

U19   *The Parish Cook Book of 1937*, 3rd Edition. The Ladies Guild of Grace Episcopal Church, Randolph, NY. (Journal Press, Inc., Jamestown, NY, 1937.

U20   *Suburban Cookie Book*. Hanover Grange #595, Forestville, NY. (n.d.).

U21   *Silver Creek's Own Book*. Woman's Association of First Presbyterian Church, Silver Creek, NY. (n.d.).

U22   *The Fredonia Cook Book*. Ladies of the Trinity Parish Guild. (Fredonia Censor Printing, 1899).

U23   *Recipes from Jack Ericson*, Westfield, NY. (1980s).

U24   *Cooperative Extension Bulletin*. (Ellicottville, NY, 1975).

U25   *American Legion Auxiliary Cook Book*. Compiled by the John W. Rogers Unit No. 327, Westfield, NY. (The Westfield Republican, 1945).

U26   *Family Favorites*. St. Hyacinth's Mother's Club, St. Hyacinth School, Dunkirk, NY. (Fundcraft Publishing, Inc., Collierville, TN, 1989-90).

U27   *C.I.A.O. Chautauqua Italian American Organization Italian Traditions Cookbook* (n.d.).

INDEX

MY FAVORITES

MY FAVORITES

MY FAVORITES

MY FAVORITES

MY FAVORITES

_____   _____

_____   _____

_____   _____

_____   _____

_____   _____

_____   _____

_____   _____

_____   _____

_____   _____

_____   _____

MY FAVORITES

Chautauqua Region Press

19 Spring Street • Westfield, NY 14787

Please send me _____ copies of CHAUTAUQUA COOKS at $17.95 per copy, plus $2.50 per copy for postage and handling to:

Name _____

Address _____

City _____ State _____ Zip _____

New York state residents, add appropriate sales tax.

- -

Chautauqua Region Press

19 Spring Street • Westfield, NY 14787

Please send me _____ copies of CHAUTAUQUA COOKS at $17.95 per copy, plus $2.50 per copy for postage and handling to:

Name _____

Address _____

City _____ State _____ Zip _____

New York state residents, add appropriate sales tax.

- -

Chautauqua Region Press

19 Spring Street • Westfield, NY 14787

Please send me _____ copies of CHAUTAUQUA COOKS at $17.95 per copy, plus $2.50 per copy for postage and handling to:

Name _____

Address _____

City _____ State _____ Zip _____

New York state residents, add appropriate sales tax.